Apostle of the Exiled

ST. DAMIEN
of Molokai

Apostle of the Exiled

St. Damien

of Molokai

Margaret R. Bunson and Matthew E. Bunson

Our Sunday Visitor Publishing Division
Our Sunday Visitor, Inc.
Huntington, Indiana 46750

Published 2009.

14 13 12 11 10 09   1 2 3 4 5 6 7 8 9

Our Sunday Visitor Publishing Division
Our Sunday Visitor, Inc.
200 Noll Plaza
Huntington, IN 46750

1-800-348-2440
bookpermissions@osv.com.

ISBN: 978-1-59276-610-9 (Inventory No. T812)
LCCN: 2009931814

Cover design by Becky Heaston
Cover art: Shutterstock
Interior design by Sherri L. Hoffman

PRINTED IN THE UNITED STATES OF AMERICA

This book is dedicated to
Stephen M. Bunson, 1962–2008

Table of Contents

I CONSIDER MYSELF THE HAPPIEST missionary in the world," wrote Damien from Molokai, the Hawaiian island where he lived and died in the service of those with leprosy. He was referring to a strange kind of happiness, given that he lived in extreme conditions, had conflicts with his companions and his superiors (because of misunderstandings and his stubborn personality), and suffered in his own body the terrible process of decay caused by leprosy, finally dying from the disease.

Who is this man whose life, in spite of the passing years, continues to impact us so powerfully? The fascination Damien produces has changed the life of many, inspiring both religious and humanitarian commitment. Damien is not just "ours." He does not just belong to the brothers of his Congregation, whom I represent. He is a universal brother, a model of humanity, apostle to those with leprosy, a hero of charity, an inspiration for every human being called to serve the outcast and forgotten. He is a source of pride for Belgians and Hawaiians and shining light to the whole Church.

Of course very few who have felt the attraction of Damien have lived as he did, in such radical service to the poorest and most forgotten of the earth. Today we no longer understand mission or the struggle against suffering as a form of proselytism going hand in hand with cultural, political, or economic colonialism as might have been the case in the nineteenth century. All that said, Damien, with his deep desire to proclaim the Gospel, his very particular kind of love for the suffering, and his profound sense of joy that no one could take from him, continues to be a powerful inspiration inviting us to give similar meaning to our own existence. What is the secret of a life like his?

Seen from the outside, Damien certainly appears to be a giant of humanity, generosity, and service to the poor and abandoned. All of that is true, and because of Damien the way the world looks at leprosy patients was transformed. Many people have found in him the inspiration to grow in human virtues such as solidarity and commitment to justice for the marginalized.

However, if you really want to know who Damien is, then you have to get "inside," where that strange happiness took form, the happiness of a man who saw himself first and foremost as a believer, a priest, a son of the Sacred Hearts of Jesus and Mary, and a missionary of the God of mercy and compassion. As he often said, he found the strength needed to remain faithful to his mission in the Eucharist and at the foot of the Lord's cross. Only if we know this secret can we understand this strong, robust, and enterprising man, who as a young religious left his Flemish homeland to go to the other side of the world, where he would give himself to the end for his most forgotten brothers and sisters.

Damien's vitality comes from within, from his heart, where God was working, creating for us an outstanding image of the merciful heart of his Son, Jesus.

This biography is being published as the Church prepares to canonize Damien, officially including him in the list of saints. The book is not just about "Father Damien of Molokai" but "Saint" Damien. From the perspective of our faith (which was the way Damien saw things), this gives us a deeper insight into the "secret" to which we referred.

For the Church, canonization is not just the exaltation of a hero or the granting of an honorific title to a group or an institution. The Church does not canonize someone to highlight certain values or some ideology. Canonization is primarily an act of praise to the God of love and mercy, who pours forth his compassion on us by transforming the lives of his saints through the power of his Spirit. So often, as in the life of Damien, God's action is hidden in the misery that is so much a part of human history.

With the canonization, the Church proclaims that Damien belongs to God. He can only be understood in terms of his belonging to the Lord of life, who shaped him and made him his own. Holiness is the work of the Lord. It is his love that justifies us.

According to brother Joseph Dutton, faithful companion of his later years, Damien had many character defects, but they were consumed like straw by the fire of his charity. That fire is God's fire, a love stronger than death, a fire that even torrential rains cannot extinguish. It is the same fire we see in images of the Heart of Jesus: a pierced and suffering heart yet overflowing with passion and life. Damien had a heart like that.

By canonization the Church honors Damien. It recognizes in a public and official way the exceptional quality of his life and work. During his life and after his death, Damien was praised and slandered, admired and condemned. In his letters, he leaves us the testimony of the suffering caused by loneliness and misunderstanding. At one point he even thinks that he might be unworthy of heaven. We could say that the canonization dissipates those doubts and proclaims the profound truth of his existence. This is a man of God. The choices he made and the things he did pleased God and gave witness to him.

The Church, by canonizing Damien, recognizes him as a model to be imitated. By doing that, it makes a judgment about what is good and what is not good. There is a difference. Abandoning people to their misery is not the same as serving the forgotten. Seeking one's own well-being is not the same as sacrificing oneself for the happiness of others. Ignoring the poor and living well is not the same as loving those living on the margin of society. Keeping one's distance from the sick for fear of contamination is not the same as touching and embracing a leper. Living as if God did not exist is not the same as seeking him daily with a humble heart. Preserving one's life is not the same as giving it away out of love.

Honoring Damien is to clearly and unequivocally state that his way is the right way, that what he did is what is good, that his everyday stubborn compassion is what God desires.

I am confident that this book will help us listen to Damien, a man who was both so ordinary and so extraordinary. What does Damien say to us today? How does he challenge us? What would he think of the consistency of our faith (if we are believers), of the generosity with which we give ourselves to others, of our love for the poor, of the constancy of our commitment to those who suffer? As the Rev. Hugh Chapman, an Anglican priest who was such a support to Damien, said, a life like Damien's *"silently accuses us of being comfortable and selfish."*

By entering into the heart of Damien, may many be inspired to serve the poorest of the poor with great generosity. May we follow the Lord who inspired Damien, so that we also might taste that great happiness that nothing could destroy. May Damien help us love more.

Javier Alvarez-Ossorio, SS.CC.
Superior General
General Government of the Brothers
Congregation of the Sacred Hearts of Jesus and Mary
May 2009

At least once in every generation a single human being challenges the accepted standards of the world to undertake a unique level of service to others. On May 10, 1873, a priest destined to be raised to the altars of the Catholic Church set foot on the shore of the island of Molokai at a remote and geographically isolated settlement called Kalaupapa. Molokai was part of the lovely chain of Pacific islands known today as Hawaii, America's fiftieth state. The priest was Damien de Veuster, SS.CC., and he was not alone but in the company of a very unusual man, called *Lui Ka Epikopo* by the Hawaiian people: "Louis the Bishop."

Gavan Daws, the noted historian, addressing a celebration of the Sesquicentennial Anniversary of the Diocese of Honolulu in 1977, offered a compelling insight into the future saint's personality when he announced: "Damien de Veuster was an ordinary man who made the most extraordinary choices again and again and again."

Damien de Veuster was a complex individual who had a distinct awareness of the relationship of one human being to another, understanding that the human heart functions at its fullest in the service of others. Even in Damien's era, people had separated themselves from one another in various ways. Humanity was used then as it is now, as an abstraction of the term human beings. Humanity was a vast entity that could be viewed from a distance, not face to face, and in order to practice charity towards humanity, many became humanitarians. They thus became impersonal abstractions of an abstract term that denoted live, hurting men and women who needed personal and compassionate care.

The young priest landing on the shores of Kalaupapa did not view human relationships in abstract terms. He was not a humanitarian but a human being faced with the presence of incredible pain and suffering, and he knew that he had come to Molokai to be of service to all exiled there. This attitude, of course, made him an enigma to some of his contemporaries, and a genuine annoyance to others. Watching his labors among the desperately ill men, women, and children deposited by the Hawaiian authorities onto the rugged coast of Molokai, the people of the islands, and then the world, began to recognize the paradoxes of his life, and they were made uneasy.

Damien de Veuster was a farm boy from Belgium, educated only through the early grades before entering the Sacred Hearts monastery. He was also stocky in build, strong and lacking the fine manners of others. He followed his brother, Pamphile, into the religious life, believing he would never match Pamphile's holiness. He was not considered a suitable candidate for the priesthood either, because he struggled with Latin, something that he remedied with his brother's patient tutelage. When Pamphile was assigned to the mission territory of Hawaii, known in that era as the Sandwich Islands, Damien watched as his brother was stricken with typhus. An older sister of the de Veuster family, Eugénie, had died of typhus years before as an Ursuline nun; and Pauline, a younger sister, had entered the cloister to take her place. Damien volunteered to go to the islands as a substitute for Pamphile.

Raised in a close-knit, devout family and community, Damien would spend the rest of his life among diverse races, beliefs, and cultures. Enjoying the company of his family and friends and then the members of his religious community, Damien would be exiled with human beings who practiced totally different traditions and customs. A man who understood the changing seasons of his homeland and a varied annual climate, he would live in a tropical paradise where the sun was bright and the winds balmy. Lastly, when Damien's life and death were reviled by a clergyman who had no clue as to the disease or its origins, the leper priest was defended by one of the world's greatest literary geniuses, *Tusitala*, Robert Louis Stevenson, whose stinging words appeared in newspapers around the world, making Damien's detractor a household word.

Thirty-three years old and a tested missionary in 1873, Damien had sailed from the nearby island of Maui, coming to Kalaupapa on a diocesan assignment. In truth, however, this priest was stepping into history when he put his booted foot firmly onto the rugged shore. With that single act, he was condemning to death both himself and a terrifying, centuries-old tradition, born of human dread. The Hawaiian residents of Kalaupapa coming to welcome the Catholic missionary and the bishop were victims of Hansen's disease: the scourge of ancient times, the biblical horror known as leprosy. He had come among them to change their way of life forever, arriving on the scene to alter for all time the way human beings would respond to the disfigurement and pain caused by that hideous affliction.

Damien de Veuster would soon be called cantankerous by those who despised the infected, and he was ferocious in the defense of his charges, individuals whom he treated with infinite courtesy and care. In other words, Damien was a totally human personality, a man who put aside his own weaknesses and problems because he saw a stark need for his particular insights and courage. He genuinely believed that one person could make a difference in the world around him, even amid the horrors of decay and slow death. He did not imitate the blind fear that had ruled human reactions in the face of lepers and their pain. He did not demonstrate the terrified response that accompanied the disease through the centuries of human existence. Their care was the priority of his life, and other emotions were not only a waste of time and energies but unproductive. He was needed by the victims who had been cruelly isolated on Molokai's stark terrain. That was motivation enough, and to this task Damien brought not only his priestly dedication but a peasant's stout heart, the canny realism of his European ancestry, and the splendors of his faith. Hawaii was a magnificent paradise in an azure sea, and he would revive the hopes and the joys of the islanders in the settlement of Kalaupapa until he died among them as a leper.

July 14, 1827: The first Catholic Mass is celebrated in Hawaii by Father Alexis Bachelot.

December 24, 1831: Fathers Bachelot and Patrick Short are exiled from Hawaii during the anti-Catholic persecution; Bachelot returns to the islands after a few years.

October 6, 1837: Father Louis Desiré Maigret, SS.CC., arrives in Hawaii and takes the dying Father Bachelot from Hawaii.

December 18, 1837: King Kamehameha III issues "An Ordinance Rejecting the Catholic Religion."

January 23, 1838: Barbara Koob (later Marianne Cope) is born in Hessen, Germany.

July 9, 1839: The French frigate, *l'Artémise*, commanded by Captain Cyrille-Pierre Theodore LaPlace, appears in Honolulu and demands an end to the anti-Catholic persecutions.

January 3, 1840: Joseph de Veuster is born in Tremelo, Belgium.

Fall 1847: Joseph de Veuster begins school; he eventually leaves to work on his father's farm.

February 1, 1848: Bishop Maigret returns to Hawaii and assumes leadership over the Catholic community in Hawaii.

January 1859: Joseph de Veuster enters the Sacred Hearts Congregation at Louvain as a postulant.

October 7, 1860: Joseph de Veuster travels to the motherhouse of the congregation on the Rue du Picpus in Paris and makes his vows; he is given the name Damien.

November 19, 1862: Barbara Koob is invested in the Sisters of Saint Francis in Syracuse, N.Y.; she becomes known as Sister Marianne.

October 1863: Joseph's brother, Father Pamphile, is unable to set out for the Sacred Hearts Mission in Hawaii because of typhus; Joseph asks to take his place.

October 20, 1863: Damien sets out on his journey to Hawaii.

March 19, 1864: Damien arrives in Hawaii.

May 21, 1864: Damien is ordained a priest in the Cathedral of Our Lady of Peace; he is soon sent to Puna on the Big Island.

January 3, 1865: King Kamehameha V issues a decree putting into law a segregation policy for lepers in the islands that included the removal of the infected, including children and infants, from their communities.

June 1865: Molokai is chosen as the site of a leprosarium, or lazaretto.

May 4, 1873: Bishop Maigret meets with several Sacred Hearts Fathers, including Damien and raises the need for a residential priest for the lepers; Father Damien immediately volunteers.

May 10, 1873: Bishop Maigret visits Molokai with Father Damien; Maigret permits Damien to stay on a permanent basis.

September 1, 1873: Damien is reprimanded by the Board of Health for visiting Catholics in areas outside the settlement; an accommodation is reached, and Damien builds various chapels for Catholics on the island.

November 1877: Damien is offered the position of assistant superintendent of the settlement and accepts to prevent someone else creating problems for the lepers; he serves until February 1878 when a permanent assistant superintendent is installed in his place at his request.

September 15, 1881: Princess Lili'uokalani visits the settlement, weeps openly, and is unable to deliver her planned address; she subsequently awards Damien the Order of the Knight Commander of the Royal Order of Kalakaua in recognition of his "efforts in alleviating the distresses and mitigating the sorrows of the unfortunate."

June 11, 1882: Bishop Maigret dies; he is succeeded by Bishop Herman Koeckemann.

October 22, 1883: Mother Marianne and six volunteer Franciscan Sisters (selected from a total of thirty-five members of the congregation who had offered to accompany her) sail for Hawaii.

December 1884: Damien discovers that he has contracted leprosy when he burns his feet with hot water and realizes he does not feel it; several days later, Dr. Arning in Honolulu officially diagnoses the leprosy.

July 19, 1886: Father Damien welcomes Joseph Dutton to Molokai.

1888: Mother Marianne settles at Kalaupapa to provide care for the lepers.

March 19, 1889: Damien falls ill and becomes bedridden.

April 2, 1889: Damien receives the last rites; he lingers for thirteen more days.

April 15, 1889: Father Damien dies; he is buried in the shade of the pandanus tree under which he had spent his first night on Molokai.

February 22, 1892: Bishop Koeckemann dies; he is succeeded by Bishop Gulstan Ropert.

December 1894: A bronze monument to Father Damien, as "Apostle of the Lepers," is erected in Louvain, Belgium.

July 16, 1908: The Great White Fleet of the United States sails past Molokai in honor of Brother Dutton and the patients.

August 9, 1918: Mother Marianne dies on Molokai.

January 27, 1936: The body of Damien is exhumed in the presence of Church and government officials; he is transported with all honors to Belgium on the ship *Mercator.*

May 3, 1936: Damien is welcomed with great festivities at Antwerp by King Leopold III; a hearse drawn by white horses carries him to Tremelo.

May 12, 1955: The decree of the official introduction of the Cause for Canonization is issued with the approval of Pope Pius XII.

1969: The mandatory isolation decreed by King Kamehameha V for all lepers is officially ended.

April 15, 1969: A statue of Damien is unveiled in the Rotunda of the Capitol, Washington, D.C.; Damien joins King Kamehameha I as one of the official representatives of the State of Hawaii in Statuary Hall.

July 7, 1977: Damien is declared Venerable by Pope Paul VI.

December 22, 1980: Kalaupapa is incorporated into the United States National Historical Park System.

June 13, 1992: Pope John Paul II approves Damien for beatification, based on the miraculous cure of a Sacred Hearts sister.

June 4, 1995: Damien is beatified in Belgium by Pope John Paul II.

July 22, 1995: A relic (Damien's right hand) is given at the beatification ceremony to the congregation and reinterred at Kalawao.

April 19, 2004: Pope John Paul II issues the decree officially granting Mother Marianne the title of Venerable.

May 14, 2005: Mother Marianne is beatified.

June 2, 2008: A second miracle is approved and accepted by Pope Benedict XVI, thereby guaranteeing the canonization of Father Damien.

October 11, 2009: Damien is canonized a saint in Rome by Pope Benedict XVI.

Hawaiian Glossary

Hawaiian is pronounced much like English, with the exception of the consonant W, which is pronounced as V after I or E. The vowels are all pronounced.

Ali'i — ruling class, nobility.
Ali'i nui — royalty.
Aloha — hello, goodbye, love.
Aloha nui loa — a great love.
Hale pili — a thatched hut.
Haole — a white, Caucasian (foreigner).
Hapa Haole — of mixed blood (half white).
Hauoli Hanau — Happy Birthday.
Hauoli Makaliiki Ho — Happy New Year.
Ho'olaule'a — a celebration.
Hukilau — a fishing festival.
Hula — to dance.
Huli-Huli — chicken roasted on a spit.
Humuhumunukunuku'apua'a — Hawaiian triggerfish.
Imu — an underground oven.
Kahuna — a Hawaiian priest.
Kapa — Hawaiian tapa-style cloth.
Kapu — forbidden or taboo.
Kama'aina — native.
Kane — male or man.
Kau-Kau — food.
Keiki — child.
Kokua — help, aid.

Lanai — porch or terrace.
Mahalo nui loa — many thanks.
Malahini — newcomer.
Mele Kalikimaka — Merry Christmas.
Pau — done, finished, ended.
Poi — taro paste.
Tutu — auntie.
Wahine — female, woman.

CHAPTER ONE

A New Faith in the Hawaiian Islands

CONSIDERED SOME OF THE most beautiful places on the face of the earth, the Hawaiian Islands offer exquisite delights for the senses and for the human spirit. Rising out of the Pacific Ocean as monuments of enduring natural splendor, and born of the molten labors of ancient volcanoes, the islands embody a healing gentleness of landscape and a certain kindness of heart among the residents that inspire visitors from around the world, year after year. Mark Twain, the celebrated American author, described Hawaii as "the loveliest fleet of islands that lies anchored in any ocean."

Hawaii's islands are truly volcanic in origin, actually the visible crests of a submerged mountain chain that stretches in a crescent shape of fifteen hundred miles. The combined land area of the islands has been measured at 6,245 square miles, but constant volcanic activity that deposits lava along the shore of Hawaii, adds footage every year. There are eight major islands and about one hundred twenty-four islets in the chain. The major islands are Kauai, Kahoolawe, Hawaii (called "the Big Island"), Lanai, Maui, Molokai, Niihau, and Oahu, which is dominated by Honolulu, the capital city. There is another member of this chain, Loihi, forming slowly off the coast of the Big Island as a result of dramatic ongoing volcanic eruptions.

The earliest inhabitants of the islands arrived possibly as early as 300 B.C., coming probably from the Marquesas, via Tahiti, although the Polynesians from the Marquesas and possibly the

Society Islands settled in a steady flow on the Hawaiian Islands between A.D. 300 and 500. The settlers of the Hawaiian Islands sailed the uncharted Pacific Ocean in large, double-hulled vessels that were designed elegantly for long voyages, carrying large crews and supplies, including coconuts, sugarcane, and dogs. Some of these vessels were fashioned to carry entire families, their household goods, and even their livestock (such as pigs) over the waves. Studying the movement of the heavenly bodies in the night sky (a skill practiced by almost all of the older seafaring civilizations of the world) and keenly alert to oceanic currents, tidal movements, and winds, the Hawaiians sailed into the unknown in search of a new land.

This ability to span the endless miles of waves and chilling depths of the ocean is not just a matter of tradition or legend among the Hawaiians. The seafaring expertise of the island people was proven in 1976. In that year a team of Hawaiians boarded the *Hokule'a*, a replica of the sixty-foot crafts used by their ancestors. On board the vessel the Hawaiians made a return trip to Tahiti. They sailed without modern navigational instruments and without all of the safety features of modern boats. The voyage demonstrated conclusively the Hawaiian skills in moving unaided and undaunted across the Pacific's vast expanse.

Having settled in the islands, the newcomers found remarkably fertile lands, which they promptly cultivated, and they prospered. Over time, the settlers established ruling clans and a complex social system that built around defined classes: the nobility (the *ali'is*), priests (*kahunas*), and commoners (*maka'ainana*). The four largest of the islands, Hawaii, Maui, Kauai and Oahu were governed by their own *Ali'i 'aimoku*, high chiefs or kings.

The islanders, however, could not remain forever isolated from the rest of the world. Europeans were intent upon extending their own holdings and in discovering uncharted sites. In the Royal Hawaiian hotel in Waikiki, a map hung on the wall at one time and illustrated the fact that the Spanish knew of the islands long before the English arrived. There apparently is no documentation of such a visit, however, and the first actually recorded Europeans arrived in the port of Waimea, on the island of Kauai, on January 20, 1778.

Captain James Cook, a celebrated explorer and navigator sailed into the island waters on that date and is thus currently credited with discovering Hawaii, at least for the Europeans. Captain Cook displayed the typical European arrogance of his era by naming the islands after his patron, the Earl of Sandwich, who is better remembered for his invention of the modern form of lunch. Whatever the islanders thought of that newly invented name did not much matter, as the designation remained for an incredibly long period afterward. Dedicating the newfound isles to his patron, Captain Cook and his crew sampled some of the island's delights and promptly sailed out of Waimea aboard the *Resolution* and the *Discovery*. Cook was bound for the north, where he hoped to discover the fabled Northwest Passage, a sea route believed to connect the Atlantic and Pacific Oceans, either across Alaska and Canada or perhaps more to the south.

The seafarers returned to Hawaii, however, when ice packs prohibited further exploration of a Northwest Passage. Captain Cook landed at Kealakekua Bay on the Big Island of Hawaii on January 17, 1779. The Hawaiians were naturally hostile when Cook and his crew disembarked. News of his visit to Waimea had raced across the islands, and the impact of Cook's arrival was not lost on the ruling clans. Over the next weeks the rage of the islanders mounted steadily as the English conducted themselves in variously condescending ways. A fierce argument started on February 14 and escalated into a bloody war between the islanders and the ship's crew. Captain James Cook died at the hands of the Hawaiians, and his remaining crew members fled on board their vessels. That was not the end of the misadventure, naturally. Word went out in all the ports of Europe about the lovely islands, which were marvelously situated in the Pacific and could be used as stopovers for various naval expeditions. Within a short time the race was on. Ships started putting into Hawaiian ports, including vessels from the robust American whaling industry.

By 1785, foreign vessels sought Hawaiian harbors on a frequent basis, leading to further confrontations that became more and more difficult for the island people. In 1789, an American ship, the *Eleanore*, arrived; and Captain Metcalf, the skipper, became involved in a dispute, killing a reported one hundred Hawaiians. He then joined the crew of his tender, the smaller vessel used to ferry supplies and passengers, a ship called the *Fair American*. The Hawaiians, seeking vengeance, stormed the tender, killing all of the crew members except one, the mate Isaac Davis. Another American, John Young of the *Eleanore*, had also been taken prisoner, and with Davis he found himself in the service of a gifted and ambitious island ruler who was bent on adapting to changing times in order to defend his people.

"Mamala-hoe Kanwai"

E na kanaka
E malama'oukou I ke akua
A e malama ho'i ke kanaka nui a me kanaka iki;
E hele ka'elemakule ka luahine, a me ke kama
A moe I ke ala
'A'ohe mea nana e ho'opilikia
Hewa no. Make.

"Law of the Splintered Paddle"

O my people,
Honor thy god;
Respect alike (the rights of) men great and humble;
See to it that our aged, our women, and our children

Lie down to sleep by the roadside
Without fear of harm.
Disobey, and die.

—*Decree of King Kamehameha I*

That monarch in power in Hawaii was King Kamehameha I. He was born an *ali'i*, or a noble, around 1758, on the Big Island, and led a difficult early life because of political unrest. Kamehameha I was tall and powerfully built; trained in war and clearly a man who could not be denied his unique destiny. Uniting the various kingdoms in raids and wars, he defeated the last opposing chiefs in the Battle of Nuuanu Pali, on the cliffs of Oahu's verdant mountain chain that cuts across the island. By 1810, Kamehameha I had marched across all of the inhabited islands of the Hawaiian chain, slaying those chiefs who opposed unification and accepting the tribute of those leaders who shared his dream and paid homage to his claims. He lived as the ruler of a united Hawaii for nine years, bequeathing to his people a system of ethical values and a stable civilization in the face of growing foreign interventions and change.

Kamehameha I had a distinct awareness of the obligations of the throne to all islanders and normally placed the welfare of his people above his own comforts or preferences. The arrival of the European vessels had quickly alerted him to the changes taking place in the world beyond Hawaii's shores. Called by some historians "the Napoleon of the Pacific," he understood the necessity of conducting business with the constant visitors, both the Europeans and the Americans. He also welcomed the products of other lands, particularly those of a military nature. Seeing their weapons, armed units, and bureaucracies, Kamehameha I launched a campaign to modernize the kingdom in order to survive the increasing presence of foreigners. Captain George Vancouver had introduced various breeds of livestock in 1794, and the American whalers discovered the delights of winters in Hawaii, staying away from their home ports for years on end. Others explained the histories of their lands, various military traditions, and the innovations being developed in the scientific fields. Kamehameha listened carefully and made note of those things that could be of use to the islanders.

During his declining years, Kamehameha also saw the arrival of the first Russian ship in Hawaiian waters. The vessel was wrecked off the coast of Kauai. A Russian encampment soon followed, with a second fort of that nation appearing at Waimea. Kamehameha exiled the Russians rather speedily, probably at the urgings of the Americans who had entered his service. The Russians would have had little appeal to the Americans as potential residents in Hawaii.

After 1812, Kamehameha's court was in Kailua, Kona, on the island of Hawaii. He reorganized his government, using capable administrators. In 1816, he had a flag designed in the style of Great Britain's banner, and that was later adopted as the state flag of Hawaii. Two years later, he dealt with the court of Russia and sat for two Russian portraits. Kamehameha I died in Kailua, Kona, on the Big Island, on May 8, 1819. He decreed that Liholiho, who became Kamehameha II, be his heir. Queen Kaahumanu, a formidable *ali'i* who had witnessed the wars and the annihilation of chiefs, was named *kuhina-nui*, coruler or regent. Kamehameha's burial was done in secret so that "only the stars know his final resting place." His statue stands beside that of St. Damien, in Statuary Hall, Washington, D.C., as one of the two representatives of the State of Hawaii, placed in the Capitol in Washington on April 15, 1969.

Three months after the death of Kamehameha I, a French ship, the *Uranie*, arrived in Honolulu as well. The vessel was captained by a man named Freycinet. On board was a notable Catholic missionary, Abbé de Quilen, who preached the Catholic faith to the *ali'is*. Two high-ranking Hawaiians were baptized during the visit of the *Uranie*, including Boki, the governor of Honolulu, who became a patron of Catholic priests when they later reached the islands.

A curious figure enters the scene at this point, a man named John Rives, from France. When Kamehameha's heir, Liholiho (Kamehameha II), decided to sail to England, Rives was on board the *l'Aigle*, the English whaler chosen as a royal vessel. Liholiho and his wife, Kamamalu, along with Governor Boki and his wife, Liliha, sailed from Honolulu in November 1823. Rives served as interpreter until the royal entourage reached London but then abandoned Liholiho and went to France. Liholiho and Queen Kamamalu caught measles and died tragically in England. Their remains were returned to the islands by the English monarch, King George IV. Unaware of attacks being made upon him by the Americans at the Hawaiian court, Rives entered into negotiations with the French government and wealthy patrons to establish a French agricultural venture in the islands. He also contacted Catholic authorities in Paris and in Rome in order to secure priests for the French mission in Hawaii. Through the offices of Cardinal Giulio Maria della Somaglia in Rome, the Sacred Hearts Fathers (also called the Picpus Fathers) were assigned to Hawaii. The Congregation of the Sacred Hearts of Jesus and Mary and of Perpetual Adoration of the Most Blessed Sacrament of the Altar held a general chapter in 1842, and three missionary priests accepted the invitations of the Holy See and set sail on *La Comète*, the result of John Rives's vision for Hawaii.

The Sacred Hearts priests were the spiritual sons of Father Pierre Marie Joseph Coudrin, who founded the congregation on Christmas Day in 1800. Coudrin was a deacon in a Catholic seminary when the French Revolution broke upon the priests and the religious of that land, bringing about the martyrdom of many and the endless sufferings of thousands. Coudrin's seminary was invaded by troops and a filthy rabble during a demonstration of anti-Christian wrath. The rioters smashed every symbol of Catholicism that they could find, and the students and faculty were forced to flee for their lives. Realizing that he could never return to the demolished seminary, or to the routines that had been preparing him for ordination, Coudrin began to search for a bishop who would ordain him. He had no desire to go into hiding and no wish to abandon his calling to the priesthood. France needed men who were willing to risk their lives to continue the sacraments and to give instructions to the faithful. He discovered the bishop of Clermont, in the Irish College, Paris, and he was ordained by the prelate in the library of the college in a secret ceremony.

The persecution of the Church was still rampant, and when the newly ordained Father Coudrin returned to his home in Coursay-les-Bois, he discovered peril there as well. He packed his belongings and set out on the roads of his native land. There were, of course, thousands of French men and women still true to the Church. Those people practiced the faith of their fathers. They hid priests and religious, and aided them in their work while the revolution spewed up new reigns of terror that devoured the brightest and best of the land. Father Coudrin was befriended by many and began his priestly work in the midst of chaos. It was during this period that the founder of the Sacred Hearts Fathers formulated the simple motto that gave his life purpose: "Rejoice to be victims ready for the sacrifice, in union with our Heavenly Spouse and upon the same Cross." He instructed his followers in yet another spiritual attitude, the one that would mold Damien on the island of Molokai in the course of time: "Nature may shudder, but grace will finally triumph!"

On Christmas Day, 1800, the Congregation of the Sacred Hearts of Jesus and Mary of the Perpetual Adoration of the

Most Blessed Sacrament was founded. In September of 1825, the Sacred Hearts Fathers received the Hawaiian mission through the offices of Cardinal della Somaglia. On October 29, 1825, Father Alexis Bachelot, with two priest companions and some lay brothers of the congregation, received their formal appointments to Hawaii. Father Bachelot was named the prefect apostolic of the mission territory and given complete charge of the endeavor. One year later, the group set out for the islands on the vessel *La Comète*. As the priests neared South America, events were taking place in Hawaii that would have a devastating effect on their missionary dreams.

One year after King Kamehameha I's death, fifteen companies of Protestant missionaries from New England reached Hawaii. The American Protestants were aggressive in the proselytizing and converted Queen Kaahumanu to their denomination. She had been crowned in the place of Liholiho, following his tragic death and now ruled the islands.

As the Sacred Hearts priests approached the islands, American ship captains warned the island government that a group of "Jesuits" was about to land in their midst. These "Jesuits" were supposed to be agents of the French authorities, the advance sent to aid and abet the French merchants in a takeover of the islands. The Americans, highly disturbed by such a prospect, met in council and advised the government of Hawaii to resist any attempt by the French and their Catholic advance guard. Queen Kaahumanu listened to her American advisors, and as a result, when *La Comète* anchored in Honolulu on July 7, 1827, Father Bachelot was stunned to discover that none of his party would be given permission to land on Oahu. The next morning, however, he did manage to gain a temporary leave so that he could accompany the ship's captain and Philippe de Morineau, an agent of the French government (and a shrewd lawyer), in visiting dignitaries of other Catholic lands. Boki, the governor of Honolulu, was also an ally. Interviews with the foreigners representing some of the South American nations resulted in the priests' receiving permission to land so that they could rest from their long voyage.

The Sacred Hearts Fathers had no intention of sitting idly by in the face of American opposition and lies. Father Bachelot started negotiations for using a mission property. Because Brother Melchior was not ordained as a Catholic priest, he was free of the "Jesuit" stigma in the eyes of the island government and able to move about. The priests were also aided by a Spaniard, Don Francisco Paula Marin, who had been in the islands since 1791 and held in esteem by one and all. The first Catholic Mass was celebrated in Hawaii on July 14, 1827, on a plot measuring some forty square acres in a wooded area. Three grass huts were on the property when it was purchased, and the priests adapted them to their own use. Circumspect in their dealings with both the native population and the foreign inhabitants, the missionaries settled into a routine and eventually built a permanent residence, again with the help of the tactful and winning Morineau. They were allowed to remain on Oahu as a result, carrying on their work with considerable discretion and care.

Hawaiian internal affairs, however, soon put the entire mission into jeopardy once again. Father Abraham Armand, one of Bachelot's original companions, recognized the inevitable and left the islands in order to join one of the congregation's missions elsewhere. He took one lay brother, Theodore, with him. As it turned out, Father Armand was an intelligent judge of the situation in the islands. Boki, the governor of Honolulu, who had openly championed the Catholic presence, had sailed to the New Hebrides in search of sandalwood, and had suffered a maritime disaster and was presumed dead. He was no longer able to intercede for the Catholics. On April 2, 1831, Father Bachelot and Father Patrick Short, his priest companion, thus received a summons to the Fort of Honolulu. They appeared there before Queen Kaahumanu and her governors, members of the Council of Chiefs, and received a decree of banishment from the Hawaiian Islands. No argument could halt the banishment. The queen and her American advisors were adamant. Word of the persecution of the French priests spread quickly across the Pacific Basin, of course, carried by the crews of the various vessels putting into ports; and the Franciscan Friars of California offered hospitality to the Sacred Hearts Fathers if they were sent into such an exile. On December 24, 1831, despite their pleas and appeals, the priests were put on board a ship and set sail. They reached the bay of San Pedro, California, aboard the *Waverly* on January 21, 1832.

Captain William Sumner, of the *Waverly*, had been paid for the passage of the priests by the Hawaiian government, and he wanted to be rid of them as soon as possible without making contact with the Spanish California authorities. Such authorities, he knew, would take a dim view of the affair. There was an abandoned stretch of beach as the ship neared the shore, and there he set the Sacred Hearts Fathers with their baggage. A local farmer and some others came upon them and sent word for the soldiers in the next village. They arrived and tried to signal to the *Waverly* and its crew, but the ship sailed out of the bay, abandoning the priests to their fate. Captain Sumner and the crew of the *Waverly* were not able to distance themselves from the matter so easily, however. A few days later, the ship put into Santa Barbara, where they were arrested, detained, and then sent packing back to Hawaii with official censures and complaints. Sumner had been astute enough to demand that Fathers Bachelot and Short sign a document attesting to the fact that they were not ill-treated before they were set down on the barren shore, and that spared him from lasting infamy and possible charges.

In the meantime, the priests had discovered another road open to them. It was *El Camino Real* ("The Royal Road"), blazed by Blessed Junípero Serra and his Franciscan companions. The Sacred Hearts Fathers made their way to Mission San Gabriel, where they worked again as missionaries in a foreign land. Situated in the flatlands of the San Gabriel Valley, near modern-day Los Angeles, Mission San Gabriel was founded in 1771. Two Franciscan priests, a small group of soldiers, and some mule drivers had chosen the site near the San Gabriel and Hondo rivers. The mission was dedicated to St. Gabriel the Archangel. This mission was the fourth in a line of Franciscan settlements, beginning in San Diego in California. It was moved to its present site in 1791. The mission's stone building is one of the oldest standing structures in the nation. Fathers Bachelot and Short served at Mission San Gabriel, and Father Bachelot also served as the first pastor of Los Angeles. Father Short founded the first college in California, at Monterey.

In Honolulu, meanwhile, another ship had entered the harbor, carrying a member of the Sacred Hearts Congregation who would be difficult for the local government officials to handle in their usual manner. His name was Father Arsenius Walsh, SS.CC., and he was not French but Irish. Father Walsh arrived with a British passport and with letters of recommendation from the American and British consuls of Valparaiso, Chile. He was not greeted with open arms, naturally, and it took the skillful and persistent services of the British consul to maintain a degree of safety for him in the Hawaiian Islands, but his status as the holder of a British passport rendered his exile or arrest wholly impractical.

This proved a timely development as the situation for Catholics in the islands had deteriorated significantly. Catholics had been forced into labor units and had been whipped for their conversion to the Church. Persecution of all such converts was routine, and many fled to the windward side of Oahu in order to be able to live in peace. On one occasion, even Father Walsh was threatened with exile. But he boarded a French ship in the harbor, laid his case before the captain, who became extremely irate over the matter, and stood with him in open defiance of the government's edict. The authorities were forced to give the Irish priest permission to remain in the islands unmolested. He resided with Brother Melchior, who had remained behind when the priests were sent to California, and with another lay brother sent by the congregation. Father Walsh's presence became one of the island's best-known jests after a time. The islanders and the foreigners, not particularly fond of the Americans in their midst, knew that the priest was converting people and going about the island to celebrate Mass and other services. Everyone smiled, but did not bring up his name in conversation, especially with any person of rank or authority. He was protected by his British passport and by the adamant support of that nation's consul who openly dared opponents to make the first diplomatic error.

In 1837, however, Fathers Bachelot and Short returned to Hawaii, having heard reports of Father Walsh's accomplishments and believing that at long last the spirit of enlightened religious toleration had come to the islands. They arrived in Honolulu on board the vessel *Clementine*, causing an immediate uproar. In the first hours, they were confined to their ship in the harbor. Foreign dignitaries, enraged by the obvious power of the American Protestants and the total disregard of traditional rules of world diplomacy, intervened before the courts, and in time, Fathers Bachelot and Short were given permission to land in the city. Father Short sailed away to seek another mission assignment, as the Congregation of the Sacred Hearts was opening missions all across Oceania at the time. Father Bachelot, too ill to travel, planned to board another vessel to sail to the Marquesas, a secondary destination, provided in case the Hawaii mission remained closed to them.

However, the arrival of the *Europa*, on October 6, 1837, brought the man who would become famous as *Lui Ka Epikopo*,

"Louis the Bishop": Father Louis Desiré Maigret, SS.CC. Father Maigret had sailed from Valparaiso, Chile, via Tahiti. While crossing the ocean, he studied the Hawaiian language and translated a dictionary of the Gospel into Mangareva, the language of another Sacred Hearts island outpost. A British man-of-war had brought advance news of Maigret's arrival, so he and his companion, Father Columba Murphy, were immediately set upon by the Hawaiian authorities. Father Murphy was allowed to land because, like Father Walsh, he was a British subject. Father Maigret was charged with attempts to hide his French nationality and his priesthood. Grasping the situation, he decided the wisest course was to hire a ship, that he renamed the *Notre Dame de Paix*, and to take Father Bachelot from Honolulu on November 17, 1837, to a haven where he could recover his strength.

Once at sea, however, it soon became obvious that Father Bachelot would not survive the voyage. Delirious with fever, the priest-founder of the Hawaiian mission died slowly as the ship sailed away from the islands, succumbing on the morning of December 5. Father Maigret had to persuade the crew of the *Notre Dame de Paix* not to throw Father Bachelot's body overboard after he died. Instead, he had the ship anchor at a small island where he buried his priest companion and built a small memorial. Father Maigret then sailed to the island of Na, where the chief of Metalanim, the eastern district of Ponape, gave him hospitable welcome. He remained there until July 29, when the *Notre Dame de Paix* returned for him and set sail for Valparaiso.

Father Bachelot's sufferings had not been in vain, however, as his death marked a turning point in the affairs of the mission in Hawaii. His expulsion again took on international importance as various foreign representatives informed their own governments about the punishment meted out to him as a result of American influences. Other diplomatic outrages would follow, all of which became the talk of the European courts. The reports were carried on the ships that plied the oceans of the world, and the authorities of the French king in Paris were given details about the judgments of the Hawaiians.

King Kamehameha III issued "An Ordinance Rejecting the Catholic Religion" on December 18, 1837, just thirteen days after Father Bachelot's death. The document attacked the "peculiarities" of the Catholic religion and reviled the priests of the Sacred Hearts. The ban against Catholicism, issued by the monarch from Lahaina, Maui, included a provision that anyone caught teaching papal dogmas should be detained, banished and fined for insulting the Hawaiian chiefs. The lack of diplomatic awareness, the insanity of assaulting the religion of other nations, and the threats against foreigners and their representatives appear remarkably naïve, even for that era in the islands. Kamehameha III added another insult to his international population by declaring Congregationalism, an American Protestant denomination, the official religion of Hawaii. Restrictions on Sabbath labor, smoking, and drinking followed swiftly. At the same time, Hawaiians who had become Catholics were subjected to imprisonment and torture.

Many in the islands were infuriated by the king's proclamations and rumors swept through Honolulu, as the experienced foreigners and islanders understood that such reckless proclamations seldom stand unchallenged. The people of Hawaii, particularly the diplomatic representatives, waited for the first response from those insulted in the process.

On the morning of July 9, 1839, a French frigate, *l'Artémise*, commanded by Captain Cyrille-Pierre Theodore LaPlace, appeared in Honolulu harbor, glistening in the sunlight with a stunning intensity. Other French warships had docked in the islands, some with demands for reparations, others merely announcing the presence of the French in the Pacific region. The island newspapers wrote articles about the arrival of the vessel, and people went to the docks to look at the symbol of French military power. Some foreign residents, including diplomatic personnel, wrote to Captain LaPlace, asking to borrow weapons in case conditions worsened in the city as a result of the ship's presence. They also inquired as to the captain's actual intentions, as this was obviously not a courtesy call, not with that many guns, visible and aimed at Honolulu.

The diplomats and others soon discovered that the *l'Artémise* had sailed from Tahiti with a message from "His Most Catholic Majesty of France," King Louis Philippe, to the authorities of Hawaii. The message was simple enough, yet carrying a tremendous threat for the island and for the American presence as well. Kamehameha III had been ill-advised in his declaration of intolerance and the subsequent abuse of Hawaiian citizens and foreign residents. Those who had counseled such a move were obviously ignorant in matters concerning human rights, international relations, and the time-honored laws governing the exchange of ambassadorial legations. Foreign dignitaries had warned Kamehameha III that such bias against "Romanism" would not go unpunished, and their dire predictions would be proven accurate. Captain LaPlace made that obvious when he declared:

> His majesty, the King of the French, having commanded me to come to Honolulu in order to put an end either by force or by persuasion to the ill-treatment of which the French are victims at the Sandwich Islands, I hasten first to employ the latter means as being more in harmony with the noble and liberal political system pursued by France towards weaker nations, hoping that I shall thus make the king and the principal chiefs of these islands understand how fatal to their interests the conduct is which

they pursue towards her, and which may cause disasters to themselves and their country should they persist in it.

Misled by perfidious counsels, deceived by the excessive indulgence of which my country has given evidence in their favor for several years, they doubtless do not know how powerful France is, and that there is no power in the world which is capable of preventing it from punishing its enemies; otherwise they would have endeavored to merit its good will, instead of displeasing it as they have done by ill treating the French; they would have faithfully kept the treaties instead of violating them, as soon as the fear whereby bad intentions had been constrained, had disappeared with the man-of-war which had caused it; in fine, they would have understood that persecuting the Catholic religion, tarnishing it with the name of idolatry, and expelling, under absurd pretext, the French from this archipelago, was to offer an insult to France and its sovereign.

It is without doubt the formal intention of France, that the king of the Sandwich Islands be powerful, independent of every foreign power, and that he consider her his ally; but she also demands that he conform to usages established by civilized nations. Now among the latter there is not one that does not permit in its territory the free exercise of all religions; and, however, in the Sandwich Islands the Catholics are not allowed to exercise theirs publicly, whilst the Methodists enjoy there the most extended privileges; for the latter all favors, for the former nothing but the most cruel persecutions. Such a state of affairs being contrary to international law, insulting to Catholic nations, cannot last any longer and I am sent to put an end to it. Consequently, I demand in the name of my Sovereign:

1. That the Catholic worship be declared free throughout the islands which are subject to the king of the Sandwich Islands. The members of this communion shall enjoy there all the privileges granted to Protestants.

2. That a site for a Catholic church be given by the government at Honolulu, a port frequented by the French, and that this church be ministered by priests of their nationality.

3. That all Catholics imprisoned on account of religion since the last persecutions inflicted upon the Catholic missionaries be at once set at liberty.

4. That the king of the Sandwich Islands deposit in the hands of the captain of *l'Artémise* the sum of twenty thousand dollars as a guarantee of his future conduct towards France, which sum will be restored to him by the government of that country as soon as it shall judge that the clauses of the accompanying treaty shall have been faithfully executed.

5. Finally that the treaty signed by the king of the Sandwich Islands, as well as the sum mentioned above, be conveyed on board *l'Artémise* by one of the principal chiefs of the country, whilst the batteries of Honolulu do salute the French flag with twenty-one guns, which will be returned by the frigate.

These are the equitable conditions, at the price of which the king of the Sandwich Islands will conserve the friendship of France. I am pleased to believe that understanding how necessary to the conservation of his people it is to be at peace with the queen of Tahiti, who has granted the free exercise of the Catholic religion in her possessions. But, if contrary to my expectations, it should be otherwise; if the king and his principal chiefs of the Sandwich Islands, misled by bad advice, should refuse to sign the treaty which

I present, war would immediately commence, and all the devastations, all the calamities which will be the unhappy but inevitable consequences, will be imputed to themselves alone; also they will have to pay the damages which the foreigners, injured under these circumstances, will have a right to claim.

Honolulu, July the 10th (for the 9th), 1839.
The naval captain commanding the French frigate
l'Artémise.
LaPlace

—LaPlace's *Circumnavigation*, vol. V, p. 531ff.

LaPlace also notified the American consul that France held the Protestant Americans counseling Kamehameha III to be the "true authors of the insults" to France, men who would have to suffer "the unhappy consequences of a war which they shall have brought upon this country." Such a notice, of course, had dreadful ramifications that would reach all the way to Washington, D.C. The United States government did not need a process that could escalate into a war with France.

The king, having been brought to Oahu from Maui, turned to his American advisors for assistance and to other foreign residents who believed that a donation was highly advisable in order to divert a disaster. Kamehameha III was thus able to deliver the sum of twenty thousand dollars to LaPlace, as a guarantee to the French government. He also issued the required proclamation decreeing religious freedom to everyone in the islands. LaPlace, who requested and received an audience with the ruler, was perhaps not convinced that the Hawaiians would honor a manifesto after the French warship had departed, and demanded that a Catholic Mass be celebrated publicly, as a gesture of true reconciliation and a return to international diplomatic standards.

It was necessary, he added, for appropriate government officials to be visible at the services. The Mass was celebrated, and a new era of Catholicism began in Hawaii.

The United States Congress and other agencies conducted a series of protests and negotiations with France, defending the activities of the Americans in the islands for as long as possible. The obvious military presence of France in the Pacific area dampened the American enthusiasm for turning the incident into a full-blown confrontation with a European superpower, however, and the matter faded from public view.

Chapter Two

Jef De Veuster

WHILE THE TRAGEDY OF the expulsion of the Sacred Hearts priests from their beloved Hawaii was taking place in the Pacific region, in Tremelo, Belgium, the family of Francis and Ann Catherine de Veuster farmed its lands and adjusted the daily routines to the seasonal processions of the earth. These were a sturdy country-folk, who understood the patience and steely courage that men and women had to bring to the tending of fields and orchards. They were devout Catholics who demonstrated the close connection between the dignity of human beings with honest labor and loyalty, and rejoiced in the harvests and in the bounties of the crops and fruits. The de Veusters were not unique in their Catholicism or in their steadfastness to the faith in their region of Belgium, as their relatives and neighbors were permeated with the same spiritual ideals and with the solid traditions that had evolved over the centuries.

A son, the next to the last child, was born to Francis and Ann Catherine (née Wauters) de Veuster on January 3, 1840, and he was baptized Joseph on the day of his birth. The other children in the de Veuster family were Eugénie, Pauline, Léonce, Gerard, Constantia, August (known today as Pamphile), and Maria. They were raised in comparative comfort, descendants of the resilient Flemish of the area, and they understood the world in which they lived and the faith that had been given to them as their everlasting heritage. Joseph was soon called "Jef" by the family, and he and his brothers and sisters grew up with Catholic teachings and images surrounding them in their normal routines. The doctrines of the Church served as signposts for the entire family, and the saints stood as symbols of dedication and right living. This Catholicism permeated the red brick home, which adjoined a barn on the property. The de Veusters prospered from their livelihood, which was the raising and selling of grain. Frans, as the father was called, conducted business in Tremelo, Louvain, Antwerp, Malines, and Brussels.

While Jef was growing up, several things happened that would alter his life and his outlook on eternal values. When he was only five years old, his sister Eugénie took her vows at the Ursuline convent. Six years later, she died there in an epidemic of typhus. Pauline went to the Ursuline convent to take her sister's place. Among the de Veusters, vocations to the religious life flowered as a result of their mother's teachings. She read to her children often from a book about the martyrs and saints of the past. Also, in that age, religious vocations were considered normal acts of generosity, not unusual sacrifices.

Jef was a normal boy growing up in his hometown. He received tender nicknames from his neighbors, such as "The Little Shepherd," because of his way with sheep and other farm animals. He was often called "Silent Joseph" because of his tendency to be somewhat reticent about expressing his opinions and because he appreciated moments of quiet and solitude, natural elements in the lives of shepherds. In every other way, however, he was very typical for his age, getting into all kinds of mischief and being the victim of childhood accidents, such as falling into the icy river, instead of skating upon it. Showing the stamina and the rugged determination that later became hallmarks of his personality, Jef de Veuster used his skate to cut away enough ice so he could make his way back to a solid piece that would hold his weight and allow him to climb to safety. He did this unaided, demonstrating signs of the tenacity and ferocious vigor that would later help him to carry out his appointed mission in life.

Jef was butted by sheep in the barnyards and chased by dogs and a runaway cart, yet his general good humor prevailed in all of these escapades and misadventures. His physical fitness and stolid strength kept him on his feet even in the face of small disasters. This does not mean that he was complacent. For example, while studying for a short time in a school outside his home district, Jef was teased by his classmates, and he quickly struck out with a ruler to silence his tormentors.

At the age of ten, Jef de Veuster made his First Communion at Tremelo, on Palm Sunday. At thirteen, he left school and started working full-time on the farm with his father and brothers. The family members remarked at the time that he was so strong he could lift one-hundred-kilo bags of grain as if they were nothing. His father decided to introduce Jef to the world of business affairs because he showed aptitude and a shrewd sense of management. He enrolled him in a school and started to teach him the ways of conducting the various aspects of the farm and granary. Jef, who had been greatly moved by a sermon at a retreat given by the Redemptorist Fathers, discussed what he felt was a call to the monastic life, but his father put the matter aside. Frans did not rule out the possibility of a religious vocation for Jef. He simply asked his son to wait before he made a decision, so that the experiences of life and the natural order of things could work their own charms on him. He did not intend to stand in the way, but he did insist that Jef understand what was involved in such a decision. Obedient, Jef waited until Christmas Day, 1858, when he announced:

> Don't think this idea of entering the religious Life is my idea! It's Providence, I tell you, that is inspiring me. Don't put any obstacles in my way.

God is calling me. I must obey. If I refuse I run the risk of going to hell. As for you, God will punish you terribly for standing in the way of His will.

The family yielded to his announcement, and one month later, he was taken to Louvain to see his brother August, who had entered the Congregation of the Sacred Hearts Fathers and was now known as Pamphile in the religious life. Jef was accepted as a postulant in the community as the result of his brother's intercession, not because he appeared as a stellar candidate. Actually, the Congregation of the Sacred Hearts Fathers was not particularly enthusiastic about Jef's application to become one of them. They approved his entrance only after weeks of hesitation. Many did not think him fit for the priesthood, and some even had reservations about allowing him into the monastery in any capacity. This was not a superficial judgment on the part of the seminary directors. Jef did not appear to be the sort of young man that they were looking for at the time. They were joined by others with the same opinion as well. A record in the American College of the Louvain stated that a young man, Jef, who was obviously an ignorant Flemish boy, had applied for admission to the American College because he had a strong desire to go to the missions in America.

He was refused because of he seemingly lacked polish in manner and appearance, and because of his obvious lack of education in Latin or in any other language. The Sacred Hearts Fathers did not refuse him, and he was allowed into the monastery to be trained for the position of choir brother. His duties were limited to cleaning, servicing the chapel areas, acting as an infirmarian (nurse) to the sick and the elderly, and working as a secretary to one of the priests. The role of choir brother was an honorable vocation, dating to the earliest eras of the monastic life in the Church. For Jef de Veuster, however, it was not appropriate.

The decision to train him in this choir-brother category was not reached lightly. The priests in charge of the seminary and educational courses of the community had to determine the fitness of all applicants and their aptitudes for the various functions of religious life. The young de Veuster, untried, rough but eager, did not demonstrate the sort of intellectual ability or educational background to make candidacy for the priesthood possible.

Jef put up no argument about his designation within the monastic community. He went about his training sessions with his normal good humor and accepted every assignment with good grace. It appears, however, as if the young man had something else on his mind. It began as a game between him and his brother Pamphile. They lived under the same roof and were allowed to talk together in the course of their daily routines. Jef asked his brother if they could translate Latin as a form of recreation. Pamphile, a scholarly sort of man, was happy to oblige him. Within days, however, Pamphile realized that Jef was no sluggard. There was evidence of a quick mind at work during their recreation. Jef was learning Latin at an astonishing rate.

When Pamphile discussed this with the seminary superiors pointing out the studies and the rapid level at which his brother was mastering the language, they decided to allow him to assume candidacy for the priesthood. Jef entered the novitiate, which was designed to train such young men. A normal novitiate, which was considered a time of probation on both sides, lasted eighteen months. In Jef's case, an additional two months were added so that everyone would be satisfied as to his suitability.

The changes that took place in Jef as a result were obvious to the staff and students of the seminary. He also had displayed a great intuition and a sense of initiative from the start. Jef seemed to possess a turn of mind that tackled problems in ways that differed from those around him but proved successful. He worked hard to overcome his rough-and-tumble ways, and to curb his brash manner of expressing himself — in other words, becoming somewhat cultured and polished as he dealt with others. Jef also set about adopting a spirit of quietude and calm at all times, actually a renewal of his manner in his youth, the one that had earned him the nickname "Silent Joseph" from his neighbors. He carved the words "silence, recollection and prayer" into his desk in order to remind himself of his spiritual goals each day. That desk is now on display in the museum at Tremelo.

He also had studies at the Louvain as part of his priestly formation program and during this period demonstrated an element of his vocation that was not yet recognized by most of his contemporaries. During his studies, Jef displayed a capacity and a flair for learning. One of his professors, astute in discerning the hearts and spirits of his students, commented about him: "Rare as his ability to work, he did not study for the pleasure of studying nor to become a professor. He was studying to become an apostle."

According to Jef's contemporaries, his favorite seminary assignment was night prayer. The Sacred Hearts Fathers began this primary devotion as part of their spirit of atonement and reparation for the sufferings and blasphemies inflicted in the world. It had been instituted by Father Coudrin in the earliest days of the congregation. In each monastic house, all members of the congregation had to take their turn in keeping vigil before the altar.

Because of his robust health, and his ability to sleep easily and soundly, the young novice drew the hour from 2:00 to 3:00 A.M. in the chapel. His companions soon discovered that he did not need to return to his bed after that hour of vigil, apparently having slept long enough before taking his turn in the tradition of Perpetual Adoration. Silence and the natural stillness in the hours before dawn had been part of his life on the farm, and it would become the same in the tropical paradise of the Hawaiian Islands.

It was also a daily period in which he and his fellow religious could think about the loss of the *Marie-Joseph* at sea and the changes taking place in their Pacific missions. The disaster, reported to the congregation when it was confirmed, had brought about a great deal of anguish over the loss of Sacred Hearts men and women. Many of his companions spent long periods of each day trying to understand the will of God in this tragedy, and Jef was not alone in his meditations about the event.

On October 7, 1860, Joseph de Veuster went to the motherhouse of the congregation on the Rue du Picpus in Paris, where he made his vows. He was given his religious title and the name Damien, although no one present at the ceremony had any inkling of what that name would come to represent in the days ahead. Damien remained at the motherhouse for the last period of training before ordination. There his companions called him *"Mon gros Damien"* ("My big Damien"), an obvious reference to his sturdy and robust frame. One of his superiors during that time later testified that Damien was quite unique in the novitiate. He said that while the other young candidates for the priesthood ran around in a constant state of confusion, Damien seemed blessed with an innate understanding of what was expected of him. He worked easily, with a basic enthusiasm that kept him going. He also used his persistent drive and energy to make up for lost time and for his lack of appropriate academic training.

Actually, what appears to have sustained him throughout this period of his life was a marvelous awareness of the presence of God in his daily affairs. It is an experience uncommon in the modern world, and yet one that his family had shared as an inheritance of their way of life. Damien was capable of seeing existence as having an intrinsic value, something to be expended in sacrifice and in the service of others with needs.

During his seminary days, he demonstrated an eager embrace of life and its obligations; but at the same time, he was characterized by a certain modesty, which won over many of his contemporaries and superiors. Damien felt humbled in the presence of more learned or more spiritualized human beings, among whom he ranked his brother, Pamphile. He was still independent by nature, however, and he could manage to do the tasks assigned to him without asking for advice. Actually, he was a born seminarian. The rules, regulations, and daily schedules pleased him and filled him with calm, perhaps because it mirrored the sustaining and renewing earth-bound routines of his farming days. Damien became more and more delighted with his religious vocation as the weeks passed, and others noticed the signs of his joy.

Part of this was the result of spiritual growth, fostered by the daily training, the hours of vigil, the silence, and the monastic routines. A good portion of his sense of well-being, however, was centered in his good health and in his natural enthusiasm for living. Damien was reported as being able to outwalk, outrun, and outwork everyone in the seminary. He is also recorded as having been five foot eight and one-half inches tall, weighing approximately one hundred seventy pounds, all of it muscle. He glowed with vitality, enthusiasm, and robust health; so much so, some of his classmates claimed, that they could actually feel his presence.

One aspect of his monastic life that did not escape notice was his continual practice of mortification. It was not something that he paraded in front of the others. His brother Pamphile, who shared a room with him after a time, testified that during most nights Damien slept on the floor, wrapped only in a thin blanket. Thus, through the daily customs and routines of the monastery, Jef, the boy, disappeared as Damien put aside his former ways and grew in the spirit of his religious life. The ceremonies of profession conducted at the congregation's motherhouse included the act of prostrating oneself, covered by a black pall, before the altar of God. This signified the oblation that each priest made, in dying to the world of men and to his own natural desires. Damien spoke of that ceremony in later years when his oblation had taken a very startling and significant turn, etched out in his flesh and in his soul.

Damien made his vows and took up residence to complete his training for the priesthood, but Providence intervened to alter his place of abode, his activities, and his interior life. The symbol of change came in the form of a letter from Hawaii, pleading with the congregation to send priests to the mission there because of the recent tragedy. The motherhouse superiors considered the needs and decided to provide six of their members to sail across the world to the Sandwich Islands. Among the priests chosen was Pamphile, Damien's brother.

Passage was booked for Pamphile, his priest companions, and ten Sisters of the Sacred Hearts. All of them probably recalled the fateful *Marie-Joseph* and yet dared to set out with the same enthusiasm that had served Bishop Rouchouze and his missing associates. Pamphile, however, was stricken with typhus before he could start his journey. He was not mortally afflicted by the disease, but it was apparent to everyone in the motherhouse that he would be unable to sail with the others chosen for the mission. Damien, recalling the death of his sister Eugénie in the Ursuline convent and how one of his other sisters, Pauline, had taken her place then, was convinced that God was asking him to make the same sacrifice in the face of Pamphile's illness.

He wrote a letter to the father general of the Sacred Hearts Congregation, proposing to do just that. Thrifty like his Flemish ancestors, Damien added that his going to the missions in the place of Pamphile would avoid the waste of his ticket price, money that was seldom refunded in those days. To the surprise of everyone, the father general decided that this sort of generosity and common sense should be rewarded. Damien was appointed to the mission team. He did not receive the news immediately.

His seminary superior came to him one day and remonstrated with him that he was too young and too reckless, attributes that would one day bring about his ultimate disaster. The lecture served as a foreword to the announcement that Damien had been chosen for the islands.

For his family at Tremelo, the news was a terrible blow. They had common sense enough to know that they would never see Damien again. Religious did not travel home from the far-flung missions and did not visit Belgium or France often. The distance involved, as well as the slowness and expense of the passage, eliminated that possibility. When Damien was given a brief leave of absence to make his farewells at home, everyone involved felt that this would be the last time they would see the Hawaii-bound missionary. An unusually touching farewell took place between Damien and his mother. They met in the shrine of Our Lady of Monatagi, in the company of another relative. It appears that the mother and son spent most of their reunion in silence. It was not the awkward, graceless absence of words that typify anger or resentment. These were two human beings who had shared decades of faith, resolve, and care. Few words are needed to bridge such souls.

CHAPTER THREE

Damien Arrives in Hawaii

THE MISSION AWAITING DAMIEN in Hawaii had been visited by a tragedy but was slowly being transformed into a remarkable family of the faith. Almost immediately after the visit of Captain Cyril P.T. LaPlace and the liberation of Catholics in the islands, Bishop Jérome Stephen Rouchouze, SS.CC., the vicar apostolic for Eastern Oceania, arrived in Honolulu with three more Sacred Hearts priests. This handsome and charming prelate was met by an estimated three hundred Catholics at the harbor, and all of them rejoiced at the new beginning. A seasoned missionary and vicar, Bishop Rouchouze instituted many practices and regulations governing the growth of the Church in the islands. The mission was emerging from its precarious infancy and was prepared to take its place in Hawaiian society.

Understanding the need for the presence of the Sacred Hearts Sisters (a congregation of women started by Father Coudrin and the Countess Henriette de la Chevalerie), Bishop Rouchouze decided to return to Europe to recruit such women religious. He left Hawaii in January 1841, traveling to the various congregational houses in Europe and recruiting for the missions with considerable success. In the latter part of 1842, ten Sisters of the Sacred Hearts joined seven priests and seven lay brothers of the congregation on board the brig *Marie-Joseph*, bound for Hawaii. Captain Eugene Sullivan, a man familiar with the Hawaiian waters, was in command of the vessel. Letters were sent ahead on traveling ships so that the Catholics in Honolulu could prepare for this new contingent of missionaries. The local Catholic population looked forward to the educational work the sisters would assume, and began to build accommodations and new facilities for the sisters' efforts.

The joy and anticipation paled, however, when it was realized that the *Marie-Joseph* was overdue. The authorities and friends of the mission began to question other ships' crews and captains when they arrived, seeking some news of the vessel. The captains of these ships could only repeat what they had heard. The *Marie-Joseph* had been sighted off the coast of Brazil. A twenty-four-year-old Sacred Hearts sister, Calliste Le Gris, died on January 20, 1843. Captain Sullivan landed at São Miguel, Brazil, and there another passenger, a lad from Mangareva, took ill and was hospitalized. The ship's master waited until the young man died, then set sail for Chile. The *Marie-Joseph* was seen by a passing vessel only one time after that, on March 13, 1843, in a storm-tossed sea, nearing Cape Horn. In those days, word of events and sightings were called from ship to ship as the vessels crossed the vast oceans, serving as the only reliable sources of information available. Tales of disaster, massacre, captivity, and even death at the hands of cannibal tribes circulated about the Sacred Hearts disaster, as word spread across the sea lanes, but no one had any definitive facts. The *Marie-Joseph* and her precious cargo vanished, never to be seen again.

When the disappearance of the vessel was confirmed by the passage of time, the need for a new vicar apostolic was recognized by the mission and by Rome. The post was offered to another Sacred Hearts priest, who refused it. Then, Father Louis Desiré Maigret was named vicar apostolic of the Sandwich Islands and titular bishop of Arathia. *Lui Ka Epikopo* ("Louis the Bishop") had come to lead the Church in Hawaii, being consecrated on October 30, 1847.

Lui Ka Epikopo, a pivotal figure in the life of Father Damien, was a remarkable man quite overlooked by history and yet always visible in the events affecting the Hawaiian mission. Then-Father Maigret was in Honolulu when the island's Catholic community waited day after day for some word of the ill-fated *Marie-Joseph*. He had come with Bishop Rouchouze and served as the administrator of the mission in the bishop's absence. Offered the post of vicar apostolic of the Sandwich Islands, he accepted the role with the same spirit that he demonstrated when he took Father Bachelot away from Protestant bigotry and persecution a decade before.

Bishop Maigret was a true wanderer for Christ, crossing the oceans of the world in search of souls. He was of a nature that endured the endless hours of voyaging and the demands of accepting foreign customs and exotic and strange domains in remote parts of the earth. During voyages, he translated the classic *Imitation of Christ* into Hawaiian, as well as a booklet describing the role of a bishop, so that the islanders would understand his decisions and instructions. Bishop Maigret was also an administrator with a perspective that allowed him to function calmly in the day-to-day confrontations and stresses of missionary life. An unsung pioneer in the Sacred Hearts Pacific mission territories, Bishop Maigret was said by those who knew him to be a brilliant scholar of a philosophical turn of mind, with a background and training in the fields of philosophy and the classics. This particular point of view made him a rather formidable figure among the boisterous Americans who had started flooding into the islands.

Lui Ka Epikopo was born Louis Desiré Maigret in Mailee, Poitou, France, in 1804. He entered the Sacred Hearts Congregation and studied at the seminary in Poitiers. Transferred to Paris, he completed his academic requirements and was ordained to the priesthood in 1829. The Sacred Hearts superiors recognized his scholarly abilities and his intellect and assigned him the position of philosophy professor, a post that he held for five years at the seminary of Rouen, France. His religious career seemed set as he assumed this role in training future priests of the congregation. He possessed a keen grasp of ancient and modern philosophies and ideologies that impacted on the faith, and he was a good teacher who was able to interest his students in the esoteric concerns of human thought.

In 1834, however, Father Maigret was asked to accompany Bishop Jérome Stephen Rouchouze to the Gambier Islands, where they labored together in the Sacred Hearts mission. Three years later, he sailed to Hawaii and performed the sorrowful task of caring for the mortally ill Father Bachelot in exile. He was the one on hand when the *Marie-Joseph* was declared lost, the one chosen to lead the Church in Hawaii, and the one — as bishop — destined to serve as mentor to Damien de Veuster.

Accepting the position of leadership, Father Maigret sailed to Santiago, Chile, where he was consecrated on the last day of October 1847 by Bishop Hilarion Itura of Augustopolis at Santiago. He thus became the vicar apostolic of Hawaii, still called the Sandwich Islands, and titular bishop of Arathia. Bishop Maigret returned to Hawaii a month later, landing in Honolulu on February 1, 1848. There he built the Catholic community in the face of bigotry (both open and subtle), countering the efforts of the Americans, who labeled the faith as something "foreign" to the islands. The American Protestant groups were solidly entrenched in Honolulu, but their position was put to the test when the Anglicans and the Mormons arrived on the scene. The Anglicans were linked to Hawaii through Britain's dominance, as even King Kamehameha I had incorporated the British Union Jack symbol into his flag. The Mormons, coming from Salt Lake City, Utah, may have lacked diplomatic support, but the ten Mormon elders who arrived in December of 1850 began work instantly in the four major islands. After initial setbacks, these Mormons claimed a large number of converts.

Watching the efforts of these separate denominations, Bishop Maigret decided that the Church had to assume a more vigorous role, using whatever modern innovations were available. He brought a printing press and began to issue pamphlets explaining the teachings of Catholicism. An astonishing two thousand such pamphlets were produced in the first run. Soon after, he bought a bigger press from France, at a cost of two thousand dollars. It was necessary to defend the Church in Hawaii, where rival groups spread rumors about Catholic ceremonies or the Church's clergy. The bishop also started a newspaper in the mission. The *Hae Kiritiatio* (or *The Christian Standard*) appeared in 1860, followed by the short-lived *Ka Hae Katolika* (*The Catholic Standard*). These newspapers rallied the faithful in special causes, kept them up to date on local and international religious affairs, and served as a weekly bulletin on Catholic services and observances. Actually, in this particular era, the Sacred Hearts priests won many admirers in the islands. They were a no-nonsense breed of men who did not concern themselves with politics or with social affairs. Several dignitaries of the time, non-Catholics, stated that the priests had only one priority: the care of those entrusted to them.

Bishop Maigret could not depend upon such praise, however, because the attacks on Catholicism were frequent and sometimes venomous. He had another weapon at hand, however, and he made free use of it when the occasion demanded such a response. It is estimated that Bishop Maigret had forty hardworking missionary priests and from thirteen thousand to over thirty thousand Catholic laymen and laywomen in his care. His weapon in their defense was the European diplomatic corps stationed in Honolulu. Such men — from France, Spain, and other older nations — well understood the American Protestant influences. They watched the Americans amassing power and land and saw clearly that the Catholic Church was an enemy of such individuals.

These diplomats moved swiftly whenever Bishop Maigret enlisted their aid. As was the case from the first days of the Hawaiian encounter with the legations of the European powers, the experienced diplomats, veterans of posts around the world, did not hesitate to inform the Hawaiian authorities when injustice and bigotry had crossed established diplomatic lines. It was one thing, they believed, to favor a particular nationality or religious persuasion but quite another to allow unfairness to interfere with the proper functions of a governmental agency.

The delays and pressures that arose whenever Catholics dealt with the Hawaiian authorities prompted visits from the European dignitaries, including the representatives of Britain on occasion; these delays and other problems disappeared almost miraculously following such visits. The memory of the French warship *l'Artémise* floated on the waters lapping the shores of Honolulu, a dire reminder of diplomatic requirements and the circumspection required when dealing with Catholics. The readiness of France and the other European nations to defend the faith with military responses slowed the pace of the bigots and the zealous Americans.

Bishop Maigret had to use whatever defenses were available, because the Church was expanding throughout the islands. He consecrated new parishes and worked to expand charitable and educational programs. The Sacred Hearts Fathers were innovative in putting up their new parish structures, actually pioneering construction techniques that were required by the geographic realities of island life. Churches and halls made of wood were built and then dismantled in Honolulu. Placed on heavy barges, these prefabricated buildings were sent to the Outer Islands (the name used for all of the islands other than Oahu) and then assembled at minimal cost. Bishop Maigret and the Sacred Hearts Fathers had also brought the sisters of their congregation to Hawaii to open schools, the first being one on Fort Street, and to provide Catholic education for the communities. There was a serious dispute over the schools, and delaying tactics were used by the opposition.

On March 19, 1864, the seminarian, Damien de Veuster, arrived in Honolulu.

Having taken leave of his family tearfully but without regret, he had joined his companions on the Paris-Cologne-Hamburg Express on October 20, 1863, to begin a twenty-nine-hour journey to Bremerhaven. There the company boarded the *R.M. Wood*, a vessel that flew the Hawaiian ensign (the red, white, and blue flag of the island kingdom).

The sea voyage from Europe to Hawaii lasted four and one-half months, giving all on board time for serious meditation, or hours of seasickness. The fare on board was corned beef and beans, which added considerably to the passengers' discomfort and nausea. The cost of the trip was one thousand gold francs, considered reasonable at the time. The captain and the crew of the ship, all Protestants, made every effort to accommodate their religious passengers. Damien, it appears, tried to convert them, with no success. He settled into the daily routine in the course of time: Mass, prayers, meditations, and conversations, all capable of enlightening the spirit during the days of slow passage on the sea. He was glimpsing the world, of course, and he must have spent hours on deck, gaping at the lush and exotic landscapes passing into view and at the parade of seabirds and other sea creatures accompanying the ship on its voyage. His companions did not fare well throughout the journey. Damien is supposed to have mentioned that one of the priests, the one appointed the temporary superior of the group, kept losing his meals and choking, until the others expected him to burst open and collapse on the deck.

Christmas was celebrated on board the *R.M. Wood* while the three-masted merchant ship sailed south of the equator. The vessel also passed through the Strait of Magellan, and there the religious recited the prayers of the Office for the Dead in honor of the pioneering members of their congregation who had apparently perished in that area. Then the vessel entered into the Pacific Ocean, moving steadily toward Hawaii.

When the ship dropped anchor in Honolulu, Damien and his fellow passengers had spent one hundred forty-six days at sea. Damien later described his voyage in letters, stating that he had been forced to live at close quarters with heretics and unbelievers, who closed their ears to spiritual truths. He resolved, amid his complaints, to dedicate himself to the people waiting for him in Hawaii. The sheer exuberance and naïveté of his letters demonstrate that Damien was very much a product of his age and environment. His holy purpose, along with his shock in coming into contact with people who did not view Catholicism or Christianity as sacred, clearly demonstrates Damien's upbringing and the insulation that he had experienced as a child and as a young man.

The young seminarian was filled with zeal and enthusiasm, both attributes that could have paled in the light of reality in the rough-and-tumble mission field of the Hawaiian Islands. He was endowed with a genuine reverence for his religious creed, something that could have turned to prejudice or animosity in the face of future trials at the hands of others. The fact that Damien never lost his joyousness or his spirit of concern about other people's earthly and eternal destinies testifies to the strength of his convictions. He was not a callow child rushing to save souls at the expense of sensitivity and kindness. His journey across the sea had opened his eyes to the fact that Catholicism was not a universally accepted pathway to heaven among all of the people of earth. He would meet other people of differing creeds, and people with no beliefs at all, and he was ready.

Actually, when Damien and his companions landed in Honolulu in 1864, an astonishing one third of the native population of the islands was Catholic. The early Sacred Hearts missionaries had performed their ministry with extraordinary zeal, winning compliments from strangers and from rival clergymen. In 1864, Honolulu was not imbued with Catholic values, however; instead, the city boasted a polyglot society and the free-wheeling ways of an international port. Whalers, merchants, explorers, plantation owners, speculators, businessmen, farmers, sailors, adventurers, and bankers rubbed elbows with thieves, smugglers, gunrunners, prostitutes, and others living on the fringe of the law. Honolulu was a port for the world, where ships of every size and description landed and unloaded exotic cargoes.

If Damien was not given leisure time in which to walk the docks and promenades of Hawaii, he did gape in astonishment at the Cathedral of Our Lady of Peace, near the old fort where Fathers Bachelot and Short had faced Queen Kaahumanu and her governors. This Catholic cathedral, a French-style structure based on the design carried across the seas by Father Bachelot, still stands, and still welcomes worshipers and visitors. The stained-glass windows of the cathedral were also remarkable for their style and beauty. On small pedestals lining the upper reaches of the nave, statues of saints and martyrs were delicately carved and painted. Golden roses studded the ceiling, and intricate designs adorned the walls. On Damien's first day in the islands, a Mass was celebrated in the cathedral, and the rest of the day was spent in festivities honoring the arrival of this long-awaited missionary team. Describing his first days in Hawaii in letters to his family, Damien wrote that he was astonished at the beautiful Catholic cathedral. He was delighted by the food, by the lovely island music, and by his welcome. He added: "It would be impossible for me to tell you of the immense joy a missionary has ... to see his new country that he must water with his sweat to gain poor souls for God."

Following the welcoming ceremonies, Damien was sent to the College of Ahiumanu, situated in Heeia (now modern-day Kaneohe). The property bordered the bluffs of the mountains on the windward side of Oahu and measured some two hundred sixteen acres. The king had ceded the land to the Church for use as a college in 1845. At Ahiumanu, Damien began his last preparation for the priesthood, including the study of the Hawaiian language and the traditional prayers in the island tradition, such as the *Ave Maria*:

Aloha oe E Malia
Ua piha oe
I ka maikai
Ua noho puka
Haku me oe
Pomaikai oe iwaena
0 na wahine a pau
Pomaikai Iesu
Ke hua o kou opu.
Malia Saneta
Makauahine o ke akua
E pule aku oe
I ka haku no makou
No ka poe kina nui
I keia manawa
A I ko makou manawa
E make ai. Amene.

THE HAIL MARY IN HAWAIIAN

Bishop Maigret had probably been dismayed to discover that Damien had not been ordained when he arrived in Honolulu. The mission territories of the Church, particularly in the

Pacific and in the New World, demanded uniquely equipped men in every post. These missionaries had to possess common sense, initiative, balance, and the resource of interior graces if they were to survive in their distant and lonely stations. Time and distance isolated them. The needs of their own regions and people dictated the sacrifices they were called upon to make for the faith. Above all, they had to be men capable of making a mistake and learning from it. In other words, they had to be seasoned enough to risk failure in order to achieve the deeds of their own pastoral assignments. The bishop had to prepare Damien, and he provided the sort of counsel needed. On Easter Vigil of that year, Damien received ordination to the diaconate, and on May 21, 1864, Damien was ordained to the priesthood by Bishop Maigret.

Immediately after ordination, Damien was given his first pastoral assignment. He could not be offered the post of assistant to some veteran priest, even though such a position would have offered him invaluable training on the scene in the mission territories. The needs of the islanders were too pressing for that luxury, and the number of priests available never quite measured up to the demands. Bishop Maigret had to assign him to the most critical region, and he had to rely on Damien's good judgment and willingness to serve all who came to him. He started out with Father Damien and Father Clement Evrard (who had accompanied Damien and had been ordained with him in the cathedral), and together they boarded a steamer one June evening, sailing to the island of Maui, where they were given time the next morning to go ashore to celebrate Mass.

Three veteran missionaries were in residence there, and Damien was delighted to be able to talk to men who had been in the field. He mentioned in a later confidence that the ship's whistle calling the passengers back blew only minutes after the conclusion of the Mass. He had been truly hoping to have time to talk with the men and to hear of their experiences among the islanders. With his usual common sense, Damien understood the fact that all the purely theological training in the world would not prepare a young man for mission work. He had to learn from the veterans, if possible, and also from the slow and torturous process of trial and error.

Damien made his farewells sadly and then discovered that the bishop, he, and his other companion would not be taken away from the veteran missionaries. The steamer had caught on fire in the hold, and flames quickly spread to the hull, rendering the vessel unseaworthy. The trio was stranded on Maui and would have to wait for another ship to put into port. Bishop Maigret was dismayed because he had to be on the Big Island for the Feast of Saints Peter and Paul, but Damien was delighted with the prospect of being able to visit with the Sacred Hearts veteran priests.

Damien spent time with one of the veteran missionaries, Father Aubert, studying Hawaiian, which was called *Kanaka* in those days (the name also applied to the islanders). He received permission from Bishop Maigret to tour the countryside as well and went out to preach to the natives, believing that he was on the verge of becoming fluent in the language. He was not a gifted linguist, especially in Hawaiian, which he viewed as a comparatively simple tongue, unaware of the nuances and emotional shades that came to light in the renditions of the Hawaiians themselves. The islanders, as patient and kind as usual, showed appreciation for his efforts in preaching to them in their tongue. Returning to the residence of the veteran missionaries, Damien discovered that Bishop Maigret and Father Clement had hailed a passing steamer and had gone on to the Big Island of Hawaii without him. He spent a few more days touring Maui, with its beautiful plains and magnificent shoreline; and then he, too, found a ship and followed his companions back to the Big Island.

On Hawaii, Damien learned that the bishop had conducted the blessing ceremony and had traveled to the area that would be entrusted to Father Clement. Damien had to travel alone over the island to make his way there, only to find that Bishop Maigret had pushed on to Puna, which was to be Damien's district. It took Damien another three and one-half days to make his last journey, and he was able to visit with the bishop briefly before assuming his own pastoral duties.

The Big Island of Hawaii is four thousand square miles of rugged terrain, with active volcanoes, gullies, ridges, black sand beaches, vast plains, and tropical gardens. Damien's district, Puna, had three hundred fifty Catholics, who lived on land formed by Kilauea volcano.

The Church had started in Hawaii during the time of Father Walsh, but by 1840 only fifteen converts were on the island. Repressive measures had been taken there by the government and by missionaries of other faiths in order to halt the spread of Catholicism. Still, the early missionary pioneers persisted, and they left behind a remarkable tapestry of service and lifestyle.

These first priests had no money, no luxuries, and just the barest of necessities as they traveled across the island on horseback or on foot. Many of them had to go barefoot through the lava fields and over the rocky crags because they could not afford boots. They lived in grass huts and ate the same food that the natives consumed to sustain themselves. *Poi* (the paste made from the taro plant), fish, and fruits made up their diets. In some years, the priests even had to refrain from celebrating Mass every day: Their meager supply of wine had to be saved for special liturgical occasions.

In the course of time, the Catholic faith spread. When the government attempted more programs to curb the growth of Catholicism, the authorities found themselves in pitched battles with communities spoiling for confrontation. Catholics were ferocious about having the right to worship in the Church, and they believed strongly that no government agent could deny them that right. The Protestants stormed against the French priests in their sermons, but Catholicism moved steadily onward because of the missionaries. The simple lives of the first priests endeared them to the Hawaiians and gave them access into the individual grass huts and into the daily existence of the people.

Damien wrote letters to his family about the immensity of the Big Island and the district of Puna. He studied Kilauea during his rounds and believed that the volcano was the entrance to hell, or at least a startling image of the site of that eternal punishment. He was also finding out that all of his premonitions about the missionary life were true. Theology had little place in the day-to-day contact with the Hawaiians, unless the doctrines and the tenets could be translated into visual rituals or used to sustain a lifestyle that was capable of winning their admiration. He tried to make the Gospels and other teachings of the Church come alive through charity and personal goodness.

Silence was again a definitive part of his priestly life even in the mission. The Big Island pervaded his entire existence with silence, broken only by the sound of the surf, the call of the small birds, and the shrill cries of the great winged predators circling overhead. Silence was also broken by the wind on the crags, the rumble of the earth giving way to molten forces, and the complaints of his donkey as it carried him on the rough trails. He did not have to seek out penance or ascetical ways of service either. Usually alone as he made his rounds through his district, he was capsized in canoes, stranded on mountains, and caught in deep ravines and gullies.

By this time, he was called *Kamiano* by the Hawaiians, who translated his name into their own language. His soft Belgian accent at times mangled their tongue, but the accent also provided a rich undertone for his sermons and his admonitions. He told everyone that he experienced only kindness from the local Hawaiians, and he found them gentle and good. Damien, of course, brought a European attitude toward the islanders, which prompted him to feel like a father toward them in one moment and then to experience dismay when he saw them reverting to their traditional ways. Very quickly the missionaries learned not to press marriage upon the young, who appeared incapable of a lasting or committed relationship. Damien and the other Europeans of the time had brought their own judgments and values into an alien landscape. They viewed the lifestyle of the islanders as primitive and amoral in most cases, something that was not true, of course (not if placed within the context of island civilization and social patterns). The Hawaiians did not share the European views about the human body or sexual contact. They also did not have the Victorian attitudes that the Europeans of that era displayed in their contacts with the islanders and with one another — attitudes that were at times hypocritical and at best unrealistic in the face of foreign views.

Eight months after the two missionaries' original posting to the districts of Hawaii, Father Clement, somewhat frail, collapsed because of overwork. It was decided that he should exchange districts with Damien, who showed no ill effects from his labors and travels. Father Clement's district of Kohala-Hamakua covered almost one quarter of the island. It included the same rugged terrain but also the snow-clad heights of Mauna Loa and the Kohala Mountains. Damien spent six weeks wandering around the more than one thousand square miles given into his care. His letters home described his thatched hut, his life on horseback, and his affection for the Hawaiians and their customs, at times interspersing his feelings of dismay because of their behavior.

He began vast building projects, as he had in Puna, and built eight chapels with his own hands. The people worked at his side as he marched up into the mountains to cut down trees and then hauled them to the construction site. Others commented that the Hawaiians were constantly confounded by the sight of him coming over a ridge with a huge tree on his shoulder.

These were to be the happiest years of his missionary life. He wrote about his diet on one occasion, stating that "the calabash of poi is always full; there is also meat; water in quantity, coffee and bread sometimes, wine or beer never...."

He also began to experience the generous assistance of his people, who were wise to the bounties that nature calmly bestowed upon the islanders. Many came to help, but they also brought him the lore of their lifestyle. Bees gave honey for Damien's table, and they provided wax for the altar candles. He grew his own tobacco and made one advantageous profit from selling a single shipment of it. He began to raise pigs and chickens; he also grew coffee and potatoes. The potatoes ended up in Honolulu on one occasion when he sent them to his superior, asking that the money gained from their sale be given to the superior of the Sacred Hearts Sisters, "to settle a bill which I owe." Sheep were also added to his supply of livestock in the course of time. While farming was part of his nature, the roles of carpenter and construction engineer took most of his time. He became known as the chapel builder of the Big Island. Each church, of course, included a celebration, something the islanders used to break the monotony of their simple routines. He described one in a letter:

> As it is the custom of the country to give a big feast after bringing an important work to conclusion... my neophytes wanted to give one for their friends from the other districts, to match the hard work we did in building and finishing the church so well. Everyone was invited for the eve of the Epiphany. A good number of fat animals had

been killed and cooked in the kanaka oven, that is to say, in red-hot stones. At a signal the crowd goes to the church, which unhappily is too small to fit everyone in. After a short prayer, I give a sermon adapted to the occasion.... Sermon and prayers over, everyone goes to the place prepared for the feast, all around the church, on the grass.

Something like a thousand people are there to celebrate. At our kanaka, even the most civilized always eat with their fingers, no trouble about knives and forks and the rest of the table setting. Everyone brings his own with him. Just like the ancient Romans, they eat on the ground, legs crossed like tailors, a very economical way. No use for tables, chairs, seats.

Damien's tireless and efficient daily routines were perfecting in him the virtues recognized by Pope Paul VI, who announced: "In the endless variety of their manifestations, those who have emerged as saintly figures have but one characteristic in common: love in its purest essence. Love expresses itself in giving. Saints have not only given of themselves, but they have given of themselves in the service of God and their brethren.

"Father Damien is certainly in that category of an extraordinary man. He lived his life of love and dedication in the most heroic yet unassuming and self-effacing way. He lived for others: those whose needs were greatest...."

On Sundays, the people usually came to the chapel at the sound of a conch shell. The Mass was celebrated with hymns and songs, and then the people stopped for a meal. When that was ended, the conch shell was blown again, and the people gathered for the rosary and prayers. Thus, the islanders spent many hours in church activities on any given feast day or Sabbath. The Mass was not just a ritual but a gathering on the slopes of a tropical paradise.

Damien had to face the relentless rivalry among the religious faiths, even in his own district, but he seemed to take delight in measuring himself against his competitors. The priest, however, had his own method of confronting the Protestants who dared to challenge his pastoral role. On one occasion, learning that a local Protestant minister had scaled a two-thousand-foot cliff in Kohala in two hours, Damien raced up its side in forty-five minutes, astounding everyone and earning the respect of the onlookers.

He did not see other priests often, and he expressed his concern about the necessity of traveling one hundred fifty miles to make his confession. His letters concerning this aspect of the mission on the Big Island prompted his superior to provide him with an assistant at a later time. He saw Bishop Maigret only on rare occasions, since it was almost impossible for the prelate to administer the affairs of the mission territory while traveling from post to post. Damien did journey to Honolulu, but that was only about once every two years, necessitated by the business of ordering supplies for his region. He stayed frugal and thrifty. In 1869, he recorded that he had received $279, had spent $271, and had the grand total of $8 in savings.

On one occasion when Bishop Maigret did visit Hawaii, he was met by Damien, who led him across streams, mountains, and vast plains. The bishop wanted to bless the people at Damien's mission and then be on his way, but the islanders told him that this was impossible. Bishop Maigret had to wait at the mission until the runners could inform the neighboring communities about the festival. As people began to flock into the area, whole herds of pigs and even oxen were slain, and a celebration took place to honor the bishop's blessing of the new chapel.

The occasion was the source of great joy to the local Hawaiians, but for Damien this was also the opportunity to spend time with another priest, a veteran missionary who had lived his entire life ministering to the needs of souls in the Pacific. Above all, he was with the man who had ordained him to the priesthood, the one who had played such a strong role in the Church's history in Hawaii. These moments were precious for Damien, most so because the challenges and demands of the missionary life made them so rare.

In 1869, Damien was joined by a new priest on the Big Island. Father Gulstan Ropert arrived to take over the area of Hamakua, and Damien had a companion within reasonable distance. He found Father Gulstan to be a dedicated priest and a gentle man, with the background of Bretagne, France. Father Gulstan served on the Big Island until 1883 and in 1892 became the vicar apostolic of Hawaii, but only after Church officials chose to ignore his own humble appeals that someone else be named a bishop. Once in charge of the missions in Hawaii, he proved equally patient and gentle during a time of great upheaval in the islands, including the overthrow of the monarchy in 1893. As for Damien, he liked Father Gulstan and wished for a dozen more such priests, claiming that the Hawaiians had need of all of them.

In 1870, Damien became ill with a fever and wasted away quickly. In no time at all, however, he was back on his feet and again 173 pounds of energy and strength. Such illnesses were rare for him, and he thrived on the hard work and the daily grind of travel and service.

There were also many periods in which he suffered from depression on the Big Island. Damien was particularly repelled by demonstrations of lust or drunken behavior. He was dismayed by it, not because he had been raised in a vastly different environment but because he believed that such behavior diminished a human being's capacity for happiness and wholeness. He was lonely a good deal of the time, deprived of the priestly companions he had hoped to find in the mission. Spiritually, however, he was growing, experiencing the various aspects of the religious vocation in all their complexities.

The degree of the changes taking place within him became evident in his correspondence with his brother Pamphile. He had asked his local Hawaiian superior to write to the mother-house to allow Pamphile to join him in his mission territory. The motherhouse responded by sending Pamphile to the university to get his doctorate degree. This startled Damien, who had come to realize that the front line of the Church was the parish, especially the mission parish in far-flung regions of the world. He rashly believed that his brother shared his health, strength, and fitness for the hardships of mission life and wrote to him to complain about Pamphile's lack of courage in accepting the true role of the congregation, stating that he was shocked that Pamphile had not responded with eagerness, "and that another man had to go in your place, as I had done in 1863!"

This complaint from Damien was prompted by his consuming desire to bring the Catholic faith to the Hawaiians and by his lack of understanding that he was uniquely fit for such labors and Pamphile did not share his physical or mental qualities. He also did not understand that there are diverse pathways open to each human being in following Divine Providence in the choice of one's vocation. Pamphile was a scholar, a philosopher, and a teacher, not equipped for pioneering parishes in remote, exotic places. He was entirely inept at actual missionary work and incapable of sustaining the energy and physical drive needed by such a solitary ministerial worker. After Damien's death, Pamphile would volunteer to work in the islands but would have to give up the assignment and return to his academic labors. When Damien wrote his complaints, Pamphile did not defend himself, knowing that Damien did not comprehend the value of a scholarly vocation, but he naturally avoided too many more confrontations by mail.

Damien had never received many letters. There was no organized postal system or tested method by which mail could reach him. Like most missionaries in Hawaii, he checked into the various posts and ports and inquired if any letters had been left for him. He went for three years without any mail from home and then wrote Pamphile an apology. His entire contact with his family rested in the hands of Pamphile, because his parents, although literate, did not write to him. They and Damien relied upon Pamphile to convey messages and news of the family. In one letter, in fact, Pamphile wrote that Pauline, who was an Ursuline nun, was gravely ill and probably dying. Damien wrote to her immediately, pouring out his affection and emotions, not knowing if he was writing to a live person or a corpse. Pauline probably received the letter, because she lingered until the next year.

In the meantime, however, things were happening on the Big Island of Hawaii that took Damien's time and energies. The government, after years of repressive measures against parochial schools, finally assumed a neutral stance concerning educational facilities of the various religious denominations. Damien began to build schools and soon had the government providing assistance in order to train young women as teachers.

Then nature struck in Hawaii, in the form of an intense hurricane that destroyed the house and two of the chapels being used by Father Gulstan. Damien had to rebuild them all. The storm, however, proved to be less of a threat than the destructive force unleashed on the island during the previous year. There had been warnings as the earth shook and groaned beneath Damien's feet for weeks on end, culminating in a series of tremors that reached three hundred violent quakes in a given twenty-four-hour period. Then, the major cataclysm struck the southern portion of the island. Early one morning, the church bells started to ring, the trees swayed to one side and plummeted to the ground, and avalanches thundered down the mountainsides. Damien and his people clung to the earth as it rolled and groaned. Huge yawning gaps appeared, taking homes and people into the depths. At one point, the ground gushed forth with mud and stones, covering an area of five miles. No one could outrun that torrent of destruction, and islanders perished while their screams were carried in the wind.

A tidal wave, or *tsunami*, was spawned by the earthquake as well. The waters receded on the coast, gathering strength and power, and then crashed down on the shore. At an estimated height of thirty-five to forty feet, the crested wave dashed against a fishing village. Animals and humans, along with all of the humans' furnishings and possessions, were caught in a terrible vortex of power and destruction, and were carried out to sea. No one in the village survived the wave and its devastating assault. This was followed by a volcanic eruption, which took place only five days after the earthquake. Rivers and lakes of molten lava poured down from the volcano, as fires and rocks spewed out of its interior. Damien and his companions watched the rivers of flaming death snaking across the landscape while fires and smoke rose on the horizon. The priest had not been injured, but many of his people had perished, and almost all of his chapels and buildings had collapsed or disappeared under the waves and the lava. He set about rescuing those he could, feeding everyone, and then rebuilding the entire district again. There was another terror coming to the mission territory, however, one that dated to biblical times.

Just as many of the native people in North and South America proved susceptible to the common diseases of the Europeans who arrived in the New World, so too were the Hawaiians vulnerable to most of the diseases common to the *haoles,* the whites, including smallpox. The isolated location of Hawaii only added to the health risks, and while Damien served on the Big Island, islanders began to show symptoms of a new and alarming illness. It was a plague that would alter Damien's life forever: leprosy.

Chapter Four

"The Separating Sickness"

THE PLAGUE THAT STRUCK the Hawaiian people appeared quite unexpectedly. It is not known exactly when the disease came into the Hawaiian Islands, but in 1823, medical personnel recorded certain medical cases that signaled the presence of the ancient terror, leprosy, now called Hansen's disease. At that time the disease had been seen and only partially recognized. An epidemic of smallpox worked in conjunction with the disease, however, and some medical people believed that the leprosy was spread from arm to arm, person to person, in vaccinations. The strict sterilization practices of modern times were slow in coming to remote areas of medical concerns. The infection rate was listed as ten to fifteen percent by 1862, and local doctors were unable to stem the tide.

By 1862, a doctor at Queen's Hospital in Honolulu was treating patients actually diagnosed with the disease. He reported his findings to the government during the following year, asking that steps be taken immediately to isolate the patients discovered to have leprosy and to institute certain medical procedures for prevention, in the face of an apparent growing and tragic epidemic. His report, accompanied by a request for basic legislation on the matter, unleashed a wholesale panic in the *haole* community of the islands. These Caucasians responded to the doctor's announcement in much the same way that the biblical men and women reacted to the sound of a silver bell in the ravaged hand of a leper in their own historical period.

There are indications that leprosy was known in Egypt as early as 1350 b.c. but was definitely known by the start of the seventh century b.c. These cases were probably drawn from the foreign population of that nation at the time, and the victims were brought before the priest-physicians, who had earned great fame in the ancient world. Forensic studies on mummified remains from the Pharaonic period of Egypt do not provide any evidence of the presence of leprosy on the Nile in the ancient period, at least not among the native populations. A Hindu document dates the presence of leprosy in India well before the time of Christ, and certainly the Roman and Hebraic communities were well acquainted with the disease.

Leprosy was well-known in the Old and New Testament periods, as is evidenced by the many references in Scripture. While the name "leprosy" is used as a translation of the Hebrew, an exact translation for the word is not a medically precise one, for it is now generally recognized by scholars that what is seen as leprosy in the Bible refers not only to leprosy but to a wide variety of skin diseases or conditions as well as lesions or infections that might occur on the skin, fabrics, and even on walls of houses. Still, the fear of leprosy is apparent in the importance placed upon the cure of the disease by Christ (Mt 8:1-4; Mk 1:40-45; Lk 5:12-16; 17:11-19) and that Our Lord gave that power to the disciples (Mt 10:8). Moreover, the great compassion displayed by Christ toward the lepers — the outcasts of the ancient world in every sense — was an important model for Damien and all who were charged with the care of lepers in their own time.

The call for compassion was echoed by the Church during the Middle Ages when leprosy became a much feared disease. Such was the prevalence of the disease that leper hospitals, called *leprosaria*, were started across Christendom. The thirteenth century Benedictine monk and chronicler Matthew Paris put the number of leprosaria at nearly 20,000 — and they were places of both isolation and mercy.

The plight of lepers in Europe was truly terrible. The poor victims were cut off from the world and viewed as enduring a kind of living death. They were required when traveling to carry a bell and clapper to alert everyone of their approach, although the alarms also helped the compassionate to bring them food and words of concern. Since leprosy was known to be contagious even in the Middle Ages, ceremonies were instituted early on to put a certain grace on the policies of strict segregation. During this grotesque ritual, the victims of the disease were covered with black palls. A priest recited prayers over the lepers and then solemnly "buried" them, placing handfuls of dirt on their heads. While they were being thus ritually entombed, the priest instructed them on the fact that they were now considered dead to the world and could only hope for rebirth in Christ. In some regions, the victims were forced to climb down into yawning empty graves so that they understood the seriousness of the community's edict against them. The lepers were given instructions about where they could hope to reside, where and when they could beg from the healthy, etc., all the while being reassured that they would always be remembered in a kindly fashion by their friends and relatives. They had to absent themselves in the flesh in order to allow the uncontaminated population to exist in peace, but their memories would certainly be reverenced by their neighbors. In some areas, huts or hovels were provided for the lepers in out-of-the-way places that were not too visible and not convenient to normal traffic, but as a rule the victims of the disease were shown the road leading out of the territory and told to take themselves hence. The young and the elderly were given the same harsh treatment as the adult lepers.

Leprosy was later associated with venereal diseases by the ignorant and even with the Greek-documented elephantiasis.

Many European countries had severe outbreaks of leprosy, and *lazarettos* (named after the biblical character whose wounds were licked by dogs) sprang up in the major cities and capitals. Religious orders, composed of courageous men and women, were even formed to care for the victims of the disease. The Order of Saint Lazarus, a hospitaller and military order of monks, began near Jerusalem in the twelfth century to provide care for lepers in a hospital and to fight for the defense of Christianity.

By the fifteenth century, however, leprosy had declined in Europe, probably as the result of the segregation policies. The disease was carried into the New World, however, by imported slaves and laborers. Leprosy is believed to have come into the Hawaiian Islands with the Chinese, who were hired for work on the plantations. In Hawaii, the disease was originally known as *Ma'i Pake*, which meant the "Chinese Sickness." In the course of time, the islanders would call leprosy *Ma'i Ho'oka' awale*, which translates as "The Separating Sickness." The *haoles* of the world knew about leprosy but no longer felt exposed to its ravages. Certainly there were still some cases in Europe, but whole communities no longer felt at risk. The disease seemed confined mostly to underdeveloped countries, where the population was poverty-stricken, in need, and prone to other physical plagues.

Leprosy thus became a specter of the past in Europe and in America. The disease was seldom discussed outside of biblical readings and not even understood by medical men. Within a decade, in 1873, Dr. Gerhard Henrik Armauer Hansen would discover the bacillus of leprosy that was later studied by Dr. Albert Neisser, but that specific knowledge was not available at the time of the outbreak of the disease in the islands. Bacteriology was still an infant science, and leprosy thus remained a horror of the ancient world. It also served marvelously well in sermons and in admonitions about riotous living, the dissipation of one's health on fleshly pleasures, and the vengeance of a very righteous God.

Actually, leprosy is a granulomatous disease that is caused by the *Mycobacterium leprae (M. leprae)*. The resulting disease can take two forms: the tuberculoid or the lepromatous. Usually the entrance of the *M. leprae* into the human system is not noticed or marked by a particular symptom. There may be occasional onsets of fever or other minor problems, but small spots usually serve as the first sign of the disease. The normal incubation period is from one to five years, although there have been recorded cases where the bacillus lies dormant for decades before demonstrating its presence in the human body. It is transmitted by close contact, or by droplets exposed to some mucous membrane or open wound.

Tuberculoid leprosy, also called cutaneous or nodular leprosy, develops if a patient has what is called high cell-mediated immunity, which results in only a few of the bacilli being present in the system. A skin rash develops, from tuberculides, and the mucous membranes become irritated. Under attack, the skin of the patient becomes remarkably smooth or covered with tiny creases. Loss of bodily hair is experienced, and nodules begin to form, which in turn become abscesses or ulcers. The nose can collapse as a result of this form of the disease, and the eyes can become bloodied and infected. The eyeballs eventually turn into pulpy masses, and the nose and the mouth become one single opening as the disease starts to eat the face away.

Some of the patients suffering from this form of the disease become disfigured as well by the thickening of their skin, which forms large furrows. In the course of time, some of the victims assume the countenance of an aged lion. Others become extremely corpselike in appearance.

Lepromatus leprosy, also called anesthetic or nerve leprosy, develops when patients have a low-cell immunity, resulting in the presence of a large number of bacilli in the system. Nodules thicken the skin and then disappear, causing the nerves to swell and to begin to lose their primary functions. The muscles and bones, no longer protected by the nerves, are open to disfigurement and damage. Fingers and feet are injured beyond repair in the later stages, and the body no longer registers alarms when such an injury takes place. Open sores develop in this form of the disease, and ulcers become gangrenous. Today, the tuberculoid form of leprosy is not considered highly contagious (although if left untreated, it can lead to the inevitable complications and to the start of the second form of the condition).

Fortunately, leprosy has been reduced considerably as a serious threat to global health. In 1985, there were 122 countries in which leprosy was still considered a public health problem. To end this situation, the 44th World Health Assembly, held in Geneva in 1991, issued a resolution to eliminate leprosy as a public health problem by the year 2000. The effort proved remarkably successful, and by 2008 the prevalence of leprosy had been reduced from the millions to 212,802 cases, while the number of new cases diagnosed in 2007 had declined to 254,525. Progress was seen especially in Africa, although the disease remains a challenge and threat in some parts of Africa, South America, and Asia.

Crucial to the success of the World Health Organization's long-term plans is ensuring that treatment is available to all of the victims of Hansen's Disease, and central to that is the use of multidrug therapy (MDT). MDT treatment has been available free of charge to all patients around the world since 1995; its importance stems from the fact that MDT is a highly effective cure for all types of leprosy, but the drugs must be used in concert with each other. The use of only drugs in the therapy is not permitted as the disease builds up resistance. The drugs used normally in MDT are a combination of rifampicin, clofazimine, and dapsone for some patients and rifampicin and dapsone for others. Rifampicin is considered the most important of the anti-leprosy drugs.

In Damien's era, of course, the medical treatment offered to lepers was not much advanced over the ones used in the Middle Ages. Oils were recommended for initial skin conditions. Some turned to baths, turtle's blood, snake venom, and the famous Chaulmoogra oil, which did offer a considerable amount of relief for a time. Other doctors prescribed carbonic acid, lead, gold, copper, iodine, and bismuth. Because the horrors of the biblical leprosy were the points of reference for the people of Damien's time (without advanced medical treatment available), the report and request of the doctor at Queen's Hospital led to an instant panic in Honolulu. Leprosy, people suddenly realized, stalked the island trails and the community. The *haoles* responded with what they believed to be well-founded terror. The entire community rose up in anger and in desperation, and the subject was discussed everywhere. The Hawaiian government was faced with an immediate and dreadful decision. King Kamehameha V issued a decree on January 3, 1865, putting into law a segregation policy for the islands that included the removal of the infected, including children and infants, from their communities. Under the edict of the king, leprosy victims were to be turned over to the authorities for examination and hospitalization.

There was no overwhelming response by the Hawaiians to the edict, naturally. The *haoles* may have been consoled by the so-called progressive legislation, but the native islanders simply hid their sick and denied their existence. Whatever the fate of their loved ones, the people vowed to care for them and to keep them out of the hands of those who would carry them away. Eventually, islanders fought the police while their diseased relatives were hunted like wild animals. Word spread rapidly across the islands about the law, and the use of force by the police, which was instituted as a result, and those who were in the process of nursing victims of the disease became cautious about approaching authorities. Parents of small afflicted children were especially afraid. It was a disease that did not discriminate by rank or wealth. It struck without warning in the homes of the rich and in the huts of the common islanders.

Molokai was chosen as the site of a leprosarium, or lazaretto, in June of 1865. The decree of King Kamehameha V had directed that special land, in a suitable location, be purchased by the board of health. On September 20 of that year, land was purchased at Kalawao and at Valies, plus some adjacent lots. The land cost eighteen hundred dollars plus some properties given in exchange. The notice posted everywhere in the Hawaiian Islands on October 25 informed sufferers of the disease that they would be transported to the new settlement and would be offered all possible care. Kalaupapa was mentioned in the original notice, but the actual landing site there was not purchased until 1873. Kalaupapa was only the point at which the patients were to be set down on the island. They were directed to live at Kalawao.

Molokai is a very beautiful island, located in the center of the Hawaiian archipelago. It is between Maui and Oahu, rising out of the sea and covered with gentle mists. Once filled with raging volcanoes that are now dormant or extinct, the island of Molokai is still mountainous. Some of these steep cliffs descend like stone walls against the ocean. The walls are sheer, stark, and beautiful. Robert Louis Stevenson (called *Tusitala* by the islanders) described the scenery of Molokai as "grand, gloomy, and bleak."

At first, the Hawaiians effectively ignored the edict and the police measures. They had no fear of the disease on the person of a family member, believing that it was far better for such a human being to live among them rather than die alone as an outcast in some far-off place. Molokai became a dreaded word among the people who hid their sick or fled into caves and stark interior regions. All the islands had wild places where people could not be hunted down with success. One missionary of the era wrote that the Hawaiians did not even consider Molokai as the ultimate destination for the afflicted. "As soon as they hear that they will be taken," he stated, "they hide themselves in the rocky cliffs. They are very numerous. I see them all of the time. I know at least twenty, several of them Catholics."

This attitude, naturally, only enraged the *haole* community and added to their terror of the disease and its victims. The further use of force by the police was the result of hysteria and anger. Each troop of police was directed to make the rounds of villages and towns, accompanied by medical men who were supposed to make on-the-spot diagnoses. Anyone found with the disease was to be forcibly removed from his or her residence. In the course of time, the police had to be armed so that they could arrest patients in the proper fashion and ward off the attacks of would-be rescuers. The populace armed itself in retaliation, and actual gun battles took place in some locations as the police went about their grisly tasks, with people dying from bullet wounds rather than the dreaded disease. By the end of 1866, however, almost one hundred fifty men and women had been rounded up and placed on board a ship that was to take them to the haven of Molokai. As the ship sailed out of Honolulu harbor, a terrible cry of agony echoed over the city.

The board of health and the government authorities had envisioned the new settlement as a place of care and concern. This area, measuring approximately ten square miles, was a promontory, or peninsula, surrounded on three sides by the ocean and cut off from the main part of the island (called "topside") by a mountain chain that rose to a height of three thousand feet in some places. A single trail crossed the mountains and descended into Kalawao at an altitude of twenty-one hundred feet. Eventually, two separate villages were placed at the disposal of the exiles: Kalaupapa on the northwest (at the foot of the mountains) and Kalawao (the original site on the northernmost point). These locations were separated by just over two and one-half miles. The area, windblown and dreary, consisted mostly of scrub.

The board of health and the government officials actually entertained the hope that the able-bodied victims would land on the island and immediately rally to the cause of their own predicament by building up a stable and self-sustained community. This dream was aided by the initial policy of allowing the spouses and parents of the patients to accompany them into exile. The relatives of the lepers were subsequently banned when the segregation policy was in full operation. The board of health sincerely believed that the victims in the course of time could fish, farm, raise their own crops, and become self-sufficient. But getting medical supplies to them proved difficult even at the start, and shipments of food were irregular and not in keeping with the needs of the inhabitants of the settlement. What the board of health and other officials did not understand (especially the *haoles* who were in charge) was the devastating effect that the forced exile had on the Hawaiians. They had been torn out of the arms of their loved ones, cast off onto a strange island, deprived of every tradition and spiritual resource that linked them to the past. They were then told by strangers to be grateful for the kindness of others, who viewed them as living corpses, as horrors that would bring destruction to the civilized communities. Above all, the *haole* officials (all of them immigrants to Hawaii, in some generation or another) did not understand the deep attachment to the land that characterized the islanders. *Haoles* could sail halfway around the world and start up new lives because they did not feel tied to the earth of their ancestors. The Hawaiians felt at one with their islands, with their districts, and with the traditions that had evolved there. When they were physically displaced and branded as outcasts, they suffered a greater torment than the ones that their disease would eventually inflict upon them.

Superintendents, some better than others, came to Kalawao and reported that the food supplies were nonexistent and that order could not be maintained there. From 1866 to 1873, almost 40 percent of the patients sent to their exile on Molokai died without care and without hope. The young ones perished quickly; forlorn, shocked by the treatment that they had received, despairing of ever seeing their parents again, and exposed to vicious treatment at the hands of their equally despairing companions. Under the direction of a superintendent named Walsh, improvements were made, including the building of a hospital for patients in the last stages of the disease. A school and a separate residence for the children were also established, but Walsh did not live long enough to ensure the continuance of these much-needed changes.

Relatives of the patients were permanently banned from making the trip to Molokai by the new board of health, which was appointed by King Lunalilo, who assumed the throne of Hawaii on January 8, 1873. Rations of meat, *poi*, rice, salt, bread, and flour were also dispensed to the parents each week in the settlement. Those who were well enough to work at various tasks were provided with money and food, and some managed to build small houses for themselves in convenient locations. Credit was also established in a settlement store, and there the patients could buy clothing and personal supplies.

All of these things looked perfectly well-planned and ideal on paper. But in actuality, the settlements had become a place of horror, where the strong could bully the dying, and where the patients reverted to their own customs and danced the nights away and brewed their own pain-killing liquors. The Hawaiians had been put into a *haole* paradise, but they might as well have been forced to climb into the gaping open graves of the Middle Ages. The *haole* community in Honolulu was gratified by the stern measures taken against the spread of the disease. With more confidence in their own safety, they could afford to take notice of the sufferings of the patients and could develop their humanitarian instincts again. Eventually, the people began to ask what could be done for the poor unfortunates. One newspaper editorial stated that it was time for a minister of the Gospel of Jesus Christ and a doctor to sacrifice themselves for the lepers. Divine Providence had already set in motion the solution to the sudden burst of *haole* concern.

Father Damien de Veuster, SS.CC., was a *haole*, a member of the community that had descended upon the islands with "progress" and "civilization." He was not a part of that society, however, inasmuch as the Sacred Hearts priests were only tolerated as necessary to the spiritual well-being of those who embraced Catholicism. He was also distinct from his own community because his way of looking at people and events was remarkably unique.

His own parishioners on the Big Island of Hawaii had been among the victims of the disease. Damien had cared for them, feeling a strange spiritual sensation when they coughed up spittle on him as he heard their confessions. He had also witnessed the terrible ordeals of separation visited upon his Catholic families, heard their lamentations and their pain, and saw the dread coming into the eyes of those being forced into exile. At the same time, however, he had been comforted by the certain knowledge that he would be reunited with those parishioners sometime in the future. In a letter written in April 1873, Damien confided to the Father General of the Sacred Hearts congregation that he could "only attribute to Almighty God the undeniable feeling that soon I shall join them." He added: "However, eight years of service among Christians you love and who love you tied us by powerful bonds. Even just joking about my going to Molokai upsets them."

This premonition was not a sudden aspect in Damien's life. The year before he had written: "Now I have enough chapels, rectories, animals and fields — I am going to be able to apply myself to taking care of the sick and studying this year. At least if Providence doesn't send me elsewhere."

On May 4, 1873, Bishop Maigret dedicated the beautiful St. Anthony Church in Wailuku, Maui, and then met with six of the Sacred Hearts Fathers, who had come for the ceremony. The new church was in the charge of Father Léonore (sometimes spelled Léonor) Fouesnel, SS.CC., who would play a prominent role in Damien's last years. After the dedication, the bishop met with the priests of the nearby districts, who had traveled from other parts of the island or had sailed by steamer from their own mission posts. These priests celebrated Mass together and talked about the territory and the needs of the various churches.

Bishop Maigret then brought up the subject of the islanders on Molokai, explaining that he had received their petition through the good offices of Brother Bertrand, who had visited the settlement as the congregation's master builder and, in six weeks, had built St. Philomena's chapel. The patients had sent word that it was not enough for them to see a priest once a year because, as they put it, there was "so much time to die in between visits." The bishop had determined that it was time to arrange for a residency program on the island. In conscience, he did not feel that he could ask any of his men to volunteer to go there on a full-time basis. They could, however, rotate, each giving three months and then being relieved by a companion. In that way, the varying districts would not be left without priests, and the patients would be given the solace they needed and deserved in their banishment.

Father Damien leaped to his feet to volunteer the instant the bishop proposed his plan. He wanted to be the one designated for the settlement, and the bishop accepted his proposal. Father Damien later confided that he made his offer because he knew that Maigret was too softhearted to order a man into such an ordeal of service. As God had chosen Damien for the priest-hood — despite his family's objections and the misgivings of his religious superiors — so was he chosen to be "the Hero of Molokai."

Damien was not the first Catholic priest to visit the settle-ment. Priests from Oahu and Maui had gone there in the past to administer the sacraments to the Catholic population. As the number of exiled islanders increased steadily, so did the visits of these priests. Records indicate that some stayed on Molokai for weeks at a time; and Father Aubert, the veteran priest with whom Damien had stayed on Maui in the first weeks after his arrival in the islands, even offered to stay at Kalawao perma-nently. It did not matter that other priests were there before him, or that priests and sisters would follow in his path after he died. Others had offered to serve on Molokai with generosity and courage. Others were perhaps more suited by temperament to endure the isolation and the martyrdom that awaited Damien de Veuster. He had been chosen as the first resident pastor, and he would never leave his post while still alive. His life and death on Molokai would signal the entire world that the disease was something separate and distinct. Leprosy was an entity apart from the human beings that it ravaged. The patients on Molokai were not wretched sinners being punished by a vengeful God. They were decent, kind, and vulnerable human beings in need of medical and spiritual care. They were, as Damien's life would give evidence, men and women who were entitled to genuine concern and respect.

Queen Kaahumanu.

Governor Boki and his wife, Liliha.

The port of Honolulu in the middle of the nineteenth century.

Father Marie Joseph Coudrin,
founder of the Sacred Hearts Fathers.

Father Alexis Bachelot, SS.CC.

Bishop Louis Maigret, SS.CC.

King Kamehameha V

Queen Kalama and King Kamehameha III

A young Damien's novitiate portrait.

Damien's family home in Tremeloo, Belgium.

Damien's brother, Father Pamphile.

The Cathedral of Our Lady of Peace, as it looked in the 1880s.

A typical rectory and church on the Big Island of Hawaii as they looked in Damien's era.

The rugged volcanic terrain of the Big Island, where Damien served as a priest.

Father Damien and the settlement choir on Molokai.

The settlement cemetery, also known as the Garden of the Dead.

St. Philomena's Church, Molokai.

The interior of St. Philomena's Church.

Damien, in a sketch by Edward Clifford.

CHAPTER FIVE

"One Who Will Be a Father to You"

ON MAY 10, 1873, the vessel *Kilauea* left Maui with a cargo of fifty lepers and some cattle for the settlement of Molokai. On board were two other passengers. When the vessel neared the shore of the island, Bishop Maigret and Damien were hailed by the settlement inhabitants, who had raced to the shore to greet them. *Lui Ka Epikopo* and Damien landed on Kalaupapa, and there the bishop introduced the young priest, telling the patients that he had brought "one who will be a father to you." He added that Damien so loved them that he was willing "to become one with you, to live and die with you."

Bishop Maigret could not have understood the prophetic nature of his words about Damien at the time. The sentiments that he expressed were probably nothing more than the formal and tender voicing of his concern for the patients, sentiments that he believed all of the priests would exhibit when they rotated in service over the years. Certainly these veterans shared Damien's generosity and devotion. He had not designated Damien as the permanent resident at Kalawao's mission post. That thought most likely had not entered into his head, particularly in view of the perils and horrors of the assignment. He was, however, speaking in such a prophetic nature that his words had great impact on the patients present and touched everyone else in the islands when they were repeated in black and white in Honolulu's newspapers.

A few days after Damien stepped ashore at Kalaupapa, one such paper in Honolulu recounted the young priest's dedication and addressed him as a Christian hero. The article stated that Father Damien was the permanent chaplain assigned to give the exiles comfort in their agonies. Father Damien, seeing what had happened, lost no time in taking advantage of the situation. He wrote immediately to Father Modeste, his kindly provincial, and asked that such a designation be made in truth. He informed his superior that he was "bent on devoting his life to the lepers." In the same letter, demonstrating his Flemish practicality, Damien asked for wine and altar breads, spiritual books, rosaries, shirts, trousers, shoes, flour, and a bell. He had left his post on Hawaii with very few personal belongings.

Damien also asked for a vast supply of lumber, intent on building himself a residence. He was currently living under a pandanus tree, the exotic plant of the region, in whose roots rodents and other creatures nested. The *Advertiser* on May 24, 1873, carried the news about his place of residence, and immediately donations and gifts were collected on all of the islands. The outpouring of generosity was phenomenal; and Damien, thrifty and cautious, began to put things aside so that emergencies could be faced with certainty in the future.

The Protestants and nonbelievers of the islands, dismayed at the acclaim and honors being paid to this young priest, began to insert their own articles into the newspaper, declaring that they had also taken care of the exiled patients in the past. Lists of the ministers who had visited Molokai appeared, and mention was given to a Mormon elder whose wife had been stricken with the disease. The board of health in Honolulu, clearly not of the Catholic persuasion and not in league with any of the Church's spiritual ambitions, protested Damien's appearance on the island without authorization from their offices. When he made the mistake of going to Honolulu in June of that same year to gather supplies and funds, the board felt that it could take revenge without appearing prejudiced against the priest because of his religion.

A declaration was given that seemed to clarify Damien's status, while clearly echoing the panic of the *haole* community over leprosy. Father Damien was given the board's most gracious permission to remain on the island (and in the face of his sudden popularity, no other decision could be forthcoming), but he would have to accept the segregation requirements of making Kalawao his place of work and residence.

The statement was clever and devastating because it banned Father Damien's apostolate from the parishes on the topside of Molokai, where the noninfected Catholics lived. At the same time, however, something that the board of health could not have realized, Damien was also restricted by the permission and segregation policy from contact with any fellow priest who could hear his confession. The Sacrament of Penance was a vital part of the religious life, not as a negative aspect but as a tool for spiritual growth and introspection. Damien, especially, relied on it for his own spiritual well-being.

If the health officials anticipated that Father Damien would shrink in terror from the edict, they were mistaken. He did not leave his assignment, and he did not feel restricted from visiting Honolulu whenever he believed that circumstances warranted such a journey. Of course, his visits to Oahu caused an upheaval among the *haoles*, but Damien was never one to be discouraged from an action just because it was unpopular. He had a unique single-mindedness in this, a fact of his personality that was judged by some to be stubborn willfulness.

The question of confessions, however, was difficult for him from the beginning. The board of health had unknowingly struck a heavy blow. Damien did not fear that he would die in the state of mortal sin, but he wanted to be able to come face-to-face with his own weaknesses in the presence of another human being. He needed the grace of absolution as well, nurtured by the sacrament that linked him to his own religious training and sustained him in the admission of his mortality.

Father Modeste understood Damien's needs and boarded a steamer one day to take him to Kalaupapa, where he intended to spend some time hearing Damien's confession and giving him a brief respite of company and conversation. He arrived at Kalaupapa on the *Kilauea*, intending to go ashore. The captain of the vessel, however, sternly forbade Father Modeste from landing. He informed the provincial that he was not allowed by the board of health and other government agencies to condone or permit any such illegal activities. Father Damien, aware of the ship's presence, had come to the dock and had witnessed Modeste's attempted landing. He quickly got into a small boat and rowed to the *Kilauea*, expecting that he might be allowed to board and be with his provincial while the vessel was unloading its cargo. The captain refused to let him on board. Anguished but undefeated, Damien asked Modeste if anyone on board the *Kilauea* appeared to understand or speak French. When Modeste assured him that this was not the case, Damien proceeded to make his confession in that language, having to shout up at his confessor. The *Kilauea* pulled away from the shore as Father Modeste was shouting Damien's absolution back at him.

A short time later, Father Aubert, that courageous and daring veteran, decided that he should go to Damien's aid. He dressed himself as a secular person and went to the mountain trail on Molokai, where he started the torturous descent. Aubert took a misstep and slid most of the way down the mountain on his backside. At the bottom, however, he rose, dusted himself off, and made his way to Damien's residence. Aubert was thrilled when he returned from Molokai, his charitable task completed. He congratulated himself that he had been able to help Damien without detection. His elation was short-lived, however, when the police arrived at his front door to demand an explanation. Someone had recognized Aubert and had reported him to the authorities.

Soon the Church was involved in a rather heated dispute over Aubert's conduct and flagrant disregard for the law. Bishop Maigret found himself involved, and he handled the situation with his usual finesse. Maigret had been in the islands in the time of the *l'Artémise* and its manifesto from the Catholic king of France. He remembered the incident and its results, and went immediately to his diplomatic friends. The French consul, upon hearing of the actions of the board of health and its police force, protested the sort of treatment that was being meted out to Damien and his fellow priests. The French consul did not, however, make his protests known to the board of health directly. He brought the matter to the attention of the king's minister for foreign affairs, an individual who was well versed with the *l'Artémise* affair and its consequences for the Hawaiian kingdom. This minister spoke to the members of the board of health about the matter. Immediately, all religious ministers were exempted from the regulations of segregation on Molokai. These ministers had only to apply to the board of health to receive permission to conduct their affairs without interference from the medical or health officials.

Damien sent in his application and was told that he could visit the lepers "from time to time," which he promptly interpreted as meaning fifty-two weeks a year, seven days a week, twenty-four hours a day. He received no further interference from the board of health concerning his desire to receive the Sacrament of Penance. Eventually, a new superintendent, a man named Rudolph Meyer, was put in charge of the settlement, a fact that brightened Damien's life considerably and made his tasks easier. Meyer, a German Protestant, placed the needs of the patients above those demanded by interdenominational squabbles. Meyer worked closely over the years with Father Damien, coming to his defense on many occasions and offering him every kindness. The changes that were taking place in the settlement because of Damien's presence could not be denied or corrupted by religious bigotry.

Damien's personality transcended the difficulties faced by the patients and those who came to their aid on the island. The horrendous tragedy is thus obscured in a way and should be understood in the stark terms of the numbers involved and their inevitable demise. The following statistics released by the settlement on Molokai reveal the actual population figures of the settlement, year by year, during Damien's term of service:

Year	Patients Admitted	Deaths
1873	415	142
1874	78	141
1875	178	149
1876	75	119
1877	122	120
1878	209	111
1879	92	204
1880	51	51
1881	195	29
1882	70	111
1883	300	150
1884	108	167
1885	103	142
1886	43	101
1887	220	111
1888	571	236
1889	307	149

The population tally of patients varied according to arrivals and deaths, and there were as many as 800 patients, including men, women, children and infants, awaiting aid in 1873 and 1,166 needing care in 1889.

When Damien first arrived on the shores of Kalaupapa, the exiled lepers boasted: *"Aole kanawai me heia wahi!"* — "Here there is no law!" He recognized what the despair of exile had done to the people, and saw the degradation and the consequences of life reduced to the levels of brute survival and animal pleasures. He understood what had prompted the revolting orgies and debaucheries that were taking place. Despite the efforts of well-meaning people and meager resources, the abandonment and the persistence of the disease in each human body poisoned hope and fostered chaos and moral decay. Patients robbed one another, abandoned the nearly dead, and corrupted the young. Damien understood the situation in a rational manner, but he did not intend that they should continue. For this reason, he and the despairing exiles were locked in a battle of the spirit from the very beginning. He was not there to fill their heads with tales about just punishments for sin, or to attempt to explain why human beings suffered unspeakable torments and were thus judged unfit for society or the comforts of their own families and homes.

Damien came to care for them for as long as he lived, and in this capacity he was unique in his era, remarkable in any age of the world. Many patients cursed him as he bandaged their sores and cleansed them, but he paid no attention to the abuse. Others remained almost comatose, traumatized by the exile and the horrors becoming visible in their own flesh. Damien did not try to engage them in conversation but washed away their filth and fed them as best he could.

In the days of early exile on the island, the lepers were given one new garment and one set of linens each year, as if that supply would ever serve them adequately. Such an allotment was totally ridiculous, of course, and the resulting nakedness and filth contributed to the quick deaths experienced during the early days of the settlement. Death wandered at will through the settlement, because of the nature of the disease; and every exile knew that eventually he or she would be carted away, or wrapped in rags, tied between two poles, and thrown into the ravine where the wild pigs would come to feast on their decomposing corpses. Damien put an end to that barbaric custom, not only being at the side of the dying but making wooden coffins for each corpse and starting a cemetery that he lovingly called his Garden of the Dead.

He did sleep under the pandanus tree on his first nights in the settlement, but he soon built a small house for himself at Kalawao. It was tiny, measuring only fifteen feet by twenty feet, but it protected him from the elements and restored a façade of civilization to his routines. He made the house by hand, finishing it in eight days and thereby astounding the native population. A storeroom was also prepared, and there Damien placed all of the gifts and donations sent to him as a result of his newspaper fame. That supply would be the only thing standing between the patients and disaster on many occasions.

There was no water available for the lepers in the early days either. In the course of time, a series of pipes was installed at Kalawao to provide the precious liquid. In the beginning, however, Damien had to walk some distance, carrying water for his own needs and for the patients. He continued to serve as a water carrier long after the pipe system was installed because so many of his patients had lost their legs and were confined to their beds, a medical condition that led to the need for soap and water.

The year after his arrival, a hurricane ravaged the coast of Molokai, and all of the houses built by the wealthier patients collapsed. Rich and poor alike were forced to sleep in the open, on sodden reed mats. Damien had already begun a vast building program, begging for lumber and other supplies from his superiors and friends. After the storm, he began another effort and, eventually, neat rows of houses appeared in the settlement. They were small and whitewashed, but they provided shelter for the patients and set a pattern of social order and civic pride.

He fought against those who brutalized the weak; he halted the drunken orgies. Damien took the weak patients away from their tormentors, and he stayed at the side of the bullies when they were dying, giving them a gift of himself when all others had fled. The building projects he started upon his arrival would continue throughout his lifetime. When Kalaupapa was opened as well for Hansen's disease patients, Damien repaired the landing-place road and started a new community of small whitewashed houses there. He worked as late as 1888 on the houses, even though the disease had crippled him and had started to drain away his remarkable stamina. By doing the work himself, Damien set an example and offered the patients the first glimmers of hope. They soon joined him, and the houses began to spring up everywhere.

He taught those patients who were well enough to farm. They raised potatoes, some of which they were able to sell to the authorities. These same officials were induced by Damien to raise the allowances of the patients from six dollars to ten dollars a year. Damien approved of the concept of paying the patients for their work and allowing them to purchase things from the local store, but he claimed that the store priced things exorbitantly. He eventually served as the banker of the community and helped many patients build their houses, establishing permanent and safe abodes. The exiles started raising flower gardens, riding on horseback, learning to sing in choirs and to play a vast assortment of musical instruments, some handmade by Damien, some purchased or received as donations. The musical accomplishments of the settlement became legendary in the course of time. The disease did not stop them from playing or singing. In later decades, visitors to the settlement were often serenaded by one hundred of the patients. Everyone remarked on the size and the skill of the band. Brother Joseph Dutton, who joined Father Damien toward the end of the priest's life, wrote that he saw patients playing as their fingers fell off. One patient lost part of his lip while he was happily tooting on his horn. Such things were part of the normal progression of the disease but did not stop the patients' enthusiasm for music.

The voices of the Pacific islanders are uniquely beautiful, and their ability to harmonize instantly has won them admiration over the decades. The choir in the settlement was particularly vibrant, and visitors came away from concerts or services with glowing accounts of the beautiful renditions performed. Hymns were sung in many parts, with the various voices blending into stunning chords of music and devotion that left spectators almost speechless. One particular hymn sung in the settlement during Damien's era was received with exceptional appreciation:

Iesu No Ke Kahuhipa
Kahuhipa maikai
E'ia makou ka ohana
Ke ho'olohe a kahai
E aloha, e aloha
Alakai a hanai mai.

Jesus, the Shepherd,
The best Shepherd,
Here we are, the family,
Obeying and following,
O love, O love;
Leader and Provider.

Damien also encouraged horse races as part of the settlement activities, because the act of riding a horse was possible for the patients in many stages of the disease. Eventually, he would have to ride on a horse or in a rickety carriage. He earned the reputation for working his horses to exhaustion, which meant that he did not put limits on his own strength. He arranged *luaus* (the Hawaiian-style barbecues and outdoor picnics), festivals, singing contests, and fishing celebrations in keeping with the Hawaiian observances of the seasons. Eventually, the choir he started gained international fame, although he always regretted the loss of so many beautiful voices as the disease took its yearly toll. He met the inter-island steamer, the *Mokalii*, each time it arrived at Kalaupapa to unload its human cargo onto the beach. There was no pier there in the early days, and several times the lepers were forced overboard and had to make their own way through the waves, the very young and the weak perishing in the waves. Damien brought coffee and hot food to each new boatload of arrivals. He also brought blankets and other small comforts down to the shore, packing up his wobbly old carriage for the trip whenever he heard the steamer making its way along the coast. In the course of time, the board of health replaced his carriage out of respect for his efforts.

All newcomers, drenched in the salty water, traumatized over the loss of their loved ones, and lamenting their banishment, were housed in Damien's own residence or in those of parishioners until adequate facilities could be found for their own comfort. He must have spent nights giving solace to weeping exiles, to men and women caught in the anguish of being placed on a strange island, without anything familiar or dear to give them encouragement and some sort of stability. Damien greeted each with compassion, offering his respect and his concern. Such activity was always conducted by Damien as an unofficial representative of the settlement. He had no authority or standing within the community as far as the board of health was concerned. In November 1877, however, he was offered the position of assistant superintendent of the lazaretto, and he accepted the role only to stop another troublesome individual from gaining responsibility and power. He had been offered the sum of ten thousand dollars a year, which was a great deal of money in those days. He accepted a salary of forty dollars a month until February 1878 when a permanent assistant superintendent was installed in his place at his request.

The political and administrative aspects of the settlement not only failed to concern him, but they held no power over his activities either. He lived only for the lepers, and he devoted his days and nights to their care. This started as concern for their spiritual well-being. But Damien was intelligent enough to know that if he did not raise their standard of living, ease their pain and suffering, and institute a stable regimen of medical care, their spirits would not survive. He visited every patient at least once a week. When he first arrived, he discovered living "corpses" lying abandoned in clumps of grass along the back trails. These victims had been dumped there by their fellow lepers or had crawled there to die alone. Some were half-eaten by worms and maggots, which were devouring their insides and slowly making their insidious way to outer layers to do the last stages of their destructive work.

The hospital, which had been established by Superintendent Walsh during his brief tenure, had little medicine and no resident doctors. Eventually, a *haole* named William Williamson arrived on the island. He had been part of the health staff at the receiving hospital in Honolulu and had contracted the disease in some fashion. A trained medical nurse, highly knowledgeable in medical care and procedures, Williamson began to teach Father Damien everything he knew about drugs, dosages, surgery, bandages, amputations, disinfectants, and general hygiene.

Damien went to the hospital every morning — gathering up the drugs, bandages, oils, and other materials sent to the settle-

ment by the board of health or by private agencies and individuals — and then he started his rounds. In some of the cabins,
he had to sweep the floors, wash the patients as well as their
bed linens, and then scrub the interiors and the furnishings. He
disinfected the sores that appeared on their bodies, bandaged
the stumps or damaged limbs, cut away rotting flesh, and even
amputated certain parts of their bodies that were in the last
stages of putrefaction.

This was not done with grace and calm from the start.
Damien admitted freely that in the first weeks he had to leave the
sides of the patients again and again, staggering outside to retch
and lose the contents of his stomach. At other times, he suffered
blinding headaches because of the stench coupled with the ner-
vous tension that developed as a result of his close contact with
the lepers in his act of ministering to them. He started wearing
heavy boots soon after his arrival, because his legs would itch in
the presence of such carnage. He also smoked a pipe, allowing
the smoke and the strong aroma of the tobacco to permeate his
clothing as a defense against the revolting smells that he faced in
every situation. An American Navy doctor, who visited the settlement later, was amazed by the tender care Damien showed to
his patients, and he went away with hearty praise for the priest's
surgical abilities and his awareness of good medical techniques.
Superintendent Rudolph Meyer added his own praise, having
witnessed Damien on his daily rounds.

Probably prompted by Williamson's knowledge of what
was available and beneficial in the care of the patients, Damien
began to write to his family and friends in Europe, asking them
to send various drugs that were being used experimentally in
other lands. He was desperate for any kind of treatment that
would alleviate the suffering that he saw each day. The patients
not only faced the disintegration of their flesh as a result of the
disease but were vulnerable to chills, fevers, germs, and injuries.

Damien and his coworkers, called *kokuas*, were careful to keep the frail out of harm's way, even though they could not secure any of them against the remorseless course of leprosy.

For a while, he used Chinese medicines that were made available to him, especially the *Hoang-Nan* pills, which appear to have brought some relief to the sufferers. Donations of the pills and other medicines continued throughout his life on Molokai, allowing him to offer some hope when he made his daily rounds. The patients lived near him and visited the storeroom often, to describe their needs, and to cajole and tease Damien into offering them sweets or some other treat along with the usual rations. In 1878, however, he abandoned his original residence and built a new one, measuring twenty-four feet by twenty-one feet and possessing a second story. He was delighted and claimed that now he could entertain his fellow priests and superiors in style.

He also took long walks in his "Garden of the Dead," the ever-expanding cemetery of the settlement. It is estimated that Father Damien built more than six hundred coffins by hand (although some former visitors claimed that the number reached fourteen hundred to sixteen hundred). He did this because he could not bear to see a body being thrown over the cliffs or just abandoned like a pile of rags at the side of the road, to serve as food for wild animals. Each dead patient deserved a coffin, a deep grave, and a religious service that would commemorate that individual's humanity and eternal destiny. Coffins were not readily available for the dead. The authorities did not consider the numbers that would be needed in the early days but, after that, Damien was taking care of the last rites for most of the inhabitants of the settlement. He also dug the graves for the coffins that he made by hand. He was the strongest human being on that part of the island. He could dig the narrow, deep trenches with ease. In the course of time, Damien would worry about having to stack coffins in the grave sites, because the cemetery area was no longer adequate. He built more boxes, placed the bodies inside, dug the graves, and lowered the remains into the ground, where they were safe from predators and scavengers roaming the area.

Within a relatively short time, Damien was no longer crawling out of the huts to throw up or to experience his own physical revulsion at the horrors around him. In the very act of ministering to the patients, he had managed to transcend the physical horror of the sores, pus, wounds, and putrefaction. Individual human beings lived in the rotting shells of flesh in his care. The masks of wretched decay hid vibrant personalities as well as gentle hearts and souls that clung to life with all the hopes and dreams shared by other beings on the earth. Damien called to the hidden spirit in these half-dead bodies. He especially felt concern for the children sent into exile and into death, alone.

The infants of Hawaii did not escape the segregation policies. After a time, mothers were forbidden to accompany their babies to Molokai. Their children were torn from their arms and carried away. Such infants, naturally, arrived in the settlement in a state of trauma, paralyzed by the loss of their mothers and by the journey in the company of equally dazed strangers.

Father Damien started the orphanages almost as soon as he settled on the island; by 1883, he had forty-four tiny lepers in his care. A home was founded for the girls, in the charge of a woman who gave them tender and maternal care. She cooked for them, crooned lullabies, and tried to replace the mothers they had lost as a result of their disease. He started a school for boys, which became such a success that patients vied for the right to live there. Religious instructions were part of the school's curriculum at the beginning, but the board of health put a stop to that in order to avoid conflict. Father Damien shared a kitchen with the boys and ate with them often.

His personal eating habits were very poor, and he was not a man given to gourmet meals or the culinary arts. Many nights, when eating alone, instead of using plates, he simply served up his stew on saloon crackers, so that he could eat the stew and the cracker "plates" at the same time. He also allowed the patients to have the free use of his tools, ate out of common *poi* bowls with them, and even exchanged a single pipe around the campfires at night. This rash indifference to the contagious nature of the disease was probably prompted by his own temperament and by his deep sense of concern for the patients.

The notorious word "unclean" had accompanied the biblical renditions about leprosy. It is a word that strikes at the very humanity of an individual, marking him for isolation, for rejection, and for terror. Damien never used that term and allowed no one else in his company to apply it to any patient. To compensate, probably, he adopted reckless abandonment as his shield against the historical precedents of the disease. He did not want the lepers to feel rejected by him in any fashion. Only when patients cooked meals — for him or his guests — did he ask them to wear gloves. During such meal preparations, the patients could have injured themselves without protection or could have contaminated the food.

Food did matter to Damien, but not for the purpose of supplying his own table. Early on, he became aware of the needs of the patients as far as nutrition and diet were concerned. He continually waged battles with the board of health over the supplies and the types of foods made available to the settlement. When the patients received only rice and potatoes, Damien wrote to remind the authorities that only the Chinese could exist on such fare and stay healthy. The Hawaiians needed *poi* as their staple, and he fought with anyone who did not make an effort to have supplies made available.

Needing milk for the children, Damien started raising cows. After a time, he managed to amass a great herd of such animals. Chickens, pigs, and fish rounded out the other essential needs.

The settlement is recorded as having consumed as much as five thousand pounds of meat each week. Keeping such amounts of food on hand was always a problem for Superintendent Meyer and Father Damien. In this capacity, the board of health did what it could to maintain a constant flow of supplies. The fact that the board had to use available means is reasonable. The *haoles* would not necessarily distinguish between types of food-stuffs. Few would recognize the need of the Hawaiians for *poi*, for example. Rice and potatoes were plentiful in some seasons, and they were sent. Also, the various channels and sea-lanes around the islands were not always clear or calm. On many occasions, the vessels carrying the supplies had to put into safe ports to wait out storms or had to delay sailing in order to avoid being smashed by giant waves.

For Damien and the patients, however, the days passed slowly and mockingly in a tropical paradise. Molokai, like the other islands, was sunny, bright, filled with soft winds, and lit at night by a canopy of stars and a moon that danced on the waters. Between the day that Damien set foot on Molokai and the day of his death, he labored silently or boisterously, alone or with a companion, unheralded or praised by the local newspapers. His routine did not change, and he accomplished his goals because he stayed at his post and carried out the monotonous, tedious small chores which made up the pattern of his caring.

Damien's work on the island was best summed up by the report he submitted to the board of health in 1886:

> By a special providence of Our Lord, who, during his life showed a particular sympathy for the lepers, my way was traced to Kalawao in May A.D. 1873. I was then 33 years of age, enjoying a robust, good health — Lunalilo being at that time King of the Hawaiian Islands and His Excellency, E.O. Hall, President of the Board of Health.

A great many lepers had arrived lately from the different islands; they numbered 816. Some of them were old acquaintances of mine from Hawaii, where I was previously stationed as a missionary priest; to the majority I was a stranger.

The Kalaupapa landing was at that time a somewhat deserted village of three or four wooden cottages and a few old grass houses. The lepers were allowed to go there only on the days when a vessel arrived; they were all living at Kalawao — about eighty of them in the hospital — in the same buildings we see there today. All the other lepers, with very few kokuas (helpers) had taken their abode further up towards the valley. They had cut down the old pandanus or puhala groves, to build their houses, though a great many had nothing but branches of castor oil trees with which to construct their small shelters. These frail frames were covered with pili-ki leaves.... or with sugar cane leaves — the best ones with pili grass. I myself was sheltered during several weeks under the single pandanus tree which is preserved up to the present in the church yard. Under such primitive roofs were living pell-mell, without distinction of age or sex, old or new cases, all more or less strangers to one another, those unfortunate outcasts of society. They passed their time with playing cards, hula (native dances), drinking fermented ki-root beer, home made alcohol, and with the sequel of all this. Their clothes were far from being clean and decent on account of the scarcity of water, which had to be brought at that time from a great distance.... For a long time, as above stated, under the influence of this pernicious liquor, they would neglect everything else, except the hula, prostitution and drinking. As they had no spiritual advisor, they would hasten along the road to complete ruin. A good many of the prostrate and sick were left lying there to take care of themselves, and several of them died for want of assistance, whilst those who should have given a helping hand were going around seeking enjoyment of the most pernicious and immoral kind.

As there were so many dying people, my priestly duty toward them often gave me the opportunity to visit them at their domiciles, and although my exhortations were especially addressed to the prostrated, often they would fall on the ears of the public sinners, who, little by little, became conscious of the consequence of their wicked lives, and began to reform, and thus with the hope in a merciful Savior, gave up their bad habits. Kindness to all, charity to the needy, a sympathizing hand to the sufferers and the dying, in conjunction with a solid religious instruction to my listeners, have been my constant means to introduce moral habits among the lepers.... I am happy to say, that, assisted by the local administration, my labors here, which seemed to be almost [in?] vain at the beginning, have, thanks to a kind Providence, been greatly crowned with success....

The years were happy ones despite the physical horrors and the presence of death, pain, and despair. Damien managed to turn the pitiful experiences of the first years into a stable and relatively calm pastoral scene. His daily routines were exhausting, but he seemed to thrive on them. His letter home about Christmas day, for example, gave an insight into the sort of life that he was sharing with his people there. Damien explained that the church bell started ringing at eleven o'clock on Christmas eve, when the moon was shining on the dark waters of the sea. The bells were answered by the sound of drums, carried by the young patients from door to door to alert the people to come in their best attire to begin the celebrations. The salutation *Mele Kalikimaka, "Merry Christmas,"* could be heard as the patients made their way to St. Philomena's Church, where the bells rang again to signal the start of community prayers. The church choir, famous across the world, began the hymns of the Christmas season, and the congregation and visitors sat enrapt.

At midnight, preceded by two acolytes, Damien approached the altar to begin Mass. He preached a thirty-minute sermon. After the Mass, he returned to his residence and took a brief rest, rising at four in the morning to return to Kalaupapa to celebrate his second Mass, most often alone, because the patients were asleep in their beds. Baptisms followed the Mass if there were candidates. A third Christmas Mass was celebrated at Kala-wao at ten o'clock, and this was attended by everyone and filled with music and the greetings of the season. A great community feast followed, with floral decorations, leis, dancing, music, and laughter. The community gathered around tables and saluted the feast and all of its joyous invitations to humans to be of good cheer and hope. The patients lingered at the tables and on the shore after the meal, listening to the music being offered and watching the stars appear in the darkening sky.

CHAPTER SIX

A Parade of Helpers

WHILE HIS LABORS TRANSFORMED the spirit and character of the settlement — providing interludes of joyous, uplifting, and healing celebration — Father Damien was being visited by an exceedingly strange parade of human beings. The lepers, the local authorities, and even the board of health had learned to respect and honor the priest and his "sympathetic hand." His torment would come from another source, and to this special breed he was particularly vulnerable.

The first of his visitors was a Father Andrew Burgermann, a Sacred Hearts priest originally from Holland. Father Burgermann had contracted elephantiasis in Tahiti and had come to the Hawaiian Islands to recuperate and to carry out his own personal dream about service to the patients on Molokai. Although not professionally educated or trained, he was a gifted medical practitioner with a solid background of caring for island people. Burgermann had read about Damien and believed that Molokai was a fine place for him to perform his specialized services. He started his sojourn on the island by coming down the trail from the topside of Molokai, the trail that Father Aubert had traveled in disguise in the past. Like Father Aubert, Burgermann lost his footing, sliding and tumbling to the bottom of the trail. He was knocked unconscious, however, and was discovered in a pitiful condition by a passing Hawaiian the next morning. The Hawaiian draped the priest over his saddle and delivered him to Father Damien's residence, where he had to be nursed for three days before he was well enough to get up and around. Damien fed him wine and hot tea, and applied compresses. Damien (always rather naïve in welcoming any priest companions who came his way) liked Burgermann and hoped that he would become his companion and would share in the work, both in the settlement and in the parishes serving nonleprous Catholics. The patients felt at home with the priest, too, relying on his medical expertise from the first day.

Damien's enthusiasm paled rather quickly, however, when he realized how troubled and obstinate Burgermann could be in his dealings with others. After a time, Damien even refused to allow Burgermann to hear his confessions, and Burgermann retaliated by not talking to his host for days on end. At the same time, it became increasingly obvious that Burgermann was ambitious and anxious to gain the upper hand in their relationship. He courted Superintendent Meyer and his wife, who could not be expected to take a dim view of the man without provocation, and then began to maneuver his way into the position of assistant superintendent of the settlement. That post was vacated just after Burgermann arrived. Damien, realizing what would happen to the patients and to his own personal apostolate, voiced his objections. The board of health, trusting Damien's sense about such things, offered him the post instead, and he accepted it on an interim basis to keep Burgermann out of power.

Burgermann, in turn, abandoned all of his non-leper-related parish duties, serving only as the settlement's medical practitioner. The religious superiors, oddly, sent Damien over the mountain trails to be the pastor in the other regions. The visitor then started to warn the mission that he might leave the congregation. On one particular occasion, he even threatened to shoot Father Damien: They quarreled over his actions, and he made the threat, exiting the room to get a gun. Father Damien fled from his house and warned a visitor whom he encountered to avoid Burgermann. The visitor, confused about what had happened, went into Burgermann's residence and found him sitting with his pipe. Burgermann showed the pipe, claiming that Damien was a bit high-strung and myopic and had dreamed up the entire incident. Burgermann stayed two years in Damien's settlement, then left, apparently discovering his vocation again in other climes.

The next visitor was Father Albert Montiton, a Frenchman who had put in twenty-four years of service in the South Pacific and was considered something of a celebrity. He had conducted a lecture tour in Europe and had met with the pope in Rome. With such credentials, Montiton was welcomed by Damien's superiors and sent to Molokai as his companion. Unknown to Damien at the time, Montiton was also entrusted with a religious assignment by the superiors in Honolulu. Rumors were rampant there about Damien's bad manners and lewd behavior. Many of the Protestants claimed that he was living an immoral life on Molokai, mingling freely with the native women in their debaucheries.

For the enemies of Damien, these were perfect charges to press upon the community. Few human beings in any age of the world will hesitate to think ill of others. Damien did not embezzle funds, did not seek power, did not court praise. He was not vulnerable in those areas, but he could be slandered effectively with the subject of sex. When his enemies could not explain his selflessness, they could compensate for their own guilt by declaring him morally vile and willing to endure segregation and the horrors of the settlement in order to have pleasures there.

His own provincial — who should have defended him or at least demanded some sort of investigation that would clear his name — instead confided all of the rumors to Father Albert Montiton. Montiton, a perfect stranger, untested and unknown, was called upon to take up the charge of overseeing Damien's morality on Molokai. Montiton (who suffered from elephantiasis, which he had contracted in his own mission work) was to become Damien's spiritual guardian. He went to Molokai and started out by preaching at Damien for three solid days. He listed the rumors that had been confided to him, related the doubts of his superiors, and pointed out the obvious ineptitude that Damien was showing as a priest and as a missionary. Stunned by the stories and the accusations, Damien listened in silence, pondering what sort of lunatic had been loosed upon him.

Montiton was remorseless in his remonstrance with Damien, adding to the priest's frustration in his apostolate. Damien finally asked to visit Honolulu in order to conduct some of his own business — and probably to be free of the man. While he was there, he received a letter from Montiton, complaining that Damien had left a carpentry chore unfinished before he left, thus causing Montiton some inconvenience and embarrassment. Returning to the settlement, Damien wrote to Bishop Herman Koeckemann, the successor to the beloved Bishop Maigret, asking that Montiton be sent elsewhere. His letter was ignored. He finally wrote that he would leave Molokai if he had to have Montiton as a companion. That threat was also unanswered.

In the end, it was Montiton's physical condition that put a stop to Damien's ordeal. Montiton had a severe skin rash, and he went to Honolulu where the doctors covered him with foul-smelling greases and tried to ease his ailment. While in the company of the priests in the mission center, Montiton made no attempt to seclude himself or to spare his hosts and their friends from the rank odor or the horrific sight of his body. One person there made the observation that he looked like a man who had been flayed alive. The fear of leprosy and the terrible stench of the man combined to make him a terror among his companions. Slowly, the superiors of the mission began to realize what Damien had been living with over the months.

Montiton returned one last time to Molokai, bringing the new rumors and sordid remarks about Damien's lifestyle as his gift. He had already caused Damien problems by firing every female worker within shouting distance of the priest's residence. He finally packed up and went back to his original mission post, hoping to settle there and to be cured in a new environment. Afterward, he sent a peculiarly worded letter of apology to Damien. For the rest of his life, strangely enough, Father Albert Montiton never allowed anyone to criticize Damien de Veuster in his presence and stoutly defended him when he heard rumors of his behavior.

The next visitor was a Father Gregory Archambault, who came to the settlement as a leper in the last stages of the disease. He was a kind and gentle man, already ravaged by the illness, and incapable of malice or envy where Damien was concerned. However, being far too ill, Father Gregory could not work with Damien or his apostolate. Rather, in his feeble condition, he added to Damien's burdens. Father Gregory was also a severe asthmatic. Damien had to sit up nights with him in order to keep him alive. The priest, courteous and good, finally begged to go to the receiving hospital in Honolulu, where he would not be a drain on Damien and where trained personnel could take over his care. He did go to Honolulu and died there shortly after.

All of these visitors should have been directed elsewhere or should have been investigated and tried before being sent to Damien's mission. His religious superiors failed miserably in this, because they did not understand his apostolate, his true character, or his physical condition. Bishop Koeckemann and Father Léonore Fouesnel, Damien's superior (who served as vice-provincial and then as provincial), appeared to consider Damien to be rash, impetuous, and rude. They probably did not attribute any immorality or willful misdeeds to him, excusing the rumors as the penalty for his brash behavior. The pair did not fend off his attackers either, and eventually they provided him with a terrible period of grief.

One last priest to enter Damien's private world came over the objections and misgivings of the bishop and the provincial. These two superiors were no match for the missionary; and his activities on Molokai and his relationship with Father Damien demonstrated the variety of opinions and approaches being used at the time. Father Léonore Fouesnel complained that by focusing exclusively on Damien and Molokai, the work of the other missionaries was overlooked and thus deemed irrelevant. He wrote frequently to the father general about his difficulties with Damien, and he tried to curb any news about Molokai and the apostolate there. The fact that Damien was not removed by the father general indicates that this superior probably understood Fouesnel very well and responded accordingly. While Fouesnel was thus undermining Damien, his letters crossed with others, coming from the motherhouse and from Rome, asking for news. Damien even had "problems" with his brother Pamphile, who shared his letters with the family and then gave them to the congregation's own publications for distribution worldwide. But because of this, more and more people in Europe understood the value in promoting Damien's life and work. Such an activity aided the congregation and put the care of lepers into an entirely different light.

Father Lambert Conrardy, a secular (or diocesan) priest, was originally from Belgium, a factor that did not please Damien's superiors. They feared the teaming of the two countrymen. Conrardy had been a noted missionary among the Native American tribes of Oregon. He had faced attacks and scalping raids, and had distinguished himself with his courage and his innovative ways. He came to Hawaii with the personal recommendation of Archbishop William Gross of Oregon City (now the Archdiocese of Portland), who praised his experience in the field, his stability, and his noble, heroic character.

Father Fouesnel and Bishop Koeckemann did not need another hero on Molokai. As a result, they were not even polite in their dealings with the priest. They viewed him as an "outsider," arriving on the scene with too much renown, too many praises, and too much political standing in Church circles. Damien had also been in contact with him, which did not add to Conrardy's stature in the eyes of the superiors. Damien finally begged for Conrardy's assignment to Molokai. Bishop Koeckemann agreed reluctantly, but he took the occasion as an excuse to write to the father general that Damien was still causing problems by circumventing his episcopal authority.

Conrardy's appearance made it look as if the Church was being forced to go to Belgium again to find a man capable of standing the horrors of the settlement. To counteract this, the bishop sent a circular letter to the priests of the Hawaiian missions, asking if any of them would volunteer for the posting. They agreed, to a man. These priests had been willing all along to serve as Damien's assistant and companion, but none of them had been sent to him. Damien thus welcomed Conrardy when that priest wrote and asked to join him there.

As a result of their initial correspondence, Conrardy wrote, in Damien's name, to Rome and to the generalate of the Sacred Hearts Congregation. Some of his letters found their way into the newspapers, with disastrous results. The conditions he described at the settlement embarrassed the Hawaiian government and the board of health in front of the entire world. When Conrardy arrived at Molokai in May 1888, the facts of the conditions there prompted him to write even more letters, which were promptly carried by newspapers everywhere.

While the priest was with Damien, the Franciscan Sisters arrived in the settlement to begin their duties. The bishop assigned Father Wendelin Moellers, SS.CC., to be their chaplain and confessor. This assignment was reasonable. (It concerned the sisters and their mission: they needed their own priest in the convent and could not rely upon Damien who was already suffering from leprosy.) Even so, it compounded Damien's internal trials. He had asked for years to have a companion, but no qualified ones had been sent to ease his burdens. Father Wendelin or any other priest would have proven invaluable in the apostolate to the patients. If such a priest had been sent, in fact, Father Conrardy would never have been considered.

Conrardy was with Damien until the end, and then he lived for six years as his successor of sorts. In the first days, Conrardy admitted to suffering severe headaches, as Damien had suffered them. After a while, however, he managed to overcome his initial repugnance, and worked in the settlement and became friends with most of the patients. The fact that Conrardy lasted six years after Damien's death is a testament to his ability to withstand the attacks of his enemies. He had another apostolate in mind, however, and went to the university in Portland, Oregon, where in a remarkably short space of time he received a medical degree. With that in mind, and with the memory of Father Damien in his mind and heart, Conrardy set out for China.

Father Conrardy founded a leprosarium in an area in Canton, where he worked for ten years among his patients, who adored him for his kindness and loyalty. All of the things he had learned on Molokai were put to use in the vast complex that served the afflicted of that foreign land. He was as reckless as Damien, by allowing the patients access to his person and his possessions, telling anyone who scolded him that he had no fear of becoming like his own people. Father Conrardy died of pneumonia on August 2, 1914. At his request, he was wrapped in a mat with two other deceased patients, and they were buried together.

CHAPTER SEVEN

"We Lepers"

ON SEPTEMBER 15, 1881, the settlement at Molokai was visited by Queen Liliuokalani, who was acting as regent for her brother, King Kalakaua, who was away from the islands on a world tour. In her entourage were Princess Likelike and other officials. When the royally bedecked steamer arrived at Kalaupapa, small boats — covered in flowers and in other designs — set out from shore to welcome the monarch and to carry the royal party to the landing site. A special pier had been fashioned for the convenience of the queen and her companions. Close by was a royal pavilion, with chairs and other adornments.

The queen landed on Kalaupapa to the ringing cheers of more than seven hundred lepers. Any of the patients who could walk or crawl to the landing managed to be on hand for the celebration. The queen intended to greet them all, but the shock of seeing the ravages of the disease upon those assembled there almost silenced her. She was not filled with a panic or with a sense of horror, nor was she particularly repelled by the disfigurements and the mutilated flesh. These were symbols of suffering, exile, abandonment, and personal grief that stalked the island in the company of lingering death. Like others in her kingdom, the queen had long been dismayed by the devastation caused not only by the disease but also by the stern methods that had to be employed in order to halt a major epidemic. She understood that such preventive measures were necessary but, as an islander herself, she understood the deep bond between her people and their own lands.

Each one of the patients had not only been afflicted with a loathsome disease but had also been taken from his or her island, where spiritual sustenance was part of life. Now they stood ravaged by a disease and by the so-called fruits of civilization. The queen would face a similar tragedy at the hands of those who had invaded her domain for land and power. The Americans would overthrow this rightful monarch in time to annex the islands. On this occasion, she wore a stately black dress, with a train, and she carried herself with the marvelous inborn dignity that characterized most Hawaiians, especially the *ali'i*. As a member of the royal family, Liliuokalani was an *Ali'i nui*.

The patients and settlement officials were entranced by her presence and deeply touched that the regent had come to visit them. Liliuokalani always held the esteem and the affection of her people. On this occasion, her subjects were quite dazzled. She was led through several triumphal arches, escorted by the patients themselves who had managed to manufacture uniforms so that they could serve as an official guard. The people spread flowers before her as she walked, and they offered her exquisite leis. The choir, which Father Damien had organized and trained, came forward at that time to serenade the queen and her court with native songs. These young patients were dressed in white, with blue and red sashes, and many of them hid their hands or their arms or took pains to stand at an angle, so that their disfigurements would not offend their regent. Liliuokalani could not speak to them after their performance. She was overcome by the sight of their agonies and by the delicate sensitivity that these children displayed in her presence. One of her officials read the speech to the gathering as she wept. Not only had she and her royal entourage been moved by the victims but they had also recognized some of their friends and relatives in the company. Princess Likelike was reduced to tears, too.

When the ceremony ended, Father Damien and Superintendent Meyer escorted Queen Liliuokalani through the entire settlement while some members of her court discovered the children that had been snatched out of their own arms by the segregation-policy police. When it was time for the retinue to depart from Molokai, the children stood on the shore, waving and sending demonstrations of affection to their mothers, many of whom fainted on the deck of the ship or collapsed sobbing.

Liliuokalani and other members of the royal family visited the settlement again at a later date as well. They toured the facilities once more, asking practical questions on all matters concerning the care of the patients. New relief measures were instituted as the result of their personal intervention in the plight of their people. When Liliuokalani returned to Hawaii after her first visit, however, she decided it was time that Father Damien be given royal recognition for his labors. The document, which was published as a form of gratitude, read as follows:

Kalakaua
King of the Hawaiian Islands
To all who shall see these Presents, Greetings:

Know ye that We have Appointed and Commissioned, and by these presents We Appoint and Commission Reverend Father Damien de Veuster to be Knight Commander of the Royal Order of Kalakaua, to exercise and enjoy all the Rights, Pre-eminences and Privileges to the same Right appertaining, and to wear the Insignia as by Decree created.

In Testimony Whereof, We have caused these Letters to be made Patent and the Seal of Our Kingdom to be hereunto affixed.

Given under Our Hand, at Our Palace, in Honolulu,
this twentieth day of September, in the Year of Our Lord,
One Thousand Eight Hundred and Eighty One.
(signed) Liliuokalani, Regent
By the King,
The Chancellor of the Royal Order of Kalakaua,
No. O. Dominis.

Queen Liliuokalani instructed Bishop Koeckemann to take the medal and the decree to Kalawao, and she sent a personal letter to Father Damien as part of the official documents. In the letter, she stated that she knew that Damien sought his reward and his inspiration only from God. Nevertheless, she felt that she had to demonstrate her own appreciation for the deeds he had accomplished in the settlement. Her visit to Molokai had enabled her to have a firsthand account of his labors and his unceasing concern for the afflicted there.

Father Damien is reported to have been a bit dismayed by the honors and the knightly commission. He had to be forced by the bishop to wear the insignia on the day that he received it. The medal and the decree remained henceforth in a drawer or cabinet, although Damien did consent to wear a token of his distinction on Hawaiian holidays. He did this in order to convey his loyalty to the Hawaiian monarchy. His reply to her was delivered by the French consul in Honolulu, who was delighted to see a demonstration of the royal regard for one of the Catholic missionaries.

The fact that Damien was not particularly thrilled over receiving recognition from the throne of Hawaii was caused in part by his natural disdain for the pomp of the world; but it was brought about mostly by his knowledge of his enemies, both inside and outside his congregation. The newspapers again printed extravagant articles that sang his praises, something that he knew would merely create more problems for him. With his usual common sense and alertness, Damien braced himself for the storm, not realizing in his heart that it would come from his own superiors. He did not look to outside problems at this stage of his life because, interiorly, he was coming to grips with the physical reality of his own existence. He was suffering the first stages of leprosy.

The symptoms started in his left foot, which pained him over the years and made walking difficult. The pain moved up into his leg, making his trek up the trail to the top of Molokai extremely arduous. All of this was happening, of course, while he was being plagued by the priestly visitors allowed or sent by his superiors in Honolulu. In the midst of this suffering, he was ordered to serve as pastor to the topside Molokai parishes.

Father Damien appears to have been in Honolulu when the incident took place that led to his diagnosis. He was visiting the mission center when he upset a bowl of boiling water on his foot. He registered no pain, did not cry out, or hop around in the usual display of suffering. Father Fouesnel witnessed the accident and the calm way in which Damien contemplated the burns that appeared on his flesh instantly. Fouesnel, who was not stupid about such things, sent for his own doctors and soon asked Dr. Eduard Christian Arning to examine Damien. Dr. Arning had come to Hawaii at the request of the board of health. He was an accredited physician who knew about the work of Dr. Hansen, having been a student of Dr. Albert Neisser, who had conducted experiments and studies on the *Mycobacterium leprae*. These advances in the scientific concern about leprosy (eventually known in the medical world as Hansen's disease) started at the same time that Father Damien began his own remarkable work with the victims of the illness. Between the scientific community's gains and Damien's lifework, the disease would never remain the same in the minds of enlightened human beings.

Dr. Arning preached to the medical community in Honolulu about the emerging germ theories in Europe, especially as they related to the disease of leprosy in the Hawaiian Islands. He refuted the often repeated beliefs of laymen, such as Dr. Charles McEwen Hyde, that leprosy was the result of debauchery and sin, or the sign of divine retribution for a failing or for an evil ancestor. Many in the islands associated leprosy with syphilis, and that belief remained a powerful impetus for the missionary clergy and others to make judgments on the moral fitness of victims. When a certain member of the Protestant missionary clergy also contracted the disease, he was sent away from the islands, so as to escape the segregating policies that would put him into the midst of the native population of the settlement and also to prevent Hyde and others from looking foolish or misled. Arning did not tolerate the repetition of such medical "knowledge" in his presence, and he set about hoping to find a way of inoculating a person with leprosy in order to study its progress and symptoms. He was offered a sacrificial victim: a criminal who, given his choice between death or medical experiments, chose the latter. But the medical community throughout the world faced problems with the disease. Leprosy could not be induced by their methods, and therefore it could not be used to provide a serum for the benefit of future immunity.

Arning saw Damien in 1884 and immediately had to give him the cruel truth about his condition. The priest also had the help of a Dr. Arthur Mouritz, who would eventually become the settlement's resident doctor. Both of these physicians realized that the typical damage to the nerves was evident in Damien's foot and legs. Dr. Mouritz described his patient at the time, saying that Damien was five feet eight inches, weighed 204 pounds, and had abundant black hair and a handsome appearance.

Later that year and also in 1885, Damien asked permission to visit Honolulu but was refused each time by Father Fouesnel.

When he persisted in his request, the provincial wrote to him, accusing him of being egotistical and certainly devoid of all tact and delicacy. A man in his condition, afflicted with his disease, was no longer welcome in polite society. Damien had asked for this permission because he wanted to try a special sort of treatment in Honolulu. Dr. Mouritz, who sincerely lamented his inability to offer Damien and the other lepers any sort of reasonable hope about their conditions, had suggested that Damien see a Dr. Masanao Goto. Rudolph Meyer, the settlement superintendent, had agreed. Father Damien arrived in Honolulu in 1886, if not in open defiance of Fouesnel, then at least "guilty" of interpreting his provincial's letter in a rather dubious manner. He set about conducting the affairs of the mission first, and this brought him in touch with Mother Marianne Cope, who would be beatified by Pope Benedict XVI in 2005.

Blessed Marianne was born in Heppenheim, Hesse-Darmstadt, Germany, in 1838. Her name was originally Barbara Koob. At the age of two, she was brought by her family to live in Utica, New York. There the family was starting life anew as immigrants to America. By the time she was a young woman, the family name had been changed to Cope. She was introduced to the religious life by the first mother general of the Third Order of the Sisters of St. Francis, in Syracuse, New York, and she entered that convent, receiving the religious name of Marianne. After making her perpetual vows in 1863, Mother Marianne was given various assignments in the congregation's area convents. She was then put in charge of the novices in the motherhouse and began to assume administrative duties as an assistant to the mother general. She displayed a remarkable intelligence, common sense, and a certain calm in all of her tasks, endearing people to her and becoming a stable influence in the community and the secular world around her. In 1877, in obvious recognition of her abilities and spiritual advancements, she was elected mother general of the congregation, a position that she held for two terms. At the request of King Kalakaua, Father Fouesnel went to Syracuse to see Mother Marianne to ask if sisters would come to the islands to conduct an apostolate to the lepers. Most of the members of the congregation were trained medical personnel. Mother Marianne could not make that commitment at the time of Fouesnel's visit, but she confided to others that she knew God was calling her to the islands, and to Molokai.

On October 22, 1883, Mother Marianne and six volunteer Franciscan Sisters (selected from a total of thirty-five members of the congregation who had offered to accompany her) sailed for Hawaii. This single act made Mother Marianne the first sister of an American foundation to start missionary work in a foreign land. (Hawaii had not been annexed to the United States at the time, and it was still an independent kingdom.) The arrival of Mother Marianne and her sisters, and their subsequent introduction to the various social groups in the islands, caused quite a stir. People were startled by the thought of such talented, educated women taking upon themselves the dreadful ordeals of service in the settlement or at the receiving hospital in Honolulu. Above all, the people of the islands, both *haoles* and Hawaiians, were quite impressed by Mother Marianne's intelligence and executive abilities.

The Franciscan Sisters started their missionary work at the receiving center for the lepers at Kakaako. As trained nurses, they brought professional standards and modern scientific procedures into the pell-mell atmosphere of the establishment. Many patients and helpers were educated by the sisters and edified at the same time. After a while, the newcomers founded a school on Maui and started Malulani Hospital on that island to provide medical care. In the meantime, the Franciscan Sisters in Syracuse requested the return of Mother Marianne, who was needed by the congregation. Both the Church officials and the Hawaiian government gave notice that they would block any attempts to deprive Hawaii of Mother Marianne's presence and labors. The congregation surrendered to the local wishes and named Mother commissary general of the mission, thereby certifying she would remain in Hawaii.

When the furor subsided, Mother Marianne set about making sure that the small girls in the settlement were well-provided for and offered protection, something that Father Damien had pressed upon everyone as a most necessary project. These youngsters were constantly endangered by the contagion of the disease and by the outbreaks of lawlessness among the patients. In 1885, Mother Marianne founded the Kapiolani Home on the grounds of the hospital in Honolulu. The government then asked her to assume the task of founding a similar establishment in the settlement.

With some of her sisters, Mother Marianne moved to Molokai, bringing with them many of their previous patients. Father Damien lived long enough to see the sisters in residence there. He asked, on one occasion three times in a row, if Mother Marianne would take care of his small boys after he died. She promised that they would be looked after, and they were. Mother Marianne of Molokai, as she is called, remained in the settlement until her death on August 9, 1918. Damien talked with her for the first time when he visited Honolulu in 1886, and he exhausted her and everyone else within earshot. He had been so deprived of conversation and personal contact with religious that he seemed to have an infinite range of subjects to discuss with all persons around him.

While in Honolulu, Damien also visited Dr. Masanao Goto. Dr. Goto had prescribed a radically new program for the benefit of leper patients, demonstrating considerable success. His patients took baths and used pills made from the substance of a Japanese tree bark. Damien experienced considerable relief from these baths and from the pills. He insisted that his own right hand was improving as a result, and that he was regaining some of his former vigor. When Damien returned to the settlement, in fact, he immediately set about building a bathhouse and ordered vast quantities of Dr. Goto's medicine. It appears that the regimen provided relief for many there. The death rate was lowered, and patients improved, at least for a time. Dr. Mouritz, however, cautioned him against taking too many baths, realizing that the priest, in his enthusiasm, was draining away his strength.

CHAPTER EIGHT

Brother Dutton

THERE HAD BEEN NO definitive announcement by officials about Damien's condition, and, reportedly, he referred to everyone in the settlement as "we lepers" long before he contracted the disease. On one particular Sunday, however, while preaching his homily, Damien used the term "we lepers" again, and the ever alert press recognized the changes in him as the first signs of the disease. The story broke with a furious roar, and newspapers around the world flashed the story that the Hero of Molokai had become a leper. It is quite possible that his bout with fever on the Big Island signaled the first signs of the disease. Damien had cared for the lepers in his congregation without fear, and they coughed while he was bandaging them and cleaning their wounds. He had certainly not maintained the sterile, sanitized sort of medical regimen that would become mandatory in the settlement in time, perhaps because he knew in his heart that he was already infected with the horrifying bringer of death.

Back in his home in Tremelo, however, his mother, who was eighty-three at the time, had been spared all knowledge of his condition by family members. Damien's own letters home had been carefully worded to hide his actual physical decline. He did write the truth to Pamphile, but he certainly would not have told their mother such grim news. Even so, someone who had seen the reports and believed his mother deserved to know the truth about her son brought her the story. She began to hunt down the various accounts of her son in the newspapers, reading them in horror. She never recovered from the shock, particularly because some of the news stories sensationalized his affliction, stating that flesh was falling off his body in huge chunks. As the Hawaiian women accompanying Queen Liliuokalani to the settlement on Molokai were agonized by the thought of their children facing disfigurement and death alone in a land of exile, so was the mother of Damien de Veuster. Her "Jef" was out in a strange land, afflicted by an appalling disease, untended, and perhaps even unloved.

She became withdrawn after the initial shock and spent her waking hours staring at a picture of "Jef" and a single letter that announced his devotion. She also sat in silence before a statue of the Blessed Virgin Mary, but uttered no word of rebellion against the Divine Will for her son. Anne Catherine de Veuster wasted away slowly; and on April 6, 1886, while staring at his picture and sighing, Damien de Veuster's mother died of a broken heart. When Damien received the news of her death, he was grief-stricken and turned to a companion for prayers and comfort.

This trusted friend was not some long-time missionary who had come to Molokai seeking cures or chasing some mysterious dream. Damien turned to the "Irrepressible Veteran," a man of infinite calm, who had come to brighten the priest's last years on the island. The Irrepressible Veteran arrived "out of nowhere" and stayed there for the rest of his life. On July 19, 1886, Damien went in his carriage to the landing area at Kalaupapa, expecting to welcome yet another load of patients forced into exile by the segregation policy of the Hawaiian government. He was already displaying symptoms of the disease and losing his energies, but he maintained his normal routines as much as possible. The welcoming of new patients was a priority with him in any case, and he managed to get to the boat landing whenever a steamer was sighted making its way to the shore. This kindness blunted the initial shock for most of the patients.

On that day, however, there was a *haole* in the group. He was an American, with brown hair and a pleasant smile. He demonstrated a military bearing; but there was a certain gentleness in his manner, and his blue-gray eyes shone with a clear and placid light. His name was Ira Barnes Dutton, but he would be known forever at Molokai as "Brother Joseph." The name was not given lightly to him by Father Damien. It had nothing to do with formal religious commitment although Dutton was a professed member of the Third Order of Saint Francis, a religious group open to those laypersons who wish to practice the art of living the spiritual life in the world, imitating St. Francis of Assisi.

In the course of time, there was another "Brother" in the residence at the settlement, an Irishman whom few hear about: James Sinnet, who had been trained in Chicago's Mercy Hospital and had been hired by the board of health. Sinnet was dubbed "Brother James" by Damien, whom Sinnet addressed rather adoringly as "Brother," too. Sinnet was with Damien when he died, after having served him faithfully for eight months. Sinnet left Molokai soon after Damien's death, unwilling to be part of the changes that inevitably took place in the settlement. There appears to have been a period of disorder and chaos following Damien's death, and sterner measures of control were put into operation as a result. Brokenhearted, Sinnet was not up to seeing the new style of government in place.

Brother Joseph Dutton, however, was made of sterner stuff and quite able to withstand the cold winds of change. He had been born on April 27, 1843, in Stowe, Vermont, moving to Janesville, Wisconsin, when he was four. The Civil War broke out as he reached maturity, and he enlisted in the City Zouave Corps of the newly formed Company B of the 13th Wisconsin Volunteer Infantry. Serving with his unit in Alabama, Kentucky, Kansas, Louisiana, and Tennessee, he was promoted in the field and ended his military career with a recommendation from Major General Granger that he be given a captaincy in the United States Army. Dutton, however, like so many of his contemporaries, had seen enough of the horrors of war and was anxious to get back into civilian life. He married a young woman who almost destroyed him. She went to live with someone else, all the time spending his money and putting him deeply into debt. Divorced from her, Dutton turned to "John Barley Corn" (as whiskey was called in those days) for consolation. He spent several years as a drunk and eventually became an alcoholic.

One day he "took the pledge" and never touched another drop and, in 1883, he converted to Catholicism. The Trappist monks offered him a haven at that point of his life, and he went to Gethsemane Monastery in Kentucky, where he pulled himself back together. Dutton was confirmed at Gethsemane, but he took no vows and made no commitment to the cloistered life. He was delighted with the monastic seclusion and the regimen of the monastery which was much like the military schedules of his service period. He left the Trappists, however, and set about discovering what it was that he was supposed to accomplish in his life.

A short time later, while visiting New Orleans in the company of a Redemptorist priest, Dutton came across a magazine article describing the life of Father Damien in the settlement of Molokai. He knew in an instant that he belonged on the same island, doing the same work. Dutton was not a man fleeing from the past or from heartache. He understood himself, in all his virtues and vices, and he knew the world well enough to be a realist. This new life that he sought was not an experiment; it was, rather, the natural outcome of his spiritual conversion and his years in the monastic routines of the cloister. With his typical caution and thoroughness, Dutton went to the University of Notre Dame to interview Dr. Charles Stoddard, a scholar who had visited the settlement and had written about his experiences there. Soon after satisfying himself about the island and about the Hero of Molokai, Dutton sailed to Hawaii.

He arrived in his traditional blue denim suit, very military in appearance, and visited Bishop Koeckemann and then Walter Murray Gibson, the head of the board of health. Both men were impressed with his manner and with his quiet resolve to serve Father Damien and the patients. Gibson (who, like Dutton, was a native of Vermont) understood the purpose of his visitor and approved of his initiative and steadfastness. Dutton had volunteered to serve without pay — which is an endearing quality in any volunteer — but he was hired with a monthly salary.

Father Damien was delighted with Brother Joseph Dutton. He built a one-room house for his companion, close to his own dwelling, and assigned him to do various tasks. Damien's faith was not in vain. Dutton proved a tireless worker. He also gained the reputation of never raising his voice and never displaying signs of irritability or frustration. In return, he was astonished by the activities and energy that he witnessed each day in Damien. He discovered that there seemed to be an endless number of projects the priest planned for them both. They normally worked from four-thirty in the morning until eleven at night; and they not only nursed the sick but also built tables, homes, and chapels together.

After a time, Dutton was in charge of the administrative aspects of the settlement and also took charge of the small orphanage. In all of these duties, he was known for being soft-spoken, amiable, well-bred, and in possession of a courteous manner. As a daily companion of Father Damien, Dutton swore a yearly vow to stay at the leprosarium. He also witnessed Damien's death and testified on his behalf, refuting every rumor and smear tactic used by the priest's enemies. After the priest's death, Brother Joseph worked under an agreement with the board of health.

By this time, he had achieved the status of a world-class celebrity in his own right. He corresponded with people on every continent, including kings, presidents, and men like Thomas Edison. His main interest, however, was with the veterans of the Civil War. He maintained close ties with the Grand Army of the Republic, the military and fraternal organization that had developed at the close of the fighting. The Grand Army, in its 47th Encampment (yearly meeting), held in Chattanooga, Tennessee, on September 18, 1913, honored Dutton as one of its own. He had sent the members his greetings from Hawaii, and they responded by forwarding an American flag for his military-style flagstaff outside of his office in the settlement. Dutton flew the American flag throughout his life, and many of the ensigns were replacements from veterans' organizations.

One of the most remarkable events that took place during Dutton's life on Molokai happened in 1908, while he was elderly but still in good health. On the morning of July 16 of that year, Dutton was raising the American flag in front of his office when the patients of the settlement came running to tell him some exciting news. They pointed to the ocean, and Dutton heard them say that ships were approaching the island, glistening like the silvery shields of warriors on the waves. Dutton hurried with the patients to the shore, almost afraid to believe that his dream had come true at last. He had written to President Theodore Roosevelt, telling him about the work of Father Damien, about the settlement and the patients. He expressed a hope in his letter that one day these patients might witness a visit from a ship of the United States Navy, so that they could experience the thrill of seeing such a great vessel of power and might.

With his usual enthusiasm, Teddy Roosevelt gave a quick response. A message was sent from the White House, through the secretary of the navy, to Rear Admiral Charles Stillman Sperry, who was serving at the time as the commander of the United States' Great White Fleet. This armada — one of the largest and most modern in the world at the time — was about to tour six continents, to assure everyone else on earth of the military prowess of America and to greet them on behalf of the people and the President of the United States. Admiral Sperry was on board the flagship of the fleet, the U.S.S. *Connecticut*, when he received the message, which read: "Divert from course. Pass Molokai Island in battle formation. Show naval power to Brother Dutton. Dip colors. Then continue to Japan."

The Great White Fleet (so called because the ships were all painted white) consisted of four destroyers and sixteen battle-ships. The fleet of United States battleships en route from San Francisco to Honolulu, turned from the course and entered the waters of the settlement. They passed in parade as the patients and Dutton stood out on the front lawn in dazed joy. The *Vermont, Kansas, Connecticut, Tennessee, Georgia, New Jersey, Rhode Island, Virginia, Maine, Minnesota, Ohio, Mississippi, Alabama, Kentucky, Illinois*, and the S.S. *Kearsarge*, sailed in precise and majestic order, displaying the might and resolve of the United States. The maritime procession took hours, and each ship made its presence known to the residents of the settlement and then sailed on to the appointed international designations.

Dutton wrote a letter to Admiral Sperry the same day, thanking him and describing the scene that unfolded before the patients and the staff. On July 22, 1908, Admiral Sperry, on board the U.S.S. *Connecticut*, wrote to Brother Joseph in reply. He expressed, on behalf of his fellow officers and the men of the Great White Fleet, best wishes to everyone involved in the "splendid work" of the settlement. He added: "... The island and the settlement were a beautiful sight as we steamed by almost under the shadow of the mountains, and I thank you for the photographs." Admiral Sperry enclosed his own picture for Brother Joseph, as "a token of respect and regard."

After Damien's death, when Church officials asked Brother Joseph to provide them with a report concerning his dealings with "the Leper Priest" and his views of Damien's apostolate, he wrote the following:

> As directed by the Fathers, I first state regarding myself that I came here from the United States to work with Father Damien, arriving at Kalawao the evening of July 29, 1886. And from that evening until his death — April 15, 1889 — I was intimately associated with him in his work among the people, particularly his orphan boys, and in having the care of his two churches (of only one church, though, in the latter part), in serving his masses, and assisting with his various ministrations, so far as a lay man could.... He had a great natural strength and vitality. These powers, coupled with his zeal, seemed to enable him to be ever ready to pursue with vigor whatever seemed to him ought to be done.... Father Damien had in his heart, when tranquil... a most tender feeling, as I often have been made to know. You will bear me out in stating the fact, that no one found it pleasant at all times to be with him for a very long period. If my intimate association with him was longer continued than that of others, it was partly because I admitted my own faults in that regard, and partly because I ever saw him place in me the most entire confidence, and have in his heart a deep love, no matter what his exterior might be. And also, I used to be quite open with him in speaking of all these things; he likewise to me, and this seemed to give confidence in each other....
>
> Father Damien was very devout, and in his tranquil moments he seemed to take a supernatural view of things, I may say of almost everything. His meditation in the morning was generally of about an hour's duration, and he had a regular practice of making a visit to the Blessed Sacrament, at night before going to bed. He offered the

Holy Sacrifice long after he seemed to be unable to do so, and recited his office nearly to the last, for some time after being dispensed, and while his one eye was hardly able to see.... It seems to me that the recitation of his office under the circumstances showed marked heroism. His devotion had many ways of showing itself in his last days; reciting the rosary, every evening asking for spiritual reading, etc.

His love for these people of the leper settlement — for all of them — was great. He gave himself freely for them. A sudden call of charity — one in distress — would cause him to drop at once what he might be engaged upon (except when at the altar) and quickly to give his aid.

In his ministrations with the natives he was untiring. Especially in attendance upon the dying was he earnest and helpful. So frequently being with him in this office, I was particularly impressed with it, and often thought that he must have been a great comfort to many souls in these moments.

When he felt that his end was approaching, and having quite a number of pieces of unfinished work about the new Church, etc., he strained every nerve and muscle to get them completed. I am sure that those engaged upon the work, all who noted his efforts in those last weeks, will join me in asserting the belief, that by these extra exertions he considerably hastened his end....

In the last months of his own life, Brother Joseph became ill and was moved to the hospital in Honolulu. He died on March 26, 1931. Dutton requested burial on Molokai, however, and his wish was carried out by the Hawaiian government. The U.S.S. *Pelican* transported his remains back to the settlement, where he was buried near his beloved colleague. Church and state dignitaries accompanied his body and attended his burial there.

CHAPTER NINE

Bishop Herman Koeckemann

WHILE THE VARIOUS POLITICAL, religious, and social groups in the islands responded to Father Damien and to his apostolate in their own particular manner, motivated by their own sense of his worth and place in the history of Hawaii, men and women across the entire world watched his progress. These people of other lands were fascinated by the courage of his landing on Molokai and intrigued by the generosity that impelled him to stay among the patients there. The world honored the Hero of Molokai in a unique fashion, inspired by the various published accounts of his life and his work.

Perhaps because the people in other nations were not involved in the day-to-day rivalries or political upheavals caused by his presence and his unflagging demands for his patients, they could judge his personality and his labors with the objectivity that summons admiration. This was particularly true of the British people. Most of them have always been prompt in determining the worth of causes and the uniqueness of an individual's character. The British people had taken Gandhi (called Mahatma, or the Great Soul) into their hearts even as he caused them economic stress, jeopardized the British Raj in India, and forced the ultimate loss of that "crown jewel" of the empire. These English were thus very much a part of Father Damien's apostolate. Because of their generosity, he was exposed to envy, political wrath, and abuse from his own superiors. Because of their kindheartedness, however, Damien was given moments of true companionship and solace. From the British, Father Damien also received the ultimate service: the defense of his good name after his death, when the grave had silenced his voice and made it impossible for him to confront his detractors.

The first Englishman to make his way into Father Damien's life was an Anglican clergyman, the Reverend Hugh B. Chapman of St. Luke's Church, Camberwell, London. He had heard about Father Damien from various articles, such as the one that appeared in *The Illustrated London Times* soon after Damien's death. The article, titled "Father Damien's Abode With The Lepers," read:

> We have been favored by Dr. E. Arning of Hamburg, a German physician who formerly resided at the Hawaiian Leper Asylum, where Father Damien's self-sacrificing labors were carried on till his death…. Most of our readers will have learned something of the history of that admirable Christian philanthropist, Joseph Damien de Veuster, a native of Belgium, who was born near Louvain…. The leper settlement which had been founded some years before on the isle of Molokai, distant a few hours' sail from Honolulu, the chief town and seaport of those islands, was then not well managed and Father Damien, from motives of pure charity, undertook to reside there, both directing the needful measures for the temporal welfare of the afflicted exiles, and ministering religion's comfort and instruction.
>
> His benevolent efforts have for some years past been known in England, where a few among the members and clergy of the English Church raised contributions to assist the work of Father Damien; and in December last he was

visited by Mr. Edward Clifford, bringing a collection of useful and pleasant gifts from his English friends.

This gentleman, who had been struck with the miserable condition of lepers in India, took a particular interest in the object of Father Damien's mission, and wrote an account of it, which was published in the Nineteenth Century, just before the news arrived that Father Damien had died, a martyr of humanity, from the disease contracted by dwelling among his fellow-creatures in Molokai.

The subject was soon afterwards brought prominently into public notice at the meeting over which the Prince of Wales presided, at Marlborough House to set on foot a worthy memorial of Father Damien, and to promote the effectual study and medical treatment of leprosy, with a special investigation concerning this malady in India and the British Empire.

Mr. Clifford's writings on this topic have been reprinted in a small volume, entitled *Father Damien*, published by Messrs. Macmillan and Company, which will certainly be read with interest. In mentioning our present correspondent, Dr. Arning, this little book gives his name slightly wrong, as "Dr. Arnini."

His views of Molokai will be acceptable to all who are more or less acquainted with the history of the Hawaiian Leper Asylum, which occupies the two villages of Kalaupapa and Kalawao, on the north coast of the island. Between them is a low hill on which is the crater of the extinct volcano, with a hole 130 feet wide and of unknown depth, full of green water. Father Damien, inhabiting a small four-roomed house next to the church and school he had erected at Kalawao, did not live quite alone but was accompanied by Father Conrardy, Brother Joseph, an American, and Brother James, an Irishman....

The Reverend Mr. Chapman first wrote to Father Damien in February 1888, offering then and there to undertake the task of collecting money to bring about a measure of relief for the settlement and its needs. He stated quite openly in his letter that he was an Anglican clergyman, not connected in any fashion with Damien's Catholic religion. Chapman, however, had no qualms about linking himself to the Catholic mission in the endeavor. He stated that he viewed Damien's life as a beautiful Christian sermon that should be studied by men of all faiths, a life capable of instructing all people of good will in the Gospel.

Such a letter was most certainly welcomed by Damien, who was entering the last stages of his life in the settlement and was quite bereft of consolation. This, coming from such an unexpected source, was not only a charming but also a delightful change. He wrote back, telling Chapman that Brother Joseph Dutton was a convert from the Anglican community. Dutton had proven himself in Damien's eyes, and, as a result, the Hero of Molokai was happy to welcome any others into the apostolate, even from a distance. In the same letter, Damien urged Chapman to seek his solace and inspiration from the Blessed Sacrament. (The Eucharist of the Mass — normally kept in reserve on the altars of Catholic churches and chapels — was the object of perpetual adoration among the Sacred Hearts Fathers; perpetual adoration was an act of reparation and loyalty, which Father Coudrin had incorporated into the congregation at its founding). In the same letter, Damien informed his would-be benefactor that there were six hundred lepers in the settlement.

Chapman needed no more encouragement! He began to talk to his own parishioners about Damien's life and work, and he also started sending articles to the London newspapers. Being an Anglican did not make him feel unqualified to lighten the load of Damien and the patients on Molokai. Others followed with the same enthusiasm, and, eventually, Anglican sisters offered to go to the settlement, in the absence of any Catholic community there at the time.

The Anglican clergyman also enlisted the aid of Cardinal Henry Manning, the distinguished Catholic archbishop of Westminster, who was honored to add his own voice to the campaign. This Catholic participation, of course, touched off the usual round of prejudice and bigotry in the newspapers.

Chapman found himself the target of many letters to the editor in the British daily press. Some went so far as to state that the lepers were better off dead or abandoned than in the hands of the diabolical Roman Catholic clergy. One letter stated that Father Damien was making moral lepers out of the patients and leading them straight into the fiery pits of hell by putting Catholic doctrines into their minds. A second furor was started by the question of the Christian's obligation to the lepers. This same battle, of course, had been conducted in the islands of Hawaii over the decades. Men like Dr. Hyde firmly taught that leprosy was the result of syphilis and debauchery. No matter what Dr. Arning and the other medical specialists declared, the Protestant clergy and their admirers clung to the belief that the lepers were sinners being punished by a just God; they felt that Jehovah, annoyed by the levels of sin among the island people, had visited upon them a righteous plague.

The people of Britain were soon embroiled in the same debate, but the empire involved more than just a small group of islands in the middle of the Pacific Ocean. The Prince of Wales and others realized that thousands of British subjects, particularly in India, were suffering as the patients on Molokai suffered, and there was no English Damien in their midst.

Chapman allowed the political and religious uproar to go its own way as he continued to collect funds for Damien's people. In only three months, he raised and sent to Father Damien more than nine hundred English pounds, which amounted to forty-eight hundred dollars in the islands. He said that he and his fellow countrymen were sending the funds in the hope that it would bring a smile to Damien's lips. Over the next three years, the Reverend Mr. Chapman raised more than twenty-six hundred English pounds for Damien's apostolate. This amount, not surprisingly, led to serious problems for the Hero of Molokai, both with his religious rivals and with his own superiors.

The island newspapers, hearing of the donations coming from England, naturally began the long bout of questions concerning the need for the funds. Reporters and editors inquired about the truth of the situation in the settlement. They asked: If the money was necessary to relieve critical situations, why did the government and the board of health not provide the same without question? If the money was not necessary, what did Damien intend to do with it? In either case, no matter what the truth of the matter, Damien and the Catholic authorities in Honolulu were put in unenviable positions. At that time, Mr. Gibson and the Hawaiian monarch were making every effort to befriend the Catholics of the islands. Both of these men recognized the signs that the hostile *haole* community had gained power in many areas. Gibson was actually put under investigation and then cleared of charges of mismanagement of funds. The king, however, faced an open *haole* rebellion and was forced to cede some of his constitutional powers as a result.

The Americans had every intention of taking over the islands in the course of time, and this was just the opening shot of their long and persistent campaign. The American plan did not include a monarchy, as it did not make any consideration of the Hawaiians' historical values or their traditions and religious beliefs. The funds received from the Reverend Hugh Chapman, of course, helped Father Damien keep the storeroom available when the supply ships were forced into ports during the storm seasons or when there was a shortage of foods and articles necessary to keep the patients clothed and fed adequately. (Damien never did accept the notion that one garment and one set of linens were sufficient for each patient per year.)

The fact that many people in the Hawaiian Islands (including members of the royal family) and in America had been sending gifts and donations did not alter the controversy. The Americans winced at the thought of the English parading America's shortcomings across Europe. They were aghast at the thought of the British having to come in to remedy a situation within America's territorial domain. With his customary charm and courtesy, the Reverend Mr. Chapman referred to the money as a "flower of love from England." He and others of his nation would befriend Damien when his own people betrayed him.

The second Englishman to come into Damien's life was Edward Clifford, a British "gentleman." Clifford was a man used to the comforts of life, used to elegance and social graces. He traveled a great deal and was happy to explore the cultures and the lifestyles of people foreign to him. He was also a gifted painter, taking up the practice to express his vision and to assume responsible working habits. Clifford read an account of the life of Father Damien in a magazine in 1887, and he heard of the Reverend Mr. Chapman's efforts soon afterward. He decided, as a result, to visit Hawaii on his return from an extended stay in India. Why he felt so drawn to Damien he did not know. He admitted freely that he had been raised as a child to think only ill of Catholics. He was especially frightened by the sight of Catholic nuns, who (so he believed) would spirit him away and possibly kill him in some hideous ritual. Clifford felt only animosity toward Catholicism as he viewed it. Still, he intended to sail to Hawaii to see this Hero of Molokai with his own eyes.

He came to the settlement in December of 1888, arriving on board a steamer which found the going difficult as it neared the shore. It took a great deal of time and skill for the crew to get

Clifford's many packages, boxes, and crates on land in a safe and reasonable condition. While he was still on deck, a crew member pointed out to him the figure of Father Damien, who was waiting on the shore with a small group of patients. Soon after, Clifford stepped on shore with Damien's hand steadying him. The priest called him "Edward" from the first moment.

Clifford brought a vast variety of gifts for the settlement, some of which were extraordinarily costly. He gave Father Damien a sum of money that had been raised by private donations. He also gave him engraved Stations of the Cross for his chapel and a "Magic Lantern," the new machine that projected slides. The projector came complete with slides of the Gospel, for the edification of the viewers. Of particular interest was a barrel organ, another new machine that played up to forty separate melodies when its handle was turned with vigor. This organ had been sent to Damien and the patients by Lady Charteris, of England; it was the delight of the settlement, especially during the Christmas celebration attended by their English guest. Clifford also brought Father Damien a valuable watercolor of the "Vision of St. Francis," depicting the saint receiving the stigmata (the wounds of Christ) into his own flesh. Damien was stunned by the value of the painting, but he was grateful for it and placed it in his own bedroom on the second floor of his residence. At the end of his life, the painting would have great significance for him.

This Franciscan memento was very appropriate, even if Clifford did not understand the profound relationship between Damien and *Il Poverello* ("The Little Poor Man") of earlier times. The Franciscan Friars of California, who had pioneered the missions on the Pacific coast of America under the leadership of Blessed Junípero Serra, had offered hospitality to the first Sacred Hearts Fathers when they were sent into exile by Queen Kaahumanu and her governors. Fathers Short and Bachelot had worked in Mission San Gabriel and in other Franciscan missions during their stay in America. The Franciscan Sisters of Syracuse, New York, were the ones who responded to the pleas of the Hawaiian government and mission by coming to Hawaii to carry on the work begun by Damien, in the settlement and elsewhere. Brother Joseph Dutton, who proved to be such a good companion for Damien in his last years, was a Third Order Franciscan, a layman seeking perfection in the world as a member of that venerable religious institution. St. Francis of Assisi had a special concern for the lepers of his age, and Damien was to carry on the same apostolate. Above all, both carried the unique insignias of love and martyrdom on their own bodies before they died, as they had shared the ridicule and the spite of fellow religious who should have honored them.

From a romantic point of view, there was another similarity, which one of Damien's contemporaries on Molokai witnessed and commented upon. Father Damien went outside once a day with seeds and other types of food. He stood perfectly still and then whistled. Birds of every description appeared suddenly and perched on his hat, his shoulders, and on his arms as he fed them. The eyewitness said that it was a very startling scene.

Edward Clifford had also brought a hymnal and a supply of gurjun oil from the Indies. The medicine was mixed with lime water to form a paste, which was noted for its soothing effects on the sores and skin irritations suffered by the lepers. Clifford did not hesitate to visit the various lazarettos during his travels. A tour conducted by Damien of the Molokai settlement touched Clifford very much, and for a particular reason: Most of the leper colonies of that era were scenes of devastation, poverty, filth, and hopelessness. In the case of Molokai, Clifford saw just the opposite: small white houses, neat gardens, farm acres, livestock, chapels, a cemetery, and tidy roads.

The sight of this fastidious community, Clifford wrote later, horrified him more than the pitiful messes of other lazarettos elsewhere. The small white houses had an air of respectability and normalcy of life. They stood in the midst of death and suffering, proudly shining in the glare of the tropical sun, beside an ocean shoreline, and under swaying palms. Damien had duplicated a natural small town in the face of disaster; to Clifford, that made the leprosy and the results of that disease even more terrifying than what was normally expected. He stayed in the guesthouse of the settlement until after Christmas, a festival made a bit more cheerful by his generous gifts and novelties. Father Damien came over to be with him on the balcony (called *lanai* by the Hawaiians), and the two men sat and talked while Clifford made portraits of his host. When Damien saw the result of Clifford's efforts, he was astonished. He had not realized that the disease had done so much damage to his appearance; he had not guessed that he was so advanced in physical decay. Edward Clifford stated later that some of the happiest moments in the islands were spent on that guesthouse *lanai* with Damien. They parted as great friends, both knowing that they would never meet again on earth. Clifford went to Honolulu, where he was welcomed as an honored guest. He stayed there for a month, writing his book, *Father Damien*, which was popular in Europe and did much to further the cause of the work on Molokai.

Clifford recorded his interviews with the patients also, remarking that they told him:

> We're well off here. The government watches over us ... and we like our pastor. He builds our houses himself, he gives us tea, bisquits, sugar, and clothes. He takes good care of us and doesn't let us need for anything. We wouldn't want to leave if it meant that we would have to leave our *Makua Kamiano*.

There was yet another Englishman who would take part in the tragedy of Father Damien. Polynesians knew him as *Tusitala*. The world remembers him as Robert Louis Stevenson.

People everywhere have enjoyed the books of Stevenson. *Treasure Island* and his other works have dazzled readers in every generation and have been translated to the screen with artistry and skill. Stevenson has been honored as an author for decades, but few of his admirers know that he spent almost the last six years of his life in the Pacific, visiting the various island nations and the peoples there. His health had never been strong, and he found that the tropical climate restored his strength and enabled him to work and to recuperate from previous illnesses. Stevenson started his voyages in the Pacific on board the chartered yacht *Casco*, arriving in Honolulu in 1889.

He spent a period of five months during that initial visit. Known as "R.L.S." around the world, he was an instant celebrity in Honolulu. He met everyone, from the members of the royal family to the simple villagers on the coasts of the Outer Islands (as all of the other islands away from Oahu were known). Stevenson was a favored guest of Princess Kaiulani, who welcomed him and his party every afternoon under a banyan tree in Waikiki. That tree stands today, and it bears a commemorative of Stevenson's many hours under its sheltering boughs.

With his wife, Stevenson came to visit the princess and spent quiet hours discussing current literary trends as well as his travels and insights. He even wrote a short poem for the princess, in the shade of the banyan. Those were happy times, as the "Merry Monarch," King Kalakaua, was on the throne, brightening the lives of his people with his warmth and kindness. Hawaii reflected grace and charm, shut off from the commercialism and so-called progress of other lands. Stevenson returned to Hawaii in 1893, staying a shorter length of time during that visit because nothing was the same in the islands.

Queen Liliuokalani, the rightful ruler of Hawaii, had inherited the throne but then had been overthrown by the American *haoles*. Hawaii was to become a territory of the United States and, years later, the fiftieth state.

Stevenson had been particularly impressed with the work of Father Damien during his first visit. He did not arrive in time to meet Damien, but his visit to the settlement introduced him to evidences of the priest's labors. Stevenson also honored Mother Marianne and wrote a poem for her. A short time later, Dr. Charles McEwen Hyde (the same man who had preached that leprosy was the result of syphilis, and the Protestant cleric who had brought Portuguese ministers to the islands to woo the Catholic immigrants) wrote to a friend in America, the Reverend H.B. Gage. Dr. Hyde claimed in the letter that Father Damien was a filthy man who had laid claim to honors not due him. He also stated that Damien had merited the disease by debauchery with women patients and with women on the island of Hawaii. He had died, Hyde said, because of his vices, his carelessness, and his corruption, and because of divine retribution.

The Reverend Mr. Gage printed the letter in American circles, and the attack became known around the world. Stevenson read of it and was horrified. He had met Dr. Hyde during his first visit to Hawaii and had seen the work of Damien. In Tahiti, when the news of Hyde's slander reached him, Stevenson set about using all of his literary craft to raise a defense for a man no longer able to clear his own good name. He wrote an open letter to Dr. Hyde that was published across the globe. In it, he took the clergyman's attacks, one by one, and began to lay down a battery of words and images that was devastating. In the first paragraphs, Stevenson ferreted out the envy, cruelty, and guilt that prompted Hyde's attack. Step by step, word by word, he then assaulted Hyde's lifestyle, hypocrisy, villainy, and injustice. He topped off the attack by claiming that Hyde had lost the last shreds of honor and decency. [The letter is included in its entirety in Appendix 2.]

Stevenson saw to it that his letter appeared in nearly every newspaper in Europe and America. Editors relished the conflict and, certainly, Dr. Hyde had no choice but to do battle with the most formidable enemy possible in that era. The debate started again in European capitals, and Hyde and his company went into seclusion to avoid further assaults. When Stevenson died four years later, they emerged unrepentant and started the story that Stevenson had recanted his position on his deathbed. Mrs. Stevenson, in turn, gave an interview and stated that R.L.S. died unhappy that he could not have brought more disgrace and damage to Hyde and his company of slanderers.

Two figures emerge in this stage of Damien's life, both having significant roles in his torments and in his martyrdom. One was a German, and the other was a Breton. They had distinguished themselves in the missions and had relationships with the monarchy and the upper-class inhabitants of Honolulu, who were normally cordial and correct. Perhaps this social ease, this ability to mingle in the salons and drawing rooms, put them at a disadvantage when it came to dealing with Damien, who was fast approaching the end of his life and had become, as Dutton explained, one of the most hideous victims of leprosy.

Herman (spelled "Hermann" in some accounts) Bernard Koeckemann has been the subject of a great deal of speculation over the years because of his part in Damien's life. He does not fare well in the historical study of the Hero of Molokai's travails, particularly in the area of offering support or consolation at a time when both would have blunted the physical ordeals of Damien as a leper. His dealings with Damien, in fact, appear to have been overshadowed by the somewhat vindictive presence of the congregation's regional provincial, Father Léonore Fouesnel, SS.CC. Bishop Koeckemann's own defensive posture, particularly in situations where his episcopal rights were concerned, added yet another complication.

It is comparatively easy for people living in later generations to view the period with a modern eye and to pass a hard judgment on Bishop Koeckemann and to question the manner in which Damien was treated by both the bishop and Fouesnel, particularly at the end of his life. Judgment on the two, however, cannot be reached in a truly objective manner because of the wider context of events and the many factors in the islands that impacted the situation. One must believe that they acted according to their consciences, especially Koeckemann, who seemed as much a victim of Damien's martyrdom as the Leper Priest himself.

Bishop Koeckemann was a German member of the Sacred Hearts Congregation. He was born in Westphalia in 1828 and went on to attend school in Munster; there he studied the classics and proved himself to be so brilliant that his professors did not require him to take examinations in order to stand as a candidate for graduation. He was able to read and write Latin, Greek, Hebrew, and French, and he was remarkably adept at science and philosophy. Eager to enter the religious life and the priesthood, Koeckemann looked at the various congregations in his native land but decided to apply to the Louvain. He offered himself to the Sacred Hearts Congregation and was accepted speedily. He made his first vows in 1851 and three years later was sent to the Hawaiian missions as an ordained priest. This assignment is the first puzzling aspect of Koeckemann's life. Certainly the man was equipped by nature and academic background for administration, and as such he would have been more at home in Europe, in the various offices of the motherhouse of the congregation. Father Pamphile, Damien's own brother, had proven his worth as a scholar. Koeckemann was sent, instead, to the islands, where his knowledge of the classical languages and all of his brilliance meant very little.

Upon Koeckmann's arrival in Honolulu, however, Bishop Maigret, *Lui Ka Epikopo*, realized the man's potential and put him to work in the administrative offices of the mission territory. Such regions were not only the arenas of rugged missionaries and parishes flung over the wild terrain; each mission had to maintain records, reports, and keep in contact with the generalate, the governing body of the congregation, and with the local authorities. Koeckemann was brilliant and could manage the social and political environment of Honolulu with a certain grace. Because he was required to conduct business with the Americans, who did not show finesse or flair in European languages, Koeckemann set about studying English; and within a few weeks' time was able to converse eloquently and fluently with the inhabitants of the island capital. It is also possible that Bishop Maigret, who was certainly a veteran in the mission field, recognized that Koeckemann would not have fitted into the parishes dotting the Hawaiian Islands. He would have certainly fared poorly among the native settlements, because the basic requirements for the pastoral assignments in the outlying areas had little to do with languages, the classics, or philosophy.

For Koeckemann, life went smoothly while working with the gentle and compassionate bishop, but everyone could see that Maigret was on the decline. His strength was failing him, and he was becoming something of a recluse, exhausted by his labors and his advancing age. For this reason, at the age of 53, Herman Koeckemann was ordered to San Francisco and on August 21, 1881, was consecrated at St. Mary's Cathedral as the titular bishop of Olba and as Maigret's coadjutor (which meant that he was Maigret's auxiliary bishop with the right of succession in the see, or diocesan area). Koeckemann received the miter but was told not to interfere in the administration of the mission while Maigret lived. He believed that the old bishop was far gone, however, and he took things into his own hands immediately.

This was probably not an easy task. Bishop Koeckemann must have felt a bit estranged from the other priests of the mission, especially the long-time veterans. He was a German and a comparative newcomer who had gained power quickly. In all honesty, he had little or no pastoral experience, being an outsider to most of the people in the Hawaiian Islands and therefore limited in his judgment about the right responses to many issues that developed.

Such a lack of hands-on experience in the outlying districts would have made Koeckemann suspect in the eyes of the veteran missionaries, who judged a man by the way he worked among the parishioners and by the hours he put in each week to spread the Gospel and to provide adequate pastoral care for the flock. Koeckemann was a prelate who was more at home in ceremonies and performing administrative duties, more assured in the middle-management level of the Church. He was a classical scholar and somewhat fastidious about his personal appearance and his routines. In contrast to the elegant bishop, pictures from the era depict his priests as rugged, almost ragged men, oblivious to the fine arts of grooming and the graces of the various Honolulu social salons.

One of his first problems as bishop was the arrival of vast numbers of Portuguese in Hawaii. The first migrations to the islands by these people had started in 1814, and by Koeckemann's time they numbered in the hundreds. Stoutly Catholic and loyal to the Church even in their new environment, these Portuguese asked for priests from their own country to serve in their parishes. Bishop Koeckemann refused their requests, building tension in the community. He had difficulties with this situation until the Sacred Hearts priests, including Father Damien, learned enough Portuguese to serve the transplanted families adequately.

In 1890, Dr. Hyde brought Portuguese Protestant ministers into Hawaii to woo the Catholics away from the Church. He was not successful because of the stalwart nature of Portuguese Catholicism and also because the Sacred Hearts Fathers had taken steps to make themselves accessible and fluent in the language of the migrants. Koeckemann also enforced the mission's policy toward the establishment of schools and institutions of learning, sometimes coming into conflict with the government and having to spend time winning foes over to his cause. Koeckemann welcomed the Marianists to the islands in 1881 (this congregation, also known as the Brothers of Mary, was founded in 1817 by Blessed William Joseph Chaminade). The Marianists were able to staff the college that Bishop Koeckemann had founded. This pleased him very much, because he knew the value of education in any endeavor and seriously wanted to equip the young islanders with the advantages of academic training.

Thus, it appears that Koeckemann wanted to conduct the mission in peace but was willing to stand and defend those policies that he knew were right for the territory. Things might have been easier for him if he had been the only one in charge of the mission. He was the bishop, but the religious aspects, including direction and discipline, were not in his hands; the congregation had provided the mission with a prelate and with a provincial.

Father Modeste Favens, who was the gentle and good provincial when Damien began his apostolate on Molokai, had been easy to work with and was a veteran of many years of pastoral life. He did not remain the religious leader, however; in the course of time, Father Léonore Fouesnel became Bishop Koeckemann's coworker in the territory. The two men presented a solid front to the enemy and appear to have managed to work in harness for the good of the Church. Fouesnel, however, told companions of various incidents in which he felt that the bishop was excessively proud of his position and envious of anyone else's good fortune. One particular event was noted by Fouesnel, who resented the interference from the bishop. Fouesnel liked to promenade around Honolulu, and was to be given a new carriage and a magnificent steed by his patrons and admirers. Koeckemann told him that such a gift was unseemly for anyone in the mission except for the bishop himself.

Father Fouesnel had been the pastor of the church dedicated on Maui by Bishop Maigret, so he had some pastoral experience before assuming his role. He would have been present at the meeting in which the bishop related the needs of the patients in the settlement on Molokai. He would also have been present to witness Father Damien's instantaneous act of volunteering for the post of chaplain there. Because Damien was young and still comparatively untried in the mission, Fouesnel might have resented his boyish enthusiasm. His opposition to Damien stemmed from an early period, whatever the case. Fouesnel, in turn, was not much liked or appreciated by his fellow missionaries in the islands. He was a social lion, given to carriage rides, parties, and the companionship of the wealthy and the powerful. He gained the patronage of the upper class rather quickly. Toward those who served under his direction, however, he was quickly labeled as harsh, vindictive, and unfeeling. Even Bishop Koeckemann felt called upon at times to intervene when Fouesnel was being unreasonable in his treatment of some local parish priest. The bishop admitted on occasion that Fouesnel did not seem particularly suited to his role and office in the congregation.

Father Fouesnel is depicted in photographs of that era as being rather stout, with a generous stomach and a long white beard. He certainly enjoyed fine food and wine, and he did gain some measure of good will for the Church in Hawaii by appearing cultured and educated, his virtues bringing praise from the local *haole* community. Both the bishop and the provincial, however, seemed particularly out of place in their offices; both seemed quick to take offense and eager to defend their respective positions and rights. Above all, the two men did not have the compassion of Maigret (or of his provincial, Father Modeste, who had heard Damien's confession in French from the bow of a ship), and the pair did not seem to have insights into the tragedy taking place within the confines of the settlement. They were involved in the political aspects of the disease and were anxious to maintain their good standing with the monarchy and with the board of health, perhaps not understanding that even these two entities were sworn enemies of each other.

Damien wrote to Koeckemann soon after volunteering to go to Molokai. The fact that he felt obliged to let him know of his plans indicates that Koeckemann had assumed many powers in his own right even before being consecrated as a bishop. Damien worked in the settlement normally without much contact with the mission headquarters, and Koeckemann complained to the father general of the congregation, that because of the geographical oddity of the mission, the many islands, and the far-flung postings, most of the mission priests were on their own. As veterans of their districts and very alert to what was going on in their own territories, these hardy men stayed close to home and did not bother the authorities with trivial problems or events. The Sacred Hearts priests, because of this tendency to work hard and stay out of politics and social gatherings, won the respect of friend and foe alike over the years.

The first clash of wills and purpose came, therefore, as a result of the parade of visitors to Molokai. Bishop Koeckemann and Father Fouesnel showed Damien little regard when they allowed Fathers Burgermann and Montiton to invade his territory and disrupt his life. Even gentle Father Gregory, with his own physical problems, proved a drain on Damien's strength and time. Burgermann solved part of the problem by fleeing the settlement. Montiton demonstrated his own peculiar mannerisms in Honolulu, which made even Fouesnel admit that Damien had put up with a great deal. Father Gregory advanced in his illness and had to be taken away. Throughout their stays on Molokai, however, Damien had begged for relief and had been ignored. He was already feeling the first symptoms of leprosy, a fact that escaped the notice of his provincial and bishop. Fouesnel wrote sermonettes to him, and Koeckemann ignored him. Both, however, wrote to the father general to complain about the priest when they judged Damien guilty of some slight or minor offense. The fact that the father general did not take any unwarranted or precipitous action indicates that he had his own sources in the islands and well understood the two men in charge.

Both Fouesnel and Koeckemann fought against Father Conrardy's presence in Molokai as well. They said that Damien and Conrardy were both Belgians, as if that particular nationality was a strike against them. The two superiors also disliked the amount of publicity that was being generated as a result of Conrardy's association with the Hero of Molokai. The fact that Conrardy outlived Damien and continued to work in the settlement stamps him as a man of resolute tenacity because he faced the enmity of two well-placed foes. The English connection, therefore, was the final episode that brought about a serious breach between Damien and his superiors. As money and gifts began to pour into the settlement, both Koeckemann and Fouesnel were hard put to ratify their own positions or to exercise any authority. The Catholics were caught in the middle of the furor that erupted in the newspapers, and Koeckemann and Fouesnel wanted only to keep the peace. The gifts made Damien and the settlement well known, but his world fame prevented them from removing him as a source of problems to the mission. They were horrified to hear Queen Liliuokalani name Damien as the "Glory of Hawaii." His medal and personal letters, all of which had to be delivered by Koeckemann himself, were almost too much for the bishop to bear.

Nevertheless, Bishop Koeckemann enjoyed his tour of Molokai, even though it meant a dangerous descent down the trail and a journey accompanied by an escort of seventy lepers on horseback, carrying banners. Koeckemann was astounded at Damien's energy and schedule, and the bishop showed consideration for him and applauded his honors from the queen after coming face-to-face with the Leper Priest. Koeckemann was given a medal by King Kalakaua and was made an officer of the Order of Kalakaua. Father Fouesnel was also given a rank and a medal for bringing the Sisters of Saint Francis back to Hawaii, under the direction of Mother Marianne. Basically, the two superiors had served the islands well, and had demonstrated innovative and practical solutions to the problems of caring for the patients on Molokai. They did not receive any public gratitude for a long period, as Damien was the center of media and foreign attention. They also had several problems with Father Damien, particularly with the Americans, and they were unable to come to grips with the reality of his illness — in all of its horrible ramifications — and unable to view Damien as one chosen by God as a special soul.

To begin with, in the view of Bishop Koeckemann and Father Fouesnel, Damien appeared to have too much publicity throughout his stay on Molokai. The fact that it was Pamphile who put Damien's letters into the congregation's own magazine did not deter Koeckemann and Fouesnel from their conclusion. The requests coming from the Sacred Hearts Congregation's own motherhouse asking for more information did not matter either. The added fact that newspapers wrote what they wanted to write held no sway with either man. Father Fouesnel appears to have been the most adamant on this subject. He felt that every time Damien received publicity, the work of the other parts of the mission was diminished as a result. He once complained that the world must believe that Damien and the settlement were the only mission territories of the congregation in Hawaii.

There is no indication that Damien's fellow missionary priests raised similar objections. Even if they did not understand his apostolate or share in his particularly intense devotion to the patients of the settlement, they certainly did not begrudge him honors or publicity. Certainly the generalate had discovered that such news brought more and more support for the mission, and more candidates for the religious life. The local missionaries would have been no less astute. That, of course, left Fouesnel to wage his war on their behalf without their support.

The disposition of the vast sums of money coming from England naturally brought the situation to a head. These funds could not be turned over to the mission headquarters because the donations had been raised for the specific purpose of bringing relief to the patients of the settlement. Father Damien received the funds because he was the mainstay of the settlement and also the man who had inspired the generosity of the British people. Fouesnel was clearly beside himself as a result. By 1888, as Damien sank deeper and deeper into the morass of pain and torment accompanying the disease ravaging his body, Fouesnel decided not to have anything to do with him at all. He was disgusted over the political dimensions of the uproar and by the increasing American demands on the Hawaiian monarchy. Father Fouesnel believed that Damien had single-handedly and deliberately brought about all the chaos. He thus informed Damien that in the future he would write to him only on mission concerns, having no other contact because he believed Damien was a self-glorifier and too proud.

This did not stop Fouesnel, of course, from complaining to the father general of the congregation, and to everyone else in the city who would listen, that Damien was self-willed, vain, and even capable of laying claims to work that he had not accomplished. The regional provincial had a particularly hard time accepting the fact that Damien nursed the sick, cleansed wounds, amputated gangrenous limbs, sutured ulcers, bathed the patients, washed their clothes, dug their graves, built their coffins, and erected their chapels. The verification of all these tasks by eyewitnesses (including Rudolph Meyer, the mission superintendent) did not convince him that Damien had accomplished such things. He wrote again and again to the motherhouse that Father Damien was beyond hope and beyond reasonable persuasion. Fouesnel allowed that he had washed his hands of the situation, because Damien no longer listened. The fact that Damien was in the last stages of leprosy did not soften his complaints or his adamant dislike of the man.

The provincial and the bishop, however, had to tread lightly in the matter, because of two separate but very real factors. First, they could not risk appearing brutal and unfeeling in the eyes of the public. Damien had international fame, and such treatment would be pounced upon by the press and elaborated upon in every European and American publication, bringing them both to ruin. Second, Damien was within his rights to request that the settlement on Molokai be removed from Koeckemann's jurisdiction and become a self-sustaining entity. If that happened, Damien would become the superior. There was a precedent for the change of jurisdiction, and both Koeckemann and Fouesnel were well aware of it. They had also heard rumors to the effect that Father Damien contemplated making just such a move. He did discuss it with Superintendent Meyer and others, and when they had made later references to the matter, he only smiled in a mysterious fashion.

What did not seem to occur to the two superiors was the fact that Damien could have retaliated against them in the generalate and in the world press. He could have appealed to the father general for better treatment, for compassion, and for an end of the accusations and abusive attacks by his superiors, particularly in that last stage of his life. The constitution of the congregation provided for just such avenues of relief. The media people would have supported him as well if he had decided to go public with his problems. Damien did not make any such appeals, however. He had no desire to belittle the two men in Honolulu, as he had no desire to remove himself from his congregation. The superiors were not the only members of the Sacred Hearts Congregation in the Hawaiian Islands. His fellow priests and women religious, like his good friend Mother Judith of the Sacred Hearts Sisters, gave him daily, endearing examples of holiness and good will. Also, it is quite conceivable that the Hero of Molokai, with his canny Belgian heritage and his spiritual sense, understood that he was in the better position. It is far easier for a spiritually advanced soul to be the injured party than to be the one doing injury. He could take the blows and rally his interior strength. If he had been the one making the attacks, he would have been unable to come to terms with himself or with God.

In all fairness, it has to be admitted that both Koeckemann and Fouesnel viewed the mission and life in Hawaii from an entirely different vantage point. They were involved in a political struggle that had international implications. Damien could defend his patients with whatever stamina and fury he possessed without worrying about the ramifications of his actions. He could receive the aid he requested without any qualms while both the local bishop and the provincial stood the chance of seeing decades of work slip away as a result of enmity from the foes of the Church. Lastly, most human beings are at times incapable of tolerating other points of view on some issues, especially those that border on the deeply spiritual or on the edge of political and social impact. Father Damien lived on this edge all of his life because that was where he was needed. It cannot be expected that his superiors would share in his enthusiasm or in his stolid defense of his own charges. They were involved in what is called the broader picture, of which Molokai was only a factor, not the hub.

With the turn of the New Year of 1889, however, Bishop Koeckemann demonstrated kindness and generosity toward Damien, on occasion and perhaps in a vague sort of way. He wrote to him then and offered gentle words and good wishes. He did not make any effort to attend Damien at his deathbed, perhaps not wishing to involve himself in any sort of publicity or in anything that could be construed as a political act by the Americans. In April, he wrote to a friend that Damien might even be dead at the time, indicating that he had no great wish to have the news sent to him immediately. Father Fouesnel showed no such indications of a truce. He wrote harsh letters to Damien as late as March 1889, one month before Damien died. By that time, Damien was barely alive.

When Dr. Hyde later accused Damien de Veuster of sin and debauchery, both Bishop Koeckemann and Father Fouesnel defended his good name. But they did not have to exert themselves on behalf of the Hero of Molokai. Robert Louis Stevenson had come down on the side of Damien in the debate, sending Hyde and his companions running for cover. Neither superior outlived Damien for long. In February 1892, Bishop Herman Koeckemann suffered a massive stroke. He was paralyzed as a result and remained in a comatose condition until his death on February 22. In that same year, Father Léonore Fouesnel went to his own reward.

CHAPTER TEN

Beneath the Pandanus Tree

AFTER THE DIAGNOSIS BY Dr. Eduard Arning, Father Damien returned to Molokai, intent upon using the rest of his strength to accomplish as much as possible before leprosy made him totally helpless. He was taking a prescribed form of arsenic, but he developed a reaction to the medicine and stopped the dosage for a time. It appears that at the settlement he was also given some sort of electrical treatments on a primitive machine which had to be repaired in order to continue its benefits. At that time, he actually prayed to be spared the ravages of the disease in order to continue working for as long as possible. He already had a deep mistrust of the sort of regimen that the patients would face after his death. The Franciscan Sisters had not yet arrived at Molokai, so Damien could not be sure of his replacement or of the attitude that new people would take in conducting the affairs of the patients. He was wise enough to know that many would seek to erase all traces of the progress made during his period of stay, as others would seek to replace his fatherly concern with a no-nonsense style of authority.

He prayed to be spared for a while longer; and yet, when a friend asked him to seek a miraculous cure from God, Damien announced solemnly that his health would be too high a price to pay if that meant he had to leave Molokai and the patients. He was just borrowing time by praying for a slow death. He was also experiencing the first taste of misery that came to each patient as a distinct "gift" of the disease. The body could not avoid a rapid surrender to the ravages of leprosy, but the human spirit could fight back in a variety of ways.

Damien's forehead was changing at that stage and a leprous sore began to develop on his right ear. His particular form of the disease would cause those dreadful alterations and more. His eyebrows fell out, and marks appeared on his cheeks — two more symptoms that clearly showed he was a leper. Within months, he was admitting to a terrible fatigue that brought him to tears at night. He was able to work steadily through each day — pushing his strength to its limits — because the tasks were enough to distract him from his own physical decline. At night, however, when the settlement became silent and dark, without lights and without the normal hustle and bustle of workers and patients, the exhaustion worked on his emotions, and he wept alone. All of this was naturally the process of burnout, the result of years of unrelenting stress and unending labor. He had been on the island for more than a decade, working seven days a weeks, fifty-two weeks a year, always maintaining a ferocious schedule. He wrote to his superiors about his condition, despite their past treatment of him and their neglect of his ailments and needs. No word of sympathy or encouragement was sent in reply, and so Damien set out to face this crisis of the spirit alone.

The activity that saved his mind and soul was a simple and customary one for him. Each night, when the tears came down his scarred cheeks, when he shook because of his sobbing, Damien went out into the Garden of the Dead to keep his beloved corpses company there. He himself had placed almost all of these bodies into their narrow graves, just as he had erected their markers to ensure that future generations would remember them in their humanity. With his rosary in hand, he walked among their final resting places and prayed for them, perhaps even asking them to intercede for him as he started on the last lap of the same torturous journey that they had taken.

What was occurring in Damien's mind and soul was the natural recognition of the disease's grim reality. Damien walked among the graves because their silent vigils commemorated in a very special fashion what he had begun to dread for himself in his own flesh. He knew the course of the disease better than any other human being on earth because he had ministered to its victims with his own hands and strength. Its hideous path of destruction had been carved into the bodies that he had washed and bandaged. While he made no complaint of his torment about the disease to his companions, he must have been staggered by the diagnosis and the realization of what he faced. Any sane human being recoils in horror from such a fate, even when religious fervor and spiritual insights have led such a person to that end for the good of others. Damien was beginning his journey into the grave, and the resting places of all those who had gone before him stood as mute signs of the agony that awaited his final days on the beautiful shore of a tropical island.

He had allowed doctors to make a final physical examination of him in order to record the fact that his body showed absolutely no indications of the presence of syphilis or any other venereal disease. That should have protected him later from the likes of Dr. Hyde and his clan of slanderers, but they put aside the medical report as erroneous because it suited them to do so.

His relationship with Bishop Koeckemann and Father Fouesnel had already deteriorated (because of his English connection) by the time the disease began to manifest itself in the normal way. That episode and the harsh letters from Fouesnel had taken their toll. His greatest worry, however, was still the Sacrament of Penance. A priest came to him every two months and heard his confession but then had to return to his own mission. He pleaded for a priest companion, but he was ignored in Honolulu. Then Brother James and Brother Joseph arrived on the scene, along with Father Conrardy, and things changed for

Damien and the settlement. He finally had coworkers, friends, and a priest companion. The fact that his body was slowly rotting away did not have an overwhelming impact on him in such company. He could face anything because he was no longer alone. He increased his labors and set out to accomplish everything, much to Brother Joseph Dutton's dismay. Such a schedule meant that Damien started many tasks and left them to Dutton to complete with efficiency.

He was still suffering from depression, caught up in tears and in the nightly walks to relieve the spiritual and mental pain. Dr. Mouritz noticed his depression but brought a medical education to bear on its diagnosis. Most victims of the disease suffered forms of melancholia, which was inevitable in the face of immense tragedy and in the sudden and brutal recognition of fleeting mortality. Father Damien, Dr. Mouritz reported, suffered two separate forms. He was given to the usual variety: staring out into space in silence for long periods of time, an activity observed in other patients in the settlement. He also suffered from a growing belief that he had failed and was neither worthy of his Lord nor of meriting heaven.

This last uneasiness about failings did not come upon Damien as a result of his disease and condition. In the past, he had been told by many that he had little value. Some people had gone out of their way, in fact, to rebuke him. The authorities in the Sacred Hearts seminary had passed judgment on his being unfit for priesthood at the start of his priestly career. From the beginning, he had also lived in the shadow of his intellectual brother, having neither the academic brightness nor the flair for words or spoken concepts. He had always been "Big Joseph," or "Silent Joseph," neither title depicting any suave manner or intellectually stimulating presence.

Damien had also felt unworthy in his pastorate on the Big Island of Hawaii, where he was stunned again and again by the simple acceptance of life and fate among his own parishioners during disasters. His first superiors, Bishop Maigret and Father Modeste, had been advanced in their missionary endeavors and in their Christian charitableness. He had learned from them both, but his last two superiors had made efforts to impress upon him the ridiculousness of his ministry and the ugliness of his temperament.

Beyond this, of course, Father Damien de Veuster had entered into a realm of the spirit that few human beings encounter in their normal lives on earth. In his endeavors, he had become one with Christ, had taken upon himself the role of the Good Shepherd to a degree unheard of in his age. As a result, Damien was aware of the presence of the Divine in his life. Such an encounter leaves a human being confounded and confused. A person is confounded because the beauty of the presence of God is so spectacularly overwhelming that one wonders how such a Pure Being could allow himself contact with such a puny and wretched creature as man. The confusion comes with the understanding of the Beatific Vision, of which no creature is truly worthy. Damien could not have been sustained in his labors among the lepers of Molokai without having entered into a realm of deep, mystical awareness. The path of good works and activities seldom remains so open, clear, and sunlit. Shadows always form, but glimpses of the Divine are always available, and the presence of the Trinitarian God is absolute. The only possible response to such confrontations and encounters in a sane human being is the recognition of unworthiness.

His life, however, was not to be lived in the splendor of the spirit alone. A new board of health was convened and empowered in Honolulu, and this board was aware of the continued presence of leprosy in the islands. For this reason, the members instituted more rigid segregation activities and sent teams of policemen into the villages and towns of the islands to enforce the regulations pertaining to lepers. The old board of health had relaxed the segregation practices, recognizing the pain caused by the isolation and separation. Some of the islands had large numbers of lepers in residence, cared for by their fearless relatives and hidden from view. These were left in peace by the board of health until the new policies were enforced. The administrators, urged on by the continuing *haole* terror of the disease, embarked on programs of strenuous hunts and relentless pursuits of the victims and their families who tried to escape detection and exile. As a result, the dreaded steamer arrived more often at the landing place of Kalaupapa, depositing boatloads of fresh victims, each bearing the same expression of terror and despair. Damien again welcomed every steamer and started his routine of housing the patients in his own small residence until they could be cared for elsewhere. He must have frightened a few of these patients, because his appearance was becoming more and more repugnant. The number of patients in the settlement increased to eleven hundred during that period of enforcement of the segregation laws.

By 1888, Damien's skin was changing radically all over his body, and small tubercles were appearing everywhere. By this time, the disease had penetrated into all of his mucous membranes, meaning that his mouth, nose, eyes, and even his larynx were swollen and infected. The damage to the larynx was particularly dangerous for him, because it hindered his ability to breathe and lessened his sleep to only two hours a night. When his depression did not lead him out into the Garden of the Dead, his sleeplessness and difficulty in breathing sent him there. He spent nights among the graves and yet managed to work the next morning as if he had been given hours of sound rest on a comfortable bed. Leprosy was starting to transform his fleshly shell into a mask of torment. He was becoming one of the disintegrating creatures he had cared for in his early days in the settlement. No one had abandoned him by the side of the road to perish alone, but he was fast making his way to the same pitiful state.

He started going blind as a result of the infection of his eyes, and his companions were asked to read to him at night. Damien continued to pray his Breviary, or Divine Office, which linked men like Father Damien to other priests and religious throughout the world. The hymns of the office echoed in vast cloisters everywhere. The stately parade of the seasonal devotions wound through each year of service to bring new dimensions of understanding and faith. Missionaries in far-flung outposts recited the same Breviary and were joined to the rows of monks in habits who stood before glorious altars and under soaring Gothic naves. When the office was read to him, along with books of spiritual instructions and hagiographies (the lives of the saints), Damien listened in silence. The disease, he knew, took away a victim's sense of sight, smell, and touch, leaving him only the ability to hear the world moving steadily, almost carelessly, around him.

His lungs were now infected, and he knew that he was approaching the end. His spiritual life appears to have changed considerably as his senses were closed by his illness. Death was not the stinging end of anything, not the prelude to harsh judgment. Damien longed for death; not as the cessation of pain and torment but rather as the entrance into a realm that he had, at last, begun to understand fully. It was a kingdom in which he had joyous entrance.

He fell ill with a dreadful bout of fever, exposed, as were all of the victims of the disease, to other germs and contracted ailments. After days of serious wasting, however, word came to him that the Franciscan Sisters, under the direction of Mother Marianne, were landing at Kalaupapa. Damien rose up out of his bed to meet them and to give them a tour of the facilities. That interlude — in which he said he could stand like the biblical Simeon to chant the *Nunc Dimittis*, because he had seen the beginning of the great apostolate — was a happy one for him and enabled him to regain his strength just because of his jubilation.

By the end of that month, in fact, he was making his rounds as usual and even putting new roofs on buildings again.

He was not interiorly blind, however, and he wrote to his provincial, Father Fouesnel, to ask for a burial pall to be made by the Sacred Hearts Sisters. Fouesnel wrote him back a particularly harsh response. The pall, however, was prepared. His right hand was now swollen beyond recognition and badly infected and his face was disfigured horribly. He had acute diarrhea all of the time and was starting to cough excessively as the disease ravaged his lungs more and more. He could no longer lie flat, and he spent time propped upon the floor or walking about with a cane in the Garden of the Dead. He took time out from his work, however, to make a will, as requested to do so by Father Fouesnel, in keeping with the tradition of the congregation and because of the vast amounts of money that were still arriving for him in the settlement. He had little time to spend any of these funds because his body was starting to collapse under the assaults of Hansen's disease. When he went about, he had to protect his eyes from direct sunlight. His right arm was in a sling and his left foot was bandaged. The bridge of his nose had collapsed and his glasses hung clumsily on his rotted ears.

On March 19, 1889, on the feast of St. Joseph, his patron, Damien fell ill and became bedridden. Some of his companions discovered him on the floor of his bedroom, on a simple pallet, with only a thin blanket, shivering as bouts of fever wracked his body. He had never used a bed in the settlement because he had not used one in the seminary. His companions, however, insisted upon his accepting a cot in order to facilitate their care for him (people could not crawl around on the floor in order to tend to his needs). He accepted a bed, and one was carried into the room for him. The sores on his body were beginning to crust over, healing a bit and then turning black. Damien did not need a medical doctor to explain to him what that development indicated. He had been at the deathbed of enough victims to know that leprosy caused those changes at the end.

Saturday, March 23, 1889, was Damien's last active day on earth. He was slowing down, being drained of the last of his energies. By March 28, he was confined to his room, where he signed his last papers, including his will. He expressed happiness over the fact that he owned nothing, not even a firm grasp of life. He made his confession on March 30, consoled by the fact that his burial pall had arrived from Honolulu. He was prepared now, and he hoped that he would die within hours. But that did not happen. His body was too disciplined, too regulated by his personal stamina, to give in to the last demands of his disease.

The patients were not restricted from attending him, and they recognized the telltale sign, as did their beloved priest. Damien pointed out the fact that his leprous wounds were closing, and the encrustations around them were turning black. The patients watched and waited. They had always enjoyed unlimited access to this priest who had come to Molokai to be a father to them. Almighty God had clearly marked Damien's flesh with the insignia of their suffering, and they recognized the final stages of the disease in the human body.

When he was not receiving the patients or other visitors, including the sisters and Father Conrardy, Damien contemplated the picture that Edward Clifford had so kindly brought him from England. That valuable watercolor given to him depicted Saint Francis of Assisi, *Il Poverello*, receiving the stigmata from Christ. The Savior came on the cross, surrounded by the wings of the seraphs of heaven. Damien's stigmata mantled his flesh and corrupted his natural physical functions. The dying priest stared at the watercolor, uniting himself with Christ in the spirit of *Il Poverello*. He made a rather odd comment once about the two companions who remained at his side in his room. No one else saw them, and Damien did not elaborate on their appearance and did not identify them. His companions, whom he recognized, kept unseen and silent vigil at his side.

The days passed in island languor, warm and lovely, and the nights were splendid. The moon rose above the dark palms and danced on the waves lapping at the shore of the settlement. On April 2, Damien received Extreme Unction (the Sacrament of the Anointing of the Sick), given to him by Father Conrardy. Afterward, Father Wendelin heard Damien declare that he was no longer needed and soon would be called away. The priest then asked Damien if he would remember those he left behind when he gained heaven. Damien replied: "If I have credit with God, I will pray for all in the Leproserie." When Father Wendelin asked if Damien would bequeath him his mantle, Damien said: "Why, what would you do with it? It is full of leprosy." [For Father Wendelin's eyewitness account of the final days, funeral, and burial of Father Damien, see Appendix 3.]

On April 13, 1889, a fever rose in Damien again, reportedly reaching 105 degrees Fahrenheit and he had to forgo the pleasure of sitting up in a chair. He received Communion one last time, and two days later, early on the morning of April 15, he died. Those around him stated that he simply gave up his life, like a child, with a slight smile on his face. Typical of his fellow lepers, Damien's countenance took on a gentle repose in death, as the ravages of the disease receded. By the time his body had been dressed in a fresh soutane, the cleric's cassock, all leprous signs were gone from his face.

Gathered around him as he lay in repose that day, Damien's patients and companions had no way of knowing that men and women all around the world awaited word of his passing. Newspapers had flashed reports of his coming death days before, and people of all faiths, or no faith at all, interrupted their own routines and watched for news from that distant Pacific island. To people in all nations, Damien had been an extraordinary ray of hope. He had been remarkable for his courage and for his stubborn defense of the afflicted. Again and again, medical and social leaders expressed their appreciation for his unique role in the battle against leprosy and other dreaded diseases. His landing on Molokai had changed the world's awareness of leprosy. It became a medical condition and not a biblical punishment. The victims of Hansen's disease stepped out from their ancient shadows of terror to be viewed as human beings who deserved care and medical aid. Damien brought the light of Christ into a scene of horror, and by bearing the ravages of that affliction, he taught the modern world to recognize leprosy as a suffering, not a curse from an angry deity.

His last days offer as well a very distinct confrontation with those who say that he was not intellectual enough or refined enough to be a true mystic. Almighty God has confounded the world many times by choosing the most unlikely candidates for profound spiritual gifts. The calendar of the saints is peopled by men and women despised or scorned by their contemporaries because of their physical appearance, their lack of social graces, or their modest intellectual displays. As he was dying, Damien rejoiced because of his vocation, contemplating *Il Poverello* in the watercolor and praying. One companion after another later spoke of Damien's joy at this time. His soul was united to Christ in poverty, in pain, and in humble resignation to the inexorable toll of the disease. There are no beautiful poems or treatises bequeathed to the world by Damien to attest his degree of union with the Sacred Heart. His sermons have not been recorded to testify to his mystical awareness. Damien left future generations the stark model of a person willing to give up his life for those in need. His patience and his joy declare that he knew Christ and had served him in a pit of terror and pain for sixteen years, without seeking release. Only grace could have steeled such resolve. Only divine nurturing could have enabled Damien to survive sane and faithful to the end. His mystic heritage can be seen on the tombstones in his Garden of the Dead and in the works that continue long after the end of his earthly sacrifice. Without artistic phrases or dramatic declarations, Damien prayed before the Holy Eucharist, cared for the abandoned, and then died of leprosy.

The church bells on Molokai rang out to announce the priest's passing, answered in time by bells across the entire world. People in far-flung places received the news of his death, and banner headlines announced the fact that he had succumbed to leprosy on his distant isle. Messages of condolence began to pour into Hawaii from heads of state and men and women everywhere who honored this man of God because of his labors among the lepers of Molokai.

The body of Father Damien was taken to St. Philomena's for burial. Normally, he went about his duties in a well-worn black cassock, wearing as well the colorful scarf given to him to serve as a sling for his wounded arm. Damien also wore the flat hat of the mission clergy, its battered rim held in place by strings. That hat has become a symbol of Damien, and it has been sculpted into the striking statues of him now on display. In his coffin, Father Damien was buried in the white vestments of the altar, marked by an embroidered cross and serving as a priestly mantle for his scarred form. He was not buried wearing his small spectacles, and his hands were folded around the crucifix that served as the insignia of his priestly vocation.

A solemn procession followed the Requiem Mass, celebrated by Father Wendelin on April 16. Eight patients carried the coffin, and the entire population of the settlement formed an honor guard as Damien was carried to the cemetery spot under his beloved pandanus tree. That tree had sheltered him during his first nights on Molokai, and now it would serve as his resting place, at least for a short while.

CHAPTER ELEVEN

Aloha Kamiano!

WHEN FATHER DAMIEN DE VEUSTER, SS.CC., was buried under his sheltering pandanus tree on Molokai, wrapped in silence and in the blessed release of death, it was expected that the world would move on to other things and soon be taken up with other concerns. It could be assumed that Damien and his memory would be enhanced by a few who knew him and by those for whom he had given his life. Others, however, had no reason to remember him in the rush of new ways and new crises. That, however, did not happen.

Damien, buried and gone from the scene of his exile and martyrdom, could have become a figure from another time and place. He did not fade from memory, however, and the word spread about his life, giving him a new luster. Even today, more than a century after his martyrdom, he shines for a young generation as a unique individual who reverenced and understood a human's relationship with others and with God. Complex, with a temperament that could have compromised his apostolate, Damien never lost sight of the bonds that hold society and mankind in order. Expressing concern for others was not a vague gesture for Damien, not something that was accomplished in a remote or secondhand fashion. He did not believe that his obligations ended with the tinkle of a few coins in a collection box. Gathering up old clothes and supplies for some humanitarian organization was not his ultimate goal in dealing with the problems of the world. For this reason, he stands before today's generation as a remarkable enigma, as a challenge to the conformity demanded to the vague and artificial standards of this age. Token gestures, slogans, applause, or silent assent in the face of overwhelming moral problems would not have been sufficient for him. He dared to show concern, to be truly human in his dealings with his fellowman, to be aware of the ultimate destiny of the world and all its inhabitants.

Such a human being does not molder in exotic settings unnoticed or unheralded. Something of him lingers there and then begins to permeate the hopes and the dreams of each new age. As the famous Indian leader Mohandas K. Gandhi announced: "The political and journalistic world can boast of very few heroes who compare with Father Damien of Molokai.... It is worthwhile to look for the sources of such heroism."

Damien's image imparts a transcending beauty to those who have nerve enough to come face-to-face with the reality of life and spiritual dimensions. Because he did not fade from our view, because his spirit and his courage could not be entombed with his rotted flesh, he remains very much a part of the contemporary scene throughout the world. Damien is alive and well in many lands, carried into new leprosariums and into new realms of the spirit by those who understood his purpose, his relentless daring, and his boisterous enthusiasm for life and God's creation.

In 1936, the Belgian government made known its desire to have the body of Father Damien exhumed from its grave on the island of Molokai and returned to his homeland. King Leopold III of Belgium made a formal request to President Franklin Delano Roosevelt for the return of the body, and on January 27, 1936, it was lifted from its grave in the presence of Church and government officials. The coffin was put on board a ship and taken to Honolulu, as the remaining patients on Molokai wept and mourned the departure of their priest and patron. The coffin rested in the Cathedral of Our Lady of Peace and was then laid in state in the state capitol. Official honors were paid to the Hero of Molokai by the people of the islands, who came to demonstrate their homage and respect during the various ceremonies.

In a solemn procession, the body was then taken to the port and placed on an American vessel, the U.S.S. *Republic*, bound for the port of Panama, after a stop in San Francisco, California. In Honolulu, the U.S. Army gave Damien a hero's farewell, with honor guards, official bands, and bombers flying overhead. During the stop in San Francisco, Archbishop John J. Mitty received permission to have the body taken briefly to St. Mary's Cathedral. A Belgian ship, the *Mercator*, waited in Panama to receive its precious cargo.

The *Mercator* sailed with Damien's remains to Antwerp, arriving in that city on May 3. King Leopold III and a full company of Belgian dignitaries, as well as high-ranking Church prelates, were on hand to witness the return of their native son in triumph. The bells of Antwerp began to ring the instant the ship was sighted entering the harbor, and thousands of Belgians went to the shore to welcome home their countryman. The parade that followed included a hearse drawn by six white horses, bearing the casket to the cathedral, where solemn funerary commemorative services were conducted in Damien's honor. After the ceremonies, the casket was placed in a limousine for the last part of the journey to Louvain. The procession passed Tremelo, Damien's hometown, and the people of that area were able to greet him in their own way. The procession also passed the cemetery where Father Damien's mother and father rest side by side. Today, the remains of the Hero of Molokai have been placed under a monument of black marble, in the chapel of the Sacred Hearts Fathers, just under the cell where Pamphile, his brother, passed away. People from all over the world visit Damien's tomb each year.

In 1964, a group of modern facilities was founded to carry on the work of Father Damien. In that year, Father Michael Kavanaugh started the Damien Social Welfare Center in Dhanbad, India, a region in which leprosy is almost endemic. The center was founded with a 150-bed hospital, two separate field hospitals, 156 clinics, a leprosy control system, and a project designed specifically to rehabilitate patients suffering from the disease.

"The Damiens," as the medical workers were called, were particularly anxious to provide shelter for the young victims of the disease. Boys and girls diagnosed with leprosy were thus housed in hostels, where they received the sort of care that Damien believed appropriate for his small charges on Molokai. The Damiens served without bonuses and worked on a twenty-four-hour basis in the various facilities. By 1981, the staff of the Damien Social Welfare Center was treating nearly twenty-four thousand patients in and around Dhanbad.

On April 15, 1969, in the Rotunda of the Capitol in Washington, D.C., Father Damien de Veuster, SS.CC., joined King Kamehameha I as one of the official "representatives" of the State of Hawaii in Statuary Hall. (The purpose of Statuary Hall is to offer Americans representatives from each of the fifty states, the most exemplary human beings to grace the history of each of the states, and human beings who embodied the virtues and the ideals of their particular era.) The designation of Father Damien, an outsider, as the companion of the Father of the Hawaiians, was a unique honor. It was signed into law by Governor John A. Burns, in Hawaii, on May 10, 1965. The legislative act declared that Father Damien's efforts among the sufferers of Hansen's disease had made him a humanitarian of international standing. In addition, his death from the disease had given great impetus to the medical efforts to discover some way of controlling and alleviating the dreadful symptoms of leprosy.

In the Rotunda, Senator Daniel K. Inouye welcomed the guests, many of whom had come from Hawaii and from Rome. The Very Reverend Henry Systermans, SS.CC., the superior general of the Sacred Hearts Congregation at the time, gave the invocation. Louis Lopez, who had been the chairman of the Hawaii Statuary Hall Commission, explained that the statues being unveiled on that occasion represented the supreme achievements of island culture and society. When the time came for the unveiling of the statue of Father Damien, which was a remarkable bronze portrait by the artist Marisol Escobar — Father Damien's relative, Father Ernest Claes, SS.CC., was asked to do the honors. Father Ernest had served in Hawaii with the same tenacity and spirit as his pioneering family member. Senator Inouye also pointed out the fact that the base of the statue contained the jeweled insignia of the Order of the Knight Commander of the Royal Order of King Kalakaua. This was a symbol of the medal that Queen Liliuokalani had sent to Father Damien after her traumatic visit to the settlement. It was proper that this insignia be incorporated into the base of his statue, because it exemplified the royal regard that Damien received during his lifetime.

Following the senator's remarks, a message from King Bauduoin was delivered by the ambassador of Belgium. The king expressed the gratitude of the Belgian people for the extraordinary honor being given to one of their countrymen. The apostolic delegate, Archbishop Luigi Raimondi, then gave the message from the Holy Father, Pope Paul VI, who congratulated the people of the United States for having dedicated such a shrine to the idealists and dreamers of the nation. Other representatives of the state government and the Church spoke about the works of the two honorees, spanning the history of the Hawaiian Islands and providing two pivotal aspects of life.

Damien represented the tragedy of the human experience and the spirit that challenged such suffering with resolve and compassion. King Kamehameha I represented victory and the unification of a people with wisdom and steadfastness. Damien served in the spirit and yet had to provide all of the physical care. The unique aspect of his ministry was the fact that in his work he echoed the "Law of the Splintered Paddle," which the king had given his own people in order to secure unification, peace, and prosperity. As Kamehameha I had feared for the young and the old, so had Damien felt the same urgency and dedication. They viewed life from different spectrums, but both of them understood the human dimensions and the role of the individual in bringing about changes.

In an address titled "Supreme Involvement," Honolulu's Bishop John J. Scanlan set the tone for the unveiling, echoing the heartfelt emotions of the island people who understood his apostolate:

> It is with mingled feelings of pride, joy, humility, even in a sense, of unworthiness, that we of the 50th State join this distinguished assemblage here today to honor Hawaii and one of its most distinguished sons. It is my particular privilege to represent over 200,000 people of Hawaii who profess the same faith which Father Damien professed. But, today, we join with all the citizens of the State, of every creed and ethnic background, and express for them our collective joy and pride that *Hawaii Nei* ("this Hawaii") has this opportunity to place here in our Nation's Capitol the statue of one who exemplified in such an utterly convincing way the spirit of Aloha.
>
> Humility takes possession of all of us on this unique occasion, for we know that the motivation which inspired the supreme involvement of Damien in the suffering and despair of Kalawao springs only from a greatness of soul which most of us do not have. We are humble in this proud

moment for Hawaii because we have realized that the dedication, the unflagging courage, and unwearying love of God and men which Damien showed are the possession of only the few.

His statue will stand here among the statues of the great men who each in his own way contributed to the building of America. This humble but sturdy farmer's son from the plains of Flanders takes his place here because his contribution to Hawaii, to America, and to all mankind was the greatest. They are faith, hope and love, but the greatest of these is love. Many of the great men who are represented here were men of faith and courage, hope and persistence. Damien was also a man of faith and hope, but especially of love.

His claim to greatness is not in the wisdom which discovered that ordered administration and proper balance of authority given to us by the founding fathers of our Republic, and neither is it to be found in the daring adventure which opened up new areas in our broad land, nor in the military victories which preserved our union and our liberties. Damien's greatness is in the heroic example of Christian living which he gave to all. Life, liberty and the pursuit of happiness are human rights. For Damien, life meant losing it for the sake of Him who said "he who loses his life for my sake shall find it." Liberty meant shutting himself up in his prison at the foot of the cliffs of Molokai for sixteen years, that he and his charges might possess the liberty of the sons of God.

His pursuit of happiness was paced for eternity, for his faith told him the age-old experience of mankind that the human spirit is not satisfied with even the best that this life can offer. Accordingly, he witnessed to his Divine Master in an extraordinary degree.

Where there was suffering, he brought alleviation. Where there was despair, he brought hope. Where there was ugliness and deformity of the flesh, he brought beauty of soul. In that place where it was said that there was no law of God or man he showed what could be gained by humble obedience to a Heavenly Father. Where the living death of leprosy made life meaningless and without purpose, he showed man the vision of life eternal and the privileged way of the suffering pilgrim.

It was written of him, by one who did not share his faith but who saw and admired his greatness of soul, that he stepped into battle under the eyes of God to succor the afflicted and console the dying. He himself was afflicted in his turn and died upon the field of honor. Greater love than this no one has.

Our country today is blessed beyond measure with the material things made possible by the intelligence, energy and industry of our people, but we need greater values for the human spirit. We need the understanding of and the dedication to the values to which the life of Damien gives witness. We need the recognition of the value of human life itself from its very beginnings. We need the recognition of the dignity of the human person, even the poorest and most wretched. We need a humanity possessed of a pity which is not condescending and of a humility which thinks of duties before rights.

We need that attitude of mind which leads to a faithful personal adherence to the blueprint for living given to us in the Ten Commandments and in the Sermon on the Mount. This blueprint includes a sense of justice. It means an intelligent patriotism. It contains the simple virtues indicated by home and altar which make for true greatness. These values are not merely ideals to be admired. It is not true that they are beyond the reach of men. They must be attained and put into practice if the civilization which built on them is to be saved.

Damien, human in his short temper and impatience, human in his stubbornness, but with the mark of divinity in his loving concern for the most wretched of men and women, speaks now from this seat of civil government of the Nation, and the word that he utters is the Hawaiian word which expresses what is noblest and greatest in us all — it is Aloha.

In August, 1977, a television play was produced by Hawaii Public Television, concerning the life and the spiritual heights of Damien de Veuster. Very rarely does a television camera lend itself to the interior landscape of the human soul. Very rarely can centuries be spanned in order to illustrate with quiet and penetrating calm the true dimensions of human tragedy and human courage. This production by Hawaii Public Television managed to accomplish all of those things, and, as a result, it became a television experience that deeply affected countless millions of viewers around the world.

The play, called simply *Damien*, was the profound demonstration of the ability to portray a single human being in all of his spiritual and intellectual facets. The play echoed the truly profound levels of mankind's longings and aspirations in the face of terror and pain.

Written as a one-man drama, *Damien* was the magnificent work of Aldyth Morris, a woman long respected in the islands for her professionalism and her craft. She had studied the life of Father Damien and believed that it was time to capture his labors and spirit in the beautiful frame of soliloquies and simple conversation. This technique, making the camera function as a receptacle for every emotion known to man, allowed the character to speak from his own heart without the staged effects of other characters or dramatic ploys. In her play, the Hero of Molokai came alive, transported out of his time in much the same way that his spirit has transcended location and decades. Nino J. Martin, a producer for Hawaii Public Television, saw the play and began to envision its production with stark sets, with authentic reproductions of the period, and with truth as the single factor that could give way to the process of bringing Damien alive to a new generation. As he envisioned the production, the play could become a magnificent insight into the human tragedy of Molokai as a place of exile; it could become a palette upon which the vibrant colors of Damien's life could be exhibited freely.

Terence Knapp, the distinguished actor who had gained a reputation on the stage, was asked to stand alone before the cameras, to re-create not just a single dramatic role but an entire era in history. He had to personify not only the Hero of Molokai but also allow Damien's contemporaries to come alive through his words. Knapp was born in London and was educated there in his craft as a performing artist at the Royal Academy of Dramatic Art. He worked with the Royal Shakespeare Company, in productions directed by the late Laurence Olivier. He was also featured in National Theater productions, including Peter O'Toole's *Hamlet*. While touring Japan, Knapp won distinction and fame as an actor and as a director. During his Asian tour, he visited a leper colony in Malaysia, where patients were being brought in for their first medical treatments to alleviate the ravages of the disease. "The visit never left my mind," he confided in an interview for *The Damien Report*, a monthly newsletter from Hawaii. "I think that I can begin to understand Damien's vocational call to be their priest and helper," he said.

Knapp arrived in Hawaii in 1970, joining the drama and theater department of the University of Hawaii where he directed two major productions annually. "I cannot say where Damien began or where I left off during the filming of the play," he confided in the interview. "It was an experience that seemed to bring me to a point of understanding him as a single human being. He was a man who took all the negative aspects of his life, including his temperament, and used them to alter the tragic destiny of the people of Molokai, and perhaps of the world."

Knapp felt that where he has a "deep and passionate love for the theater," Father Damien possessed "that sort of love for God." He found that the role of Damien in the television production was an "exhilarating experience, because of his forceful personality and the psychic energy which stemmed from Damien's deep, spiritual persuasion." Knapp added: "I firmly believe that one must find the courage and foolhardiness within oneself to explore and to allow one's personality to be the basis of the character. The character created by the playwright must be allowed to reform and mold one's nature." Knapp also said that while Damien's intensity was always an internal one, he had to be aware during the production that the audience was a dispassionate camera, and that even the humor in the play would receive no responding laughter in the studio.

The play *Damien* transported the television audience into a miniature world that encompassed Damien's physical life and his spiritual aspirations, depicting the Hero of Molokai as an enigma to his own generation and to generations yet unborn. As such, the play was a triumph for the Hawaii Public Television staff. With Aldyth Morris's searing portrait, with Martin's direction, and Knapp's insight into the heart of Damien, the play soared into the realm of the spirit, where all human beings function on a different level. Even as the tragedy of Molokai unfolds, and as the disease begins to wrap Damien in its eternal and terrifying embrace, he comes alive on stage and proposes a challenge of the spirit that scorns the limits of cameras and the distances of time.

Shortly after its first airing, Bishop John J. Scanlan sent a tape of the production to Pope Paul VI.

Around the same time that the play *Damien* was first produced, an effort was begun to establish the Damien Museum, a place for visitors to learn more about the Leper Priest and appreciate his personal effects. Through the work of volunteers, the Sacred Hearts Fathers, and the Diocese of Honolulu, the museum was opened in 1977 at St. Patrick's Church in Honolulu. Among the most notable artifacts from Damien's life are a hand-carved *prie-dieu* (kneeling bench), his chalice and crucifix, and a cassock. Parish records, reports, and even his eyeglasses, are on display. The museum is located in Waikiki, near St. Augustine's Church, and is open to individual visitors and available for group tours.

In Tremelo — Damien's hometown, where he roamed the streets with his flocks of sheep, fell through the ice, and grew up as a happy child — a museum has also been opened at the Damien family home to commemorate his life and work. Many of his personal effects and those of his family are on display.

On Molokai, meanwhile, the settlement areas for the lepers became the subject of much discussion in 1969 when the mandatory isolation decreed by King Kamehameha V was officially ended. The Hawaii State Legislature considered closing the facility, but a movement in the islands succeeded in securing the right of the residents to remain there for life if they so chose. The decision was seen as a humane offer to the patients; many were severely disfigured by the disease and had lived on the island for most of their lives. Integration into society might thus have been a very difficult challenge. To provide a permanent designation to the land that had been the site of such suffering and heroism, Kalaupapa was incorporated into the United States National Historical Park System. The park was officially established by

Public Law 96-565 that was signed by President Jimmy Carter on December 22, 1980.

Given his labors on behalf of those suffering from a disease that brought with it severe social stigmas and irrational fears, it was not surprising — and indeed entirely fitting — that Damien should be embraced as an unofficial patron of those afflicted with HIV/AIDS. In 1987, for example, two centers were established to respond to the needs of AIDS patients in Washington, D.C., and Indianapolis, Indiana. The centers, and other like them that have been started since then around the country, were places of welcome and care for AIDS patients at a time when the diagnosis was as grim a death sentence as that given to the lepers sent to Molokai. Damien's status as unofficial patron was noted in 1995 when the memorial chapel to those who have died of the disease at the Église Saint-Pierre-Apôtre in Montreal was consecrated and named in his honor.

One additional honor was given to Father Damien in 2005. The Belgian public television channel Canvas asked Belgians who in their opinion was *De Grootste Belg* (The Greatest Belgian) of all time. The list encompassed any Belgian between 50 B.C. and the modern era living within the borders of present day Belgium. The Top Ten list of the 111 Greatest Belgians included the painter Peter Paul Rubens (d. 1640), the first-century B.C. tribal leader Ambiorix, and the pharmaceutical founder Paul Janssen (d. 2003). At the top of the list was the beloved *Pater Damiaan*.

The ruggedly beautiful landscape of the Kalaupapa region, captured in a photograph taken during the celebration of Damien's beatification.

Bishop Herman Koeckemann, SS.CC.

An early photo of the settlement on Molokai.

The leper settlement on Molokai.

A photo of Brother Joseph Dutton. He signed it,
"With compliments of the original."

Brother Dutton walking in the settlement.

Father Damien in the later stages of his leprosy.

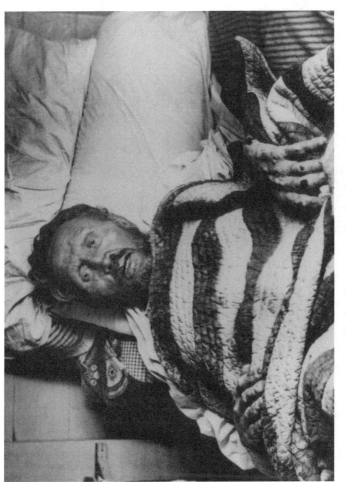

Father Damien in his last hours.

*The empty resting place of St. Damien on Molokai
remains a pilgrimage place on Molokai.*

Procession on Bishop Street, Honolulu, when Father Damien's remains were sent to Belgium, 1936.

Body of Martyr Arrives

SOLEMN TRIBUTE PAID FATHER DAMIEN HERE

RECEIVED WITH HONORS OF THE CHURCH

BODY OF LEPER COLONY'S HEROIC PRIEST IS REMOVED FROM ARMY SHIP

CASKET TAKEN TO CATHEDRAL

Clergy and Laymen Join Homage to Leper Priest

Damien, martyred priest of the lepers and uncanonized saint, arrived yesterday in San Francisco.

The body of the man who gave his life to bring spiritual hope and physical care to the lepers of the once dreadful colony of Molokai arrived here aboard the United States Army transport Republic. It was received here with the most impressive ceremonies of the Roman Catholic Church and will lie in state at St. Mary's Cathedral until Friday afternoon.

Going Home

The body of the man born as Joseph de Veuster, later known throughout the world as Father Damien, is on its way to Louvain, Belgium, near where Father Damien was born. It was the plea of King Leopold to President Roosevelt which resulted in the return of the body to its native soil, where an elaborate shrine in his memory is being erected.

The body was received here at an impressive ceremony in which thousands participated. Archbishop John J. Mitty headed the hundreds of priests and laymen who received the body at the transport dock at Fort Mason.

Sun Appears

Lowering skies and a drizzle of rain did not keep the throngs away. But as the massive koa wood casket was lowered to the pier from the hold of the Republic, a winter sun broke through the raining heavens. And though the rain continued, a pale golden light shone on the glistening box and the tri-colored Belgian flag that draped it.

Archbishop Mitty blessed the box with holy water and prayer as the throng—even to the stevedores who handled the box—stood bare-headed in the rain. It was placed on an army gun carriage. White clad priests, monsignori in crimson, the mitred archbishop in deep black, marched slowly out of the cathedral-tail pier warehouse.

Majestic Chant

The slow, majestic strains of "De Profundis" arose in a chant from the throats of hundreds of priests and choir boys. To the music of this chant of death and the life beyond, the procession moved to the gates of this military reservation.

There the procession became an automobile cortege which stretched more than a mile along Van Ness avenue. And as the hearse, with its escort of a dozen motorcycles, moved slowly along the broad avenue more thousands stood at the curbs in reverent silence, heads bared, to honor the man of lowly farm origin who is now close to the role of holy men which includes John the Baptist, Peter, Paul, Joseph, and those others who knew the Savior and practiced his preachings so well.

Throng in Cathedral

At the Cathedral were other thousands for the Office of the Dead. Again the chants, in stately threnody, filled the arching temple, as all prayed for the safety of that soul which every man believes is safe.

There were surprising numbers of reverent children in the church, youngsters who had taken time from their play, parked bicycles and skates outside, and come into the cathedral to honor this sainted man who died long before any of them were born. There were almost as many men as women, too, taking time from their busy day to pay this man homage.

After the service the thousands filed by the bright hued casket. Each placed his hand, his rosary, some their lips to the wood.

Guard of Honor

At head and foot stood an honor guard of two soldiers, two policemen and two firemen, tall flickering candles lighting their features. And between them lay the martyred Damien, dead only 47 years but already almost at the point of canonization.

It was such a spiritual experience as San Francisco has seldom seen in all her history, the privilege of paying homage to an uncrowned saint, and it is one which San Francisco will treasure as long as men lift their eyes and their hands to Heaven in prayer.

The San Francisco Examiner's coverage of Damien's journey to Belgium in 1936.

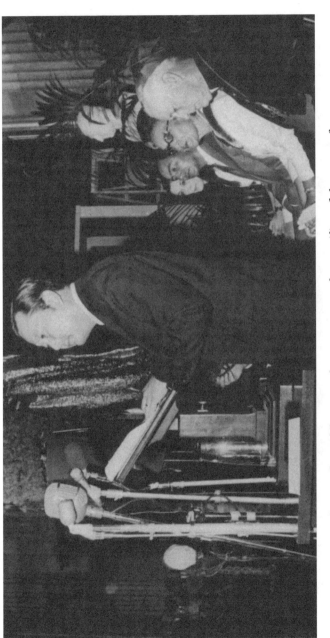

Senator Daniel Inouye welcomes guests at the unveiling of the statue of Father Damien in the Capitol, Washington, D.C., on April 15, 1969.

*Ernest Claes, SS.CC., unveils Damien's statue
in Washington, D.C.*

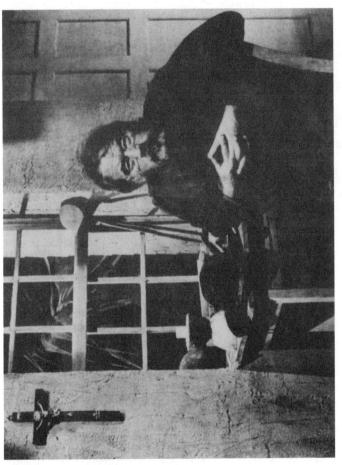

Terence Knapp in his memorable performance as Damien.

Bishop Francis X. DiLorenzo of Honolulu is shown on Molokai at a celebration of Damien's beatification.

The Statue of Damien in the state capitol in Honolulu in 1969.

CHAPTER TWELVE

The Apostle of the Lepers

IN WORDS THAT PROVED strikingly prophetic, Robert Louis Stevenson wrote in his famed defense of Damien against the calumny of Rev. Hyde:

> You know enough, doubtless, of the process of canonisation to be aware that, a hundred years after the death of Damien, there will appear a man charged with the painful office of the DEVIL'S ADVOCATE. After that noble brother of mine, and of all frail clay, shall have lain a century at rest, one shall accuse, one defend him. The circumstance is unusual that the devil's advocate should be a volunteer, should be a member of a sect immediately rival, and should make haste to take upon himself his ugly office ere the bones are cold.

As Stevenson anticipated, the movement to promote the cause of canonization for Father Damien de Veuster, SS.CC., began in the years after the priest's death, including one as early as 1924. On January 31, 1938, the ordinary process was started in Malines, Belgium, with the approval of ecclesiastical authorities. Giving impetus to the effort was the moving of Father Damien's body to Louvain, although at the same time, various investigations of his holiness were undertaken in Hainan, in Hawaii, in Paris, and in Northampton, England. Father Marie-Joseph Miguel was named postulator general.

By 1941, the Malines Process was completed and sent to the Congregation of Rites in Rome. Work continued until May 12, 1955, when a decree of the official Introduction of the Cause was issued with the approval of Pope Pius XII. This phase was a step forward, because the apostolic processes now undertaken were sponsored by the Holy See. These investigations were conducted until May 2, 1959, when a decree was issued to the Congregation for the Causes of Saints. A *positio*, or an exposition of Damien's life and virtues, contained several thousand pages of documentation. Father Angel Lucas, SS.CC., became the postulator in 1968. He was asked to find a *Cardinal Ponente* (an official presenter), and Cardinal Michael Browne, an Irish Dominican, accepted the role.

Years were spent in this phase of the investigation, and on July 7, 1977, Pope Paul VI declared that Father Damien was of "Heroic Virtue," giving him the title of Venerable. [See Appendix 4.] The cause was entering yet another phase, this one concerning miracles. Cardinal Pietro Palazzini served as *Cardinal Ponente* of Damien's cause before becoming Prefect of the Congregation for the Causes of Saints.

At the same time, a book containing the signatures of thirty-three thousand lepers from around the world was presented to the Holy Father. Among those signing this petition for the furtherance of the cause, only nine thousand of the thirty-three thousand were Catholics. People of all religious faiths joined to honor the Hero of Molokai, including thousands of Hindus.

Another ardent admirer of Father Damien was Blessed Teresa of Calcutta. She joined the people of all faiths in urging the Church to honor Damien as a model for the entire world.

As a venerable of the Church, Damien was given a new distinction by Pope John Paul II who issued the following decree:

> Responding to the desire of our brother Francis Xavierus DiLorenzo, Bishop of Honolulu, and many brothers in the

Episcopate and of many of the faithful, and after having received the favorable response of the Congregation for the Causes of Saints, we with our apostolic authority inscribe the book of the blessed the Venerable Servant of God, Damien de Veuster, and we give permission to celebrate his Feast Day every year on the 10th of May, in the places and according to the norms established by Church law.

In the name of the Father, and of the Son, and of the Holy Spirit. Amen.

This decree, of course, was the curtain raiser on the spectacular beatification of Damien, which started with a decree from the *Congregatio de Cultu Divino et Disciplina Sacramentorum*, or Congregation of Divine Worship and the Discipline of the Sacraments, in Rome. The miracle that led to Pope John Paul II issuing a decree of beatification on June 13, 1992, was the cure of a nun in France in 1895. Sister Simplicia Hue had been given no hope of surviving a slow and agonizing intestinal illness. She began a novena to Father Damien and asked for his intercession. The pain and the symptoms of the illness disappeared overnight, and the nun was declared free of the disease.

Damien's beatification was held in Brussels, Belgium, on June 4, 1995. In a drenching rain, Pope John Paul II celebrated Mass for five hundred Sacred Hearts priests, brothers, and nuns, and declared Damien "Blessed Servant of Humanity" in the plaza before the basilica of the Sacred Heart. The day before, the Sacred Hearts Congregation observed the beatification in St. Anthony's Church in Louvain, where Damien's remains are now enshrined. The crypt was covered with leis (Hawaiian garlands) and with floral arrangements sent from devotees around the world.

The Holy Father spent several days in Belgium, making a pastoral visit and greeting the Belgian people. At the beatification vigil at the church of Notre Dame du Chant d'Oiseau, on June

3, 1995, the Holy Father spoke of Father Damien's dedication to the Blessed Virgin Mary:

> Mary the model of faith and love, helped him to make himself available, to remain, like her, upright at the foot of the Cross, and to be a missionary of the Gospel. With her, he was able to say "yes" to the Savior, receive from him the force of witnessing and the grace of eternal life.

> At the end of this prayer to Mary, I welcome with joy all the Belgians who are present, in particular the faithful of this parish who receive us. I warmly greet all those who join us via radio. Inspired by the example of the apostle of the lepers, I invite all Christians to constantly confide in Our Lady. Brothers and Sisters of Belgium, let your attachment to Mary grow, in order to revive within yourselves the gift of God! She will lead you to Christ.... The Lord has cast his eye upon you and repeats constantly: "Come, follow me" (Mt. 19:21). In fact, true happiness comes from the infinite love of God, who does not look at a person's appearance, but at his heart which — in spite of sin — remains forever marked by the beauty of God. Allow yourself to be loved by Christ, and to respond in turn, courageously, by loving him and by loving your brothers!

> When Jesus calls, it is not to put limits on a personality, but rather to help it blossom in truth of being, in order to realize the ideal that inspires it. When he demands a more specific commitment and chooses someone for a particular mission within the Church, as was the case with Father Damien, the Savior heaps his gifts on the one who responds and makes him completely free. What thus seems impossible to human beings becomes possible with the help of God (see Mt. 19:26). On the other hand, far from withdrawing from the world and impoverishing the personality, the

consecration to the Lord permits each person to find his true place in accordance with the liberty to which each person is invited, to serve his brothers, for the glory of God and the salvation of the world. The Church has faith in you. It rejoices in your desire to live fully. Do not let yourself be swept away by the fascinating temptations and seductions that the world can offer. True life is a progressive conquest of self-mastery. Root hope and faith firmly in Christ, in the hope and in the faith of the Church! The Lord will help you to become better each day, and he will fulfill your most profound desires. Draw from the spring of life, in particular by frequent participation in the sacraments of the Eucharist and penance. Allow yourself to be reconciled by Christ, who will make you new human beings!

The actual Mass of the beatification was a blend of cultures and human experience. Blessed Damien had followed Christ not only halfway around the world but into a fabulous lifestyle that was foreign and strange. This rugged Belgian farm boy had become a hero on a distant Pacific island. Now the people of his homeland and Hawaiian islanders joined with the Holy Father to honor him as the Hero of Molokai.

Part of the service was the return of a relic of Father Damien to the Hawaiian people. This relic, enshrined in precious koa wood, was brought into the service, as Cardinal Godfried Danneels, the Archbishop of Mechelen-Brussels, addressed the assembly, saying:

> Brothers and sisters of Hawaii —
>
> We return to you the relic of the right hand of Father Damien who blessed and healed so many people in your country. May it continue to be a source of blessing and comfort and a symbol of our love and solidarity with all of you.
>
> Brothers and sisters of Hawaii —

The body of blessed Father Damien is among us. He rests in the soil of our land but the soul of Damien belongs to the whole Church.

The body of Damien has a special link with the people with whom he identified himself: the lepers of Molokai. It is a joy that we now give to the bishop of Honolulu, the relic of the right hand of Damien. That this hand which has blessed and healed so many sick, return there now to be venerated as a source and symbol of blessing and healing.

Young Belgians marched proudly into the arena with pennants. At the close of the liturgical service, dancers and drummers from Hawaii stunned the assembly as they saluted *Kamiano* with traditional Hawaiian music and dances, bringing back the vivid images of Damien in his labors on Molokai. Cultures had blended to form this Blessed Servant of Humanity, now a joyous symbol for the world.

As Pope John Paul II exclaimed in his address at evening prayer on June 4, 1995, during the meeting with the Congregation of the Sacred Hearts and the delegations from the Hawaiian Islands, the Association of Friends of Father Damien, and the faithful from Tremelo:

Dear Brothers and Sisters of the Congregation of the Sacred Hearts,

Father Damien has given you an example for your religious life. He is a model for your radical and irreversible consecration to Christ, who calls upon you to follow with renewed vigor. Where did the clarity and the happiness which Damien so often displayed in difficult situations come from? He drew his strength from the spirituality of this congregation: the contemplation of the Eucharist, the mystery of love in which Christ truly communicates himself to those who receive him by committing themselves completely to him. "I find my consolation in my only Companion who never leaves me," he said, in speaking of the actual presence of Christ in the tabernacle. The Eucharist is the daily bread for the priests and the consecrated, the strength of one who wants to be a missionary.

It is in Damien's heart to heart with Christ, in the faithful meetings of the liturgy of the Hours, the *lectio divina* and in contemplation, that his actions found their meanings, and their completion. Through the *lectio divina*, the religious and faithful can "discover the Heart of God in the word of God" (Saint Gregory the Great, Letter, 4, 31). Strong in that spiritual intimacy, Damien could write to his parents after his ordination as a priest, "Do not worry about me. If one serves God, one is happy anywhere." Contemplation does not make men remote and is not wasted time. In turning his thought to the heart of Christ as a well-loved disciple, the apostle of the lepers found the energy he needed for his countless activities.

Damien also experienced the love of his Lord in the sacrament of penitence, which he frequently wished to receive, he who gladly said: "Poor sinner that I am" (*Helaas armen zondaer dat ik ben*) and who signed one of his letters "de Veuster, the leprous sinner who confesses too rarely."

To acknowledge oneself as a sinner is first of all to ask God to show His power and His love that can do marvels in the one who repents and to discover that pardon is the perfect gift of love; love does not lock the sinner up in his fault, but raises him up to continue his way with confidence in his heart that a person is worth more than what he has done.

Flanders gave one of its sons to the remote inhabitants of the Pacific: in exchange, the apostle of Molokai endowed his country with the merits and sufferings of those distant peoples, sufferings which, in the mystery of divine love, raise up the world. As the Apostle Paul said: "I find my joy in the sufferings I bear for you, for what still remains to be suffered of the trials of Christ, I suffer in my own flesh" (Col 1.24).

This great exchange of gifts between the communities of the Church is an incalculable benefit from the activities of the missionary communities. It is born of the mystery of God, Trinity of Love. The fact that the congregation to which Father Damien belongs is consecrated to the Hearts of Jesus and his Mother is eloquent. Between these two hearts there is an exchange of gifts in the mystery of the Incarnation and the Redemption. Father Damien drew his from this exchange, and he followed it to the end. "How sweet it is to die as a child of the Sacred Hearts," he said on the day of his death, Easter Monday 1889.

Today his gift is returned to the hands of that same mother whom he entrusted and gave himself, from the first day of his vocation; the gift becomes total in the glory of God.

Rejoice, Heavenly Mother! Be joyful, motherland of Father Damien! Joy to the people of the Hawaiian Islands! In your land Father Damien sowed the Word of God, whose love is manifest in the Gospel and in the life of his disciples.

In today's world, it is important to put before young people of every land an ideal of the religious and the missionary life. By the gift of themselves, the young will discover the joy of putting themselves at the service of Christ and man. Thus their lives, which may seem ordinary, will be extraordinary, because they contribute to the glory of God and the greatness of man. In fact, an extract from one of Father Damien's letters which adorn his grave, recalls the true mission: "I am the happiest of men for I serve the Lord through the poor and sick children rejected by everyone else." "This is my commandment: Love one another as I have loved you" (Jn 15.12). A gift is born of love. The love which comes from God creates in man the capability of giving himself over to others and, through that giving of himself, enables him to achieve his own humanity; love makes goodness grow in the world, which starts building the Reign of God. May Father Damien's example, raised today on the altars, be a witness to present and future generations! May it serve as an invitation to the young to become, in their turn, apostles of their brothers.

Through the intercession of blessed Damien, I pray especially today to God for the religious Congregation of the Sacred Hearts. May they be worthy heirs of the apostle of Molokai, carrying the Gospel untiringly into places where they are sent! Their actions will thus enlarge the ecclesial communion, in which there is a constant exchange of gifts. By their life of prayer and fraternity and by their works, may they be conscious of participating in the mission of the Church, as their founders were charged by the Holy See and as it is recalled in the stained glass windows of the Saint Anthony Chapel: to contemplate, live and announce the love of God revealed in Jesus Christ! The mystery of the Eucharist and the love of the Sacred Hearts must remain as the pillars and foundations of the congregation's spirituality.

I gladly grant my Apostolic Benediction to all the members of the Congregation of the Fathers and Sisters of the Sacred Hearts. I hope they allow themselves to be seized by Christ and to commit themselves wholly to the missions entrusted to them on every continent. My Blessings also upon the delegates from the Hawaiian Islands and all their compatriots, the faithful of Tremelo and to those who continue the work of the apostle to the lepers in the association of Friends of Father Damien.

The following is adapted from the English edition of *L'Osservatore Romano*, June 7, 1995:

Pentecost Sunday, June 4, 1995
Dear Brothers and Sisters,

1. *"As the Father has sent me, even so I send you.... Receive the Holy Spirit"* (Jn 20:21-22).

The Apostles heard these words from the lips of the risen Christ, on the evening of the Resurrection. On the morning of the first day of the week, the women, *then Peter and John, saw that the tomb* where Jesus had been laid was empty. The evening of the same day, Jesus appeared in their midst. It was *the same Jesus they had known before, but, at the same time, he was different.* On his body he bore the marks of the crucifixion and, at the same time, he was risen. No longer bound by the present laws of matter, he could enter the Upper Room while all the doors were locked. After greeting the Apostles with "Peace be with you," the risen Jesus spoke words of decisive importance for the Church's future: " 'As the Father has sent me, so I send you.' Then he breathed on them and said: 'Receive the Holy Spirit. If you forgive men's sins, they are forgiven them; if you hold them bound, they are held bound' " (Jn 20:22-23).

The real moment of the Holy Spirit's descent occurred on the evening of the Resurrection. Jesus, the Son consubstantial with the Father, breathed on the Apostles. This breath shows forth the origin of the Holy Spirit, who comes from the Father and the Son. *This breath is salvific: it contains all the power of the Redemption accomplished by Christ.* We understand that Christ, after saying to the Apostles:

"Receive the Holy Spirit," immediately spoke of the forgiveness of sins. He gave them the power to forgive sins, a power that comes from God. He imparted it to them together with the redeeming breath that announces the definitive coming of the Holy Spirit. On the day of Pentecost, the descent of the Holy Spirit on the Apostles led to the Baptism of those who believed in Christ at Peter's word and who wanted the salvation given to all humanity through the Cross and Resurrection of Christ.

2. The Acts of the Apostles gives a detailed description of the Pentecost event. The Holy Spirit, the breath of the Father and the Son, revealed his presence through *a violent gust of wind.* At the same time, the Holy Spirit made himself known through *the medium of fire.* See, above the Apostles gathered in the Upper Room he appeared as a fire which parted in tongues; it came to rest on each one's head. Wind and fire, natural elements, thus testify to the coming of the Holy Spirit.

Nevertheless, these manifestations are accompanied by a supernatural phenomenon. The Apostles, filled with the Holy Spirit, *began to speak in other languages* as the Spirit prompted them. This event caused great amazement among all who were staying in Jerusalem at the time, "devout Jews of every nation under heaven" (Acts 2:5). Filled with astonishment and wonder, they exclaimed: "Are not all of these men who are speaking Galileans? How is it that each of us hears them in his native language?" (Acts 2:7-8).

When the author of the Acts of the Apostles listed the countries of the world known at that time, from where the pilgrims witnessing the Pentecost event had come, he drew up a virtual *geography of the first evangelization,* which the Apostles would accomplish as they proclaimed in various languages "the marvels God has wrought." Except for

Rome, no mention was made of any country in Western, Central, Northern or Eastern Europe. *Belgium was not named, much less the islands in the archipelago of Molokai* in the distant Pacific. It is not a question of Father Damien de Veuster's homeland, nor of the country where he was to go on mission and give his life for Christ, thus fulfilling his service of love for neighbor.

3. In recalling the places dear to Father Damien's heart, I greet Their Majesties the King of the Belgians and the Queen, Her Majesty Queen Fabiola, as well as the members of the Diplomatic Corps and the civil authorities. I extend my fraternal best wishes to Cardinal Danneels on his anniversary and my warm greetings to Cardinal Suenens, who will celebrate his anniversary in a few days. I cordially greet all the Bishops. I am delighted at the presence of Father Damien's family, the many missionaries and the delegations from the towns of Tremelo, Malonne and Leuven, and at the association of the Friends of Father Damien.

I am pleased to welcome the delegates from the Hawaiian Islands: *Walena aloha okou. Ma kakou pakahe a pau ka maluhla a ma ka aloha o Iesu Chresto!* [To all of you, my warmest and most sincere wishes. May the peace and love of Jesus Christ be with you!]

4. Down the centuries the Church has never ceased growing and bringing the Gospel to the ends of the earth, in response to Christ himself, who gave the Holy Spirit, the indispensable strength for men to carry out the task of evangelization. The Church *gives thanks to the Holy Spirit for Father Damien,* since it is the Spirit who inspired him with the desire to devote himself unreservedly to lepers on the islands of the Pacific, particularly on Molokai. Today, through me, *the Church acknowledges and confirms the value*

of Father Damien's example along the path of holiness, praising God for having guided him to the end of his life on an often difficult journey. She *joyfully contemplates what God can achieve through human weakness,* for "it is he who gives us holiness and it is man who receives it" (*Homilies on Samuel* I, 11, 11).

Father Damien displayed a particular form of holiness in his ministry; *he was at once a priest, religious and missionary.* With these three qualities, he *revealed the face of Christ,* showing the path of salvation, teaching the Gospel and working tirelessly for development. He organized the religious, social and fraternal life on Molokai, at the time an island of banishment from society; with him everyone had a place, each one was recognized and loved by his brothers and sisters.

On this day of Pentecost, we ask *the assistance of the Holy Spirit* for ourselves and for all men, *so that we can let him take hold of us.* We are certain that he imposes nothing unattainable on us, but that by sometimes steep paths he leads our being and our existence to their perfection. This celebration is also an appeal to deepen our spiritual life, whether we are sick or healthy, regardless of our social status.

Dear brothers and sisters of Belgium, each of you is called to holiness: put your talents at the service of Christ, the Church and your brothers and sisters; let yourself be humbly and patiently molded by the Spirit! *Holiness is not perfection according to human criteria;* it is not reserved for a small number of exceptional persons. It is for everyone; it is the Lord who brings us to holiness, when we are willing to collaborate in the salvation of the world for the glory of God, despite our sin and our sometimes rebellious temperament. In your daily life, you are called to make choices that "occasionally demand uncommon sacrifices" (*Veritatis splendor*, n. 102). This is the price of true happiness. The apostle of the lepers is witness to that.

5. Today's celebration is also a *call to solidarity*. While Damien was among the sick, he could say in his heart: "Our Lord will give me the graces I need to carry my cross and follow him, even to our special Calvary at Kalawao." The certainty that *the only things that count are love and the gift of self* was his inspiration and the source of his happiness. The apostle of the lepers is a shining example of how the love for God does not take us away from the world. Far from it: the love of Christ makes us love our brothers and sisters even to the point of giving up our lives for them.

I am pleased to greet the Bishop of Honolulu, who accompanies the pilgrims of Hawaii to this solemn and joyful celebration.

6. Today, dear brothers and sisters of Belgium, it is your responsibility to take up the torch of Father Damien. His witness is an appeal to you, particularly to you, young people, so that you can know him and, *through his sacrifice, you will grow in your desire to love God, the source of all true love and of all true success, and in your desire to make a real offering of your life.*

7. *My heart turns to those who today are still suffering from leprosy.* In Damien they now have an intercessor, because, before contracting the disease, he had already identified with them and often said: "We others, the lepers." In urging his cause for beatification with Paul VI, Raoul Follereau had a glimpse of the spiritual influence that Damien could have after his death. My prayer is for all those who are stricken by *grave and incurable diseases,* or are *close to death.* However, prayer also unites all who are afflicted with *serious, incurable illnesses,* or who *are at the point of death.* As the bishops of your country have recalled, all men have the right to receive

from their brothers and sisters a hand extended, a word, a glance, a patient and loving presence, even if they have no hope of being cured. *Brothers and sisters who are ill, you are loved by God and the Church!* For the human race, suffering is an inexplicable mystery; if it crushes the man left to his own forces, it finds meaning in the mystery of Christ who died and rose again, who remains close to every person and whispers to him: "Take courage! I have overcome the world" (Jn 16:33). I thank the Lord for *those who accompany and assist the sick, the young, the weak and defenseless, the outcasts:* I am thinking especially of health-care professionals, priests and laypeople in pastoral care, hospital visitors and those dedicated to the cause of life, to the protection of children and to providing each individual with shelter and a place in society. By their deeds, they call to mind the incomparable dignity of our brothers and sisters who suffer in mind or body; they show that every life, even the most frail and suffering, has importance and value in God's sight. With the eyes of faith, beyond appearances, we can see that every person bears the rich treasure of his humanity and the presence of God, who fashioned him from the beginning (cf. Ps 139 [138]).

8. In the First Letter to the Corinthians, Saint Paul writes: *"No one can say: 'Jesus is Lord,' except in the Holy Spirit"* (1 Cor 12:3). In fact, to say "Jesus is Lord" means *professing his divinity,* as Saint Peter professed in the Apostles' name at Caesarea Phillipi. "The Lord" — *Kyrios* in Greek — is he who rules over all creation, he to whom the Psalm we have heard is addressed: "Bless the Lord, O my soul! O Lord, my God, you are great indeed!... How manifold are your works, O Lord! The earth is full of your creatures. If you take away their breath, they perish and return to their dust. When you send forth your Spirit, they are created, and you renew the face of the earth" (Ps 103:1; 104:24, 29-30).

These verses of the liturgy speak of God's power over all creation. They concern *the Holy Spirit, who is God and who gives life with the Father and the Son.* And so today the Church prays: "O Lord, send forth your Spirit who renews the face of the earth!" *The Holy Spirit enables man to come to know Christ and to profess his divinity: "Jesus is Lord"* — "*Kyrios!*"

In a certain way, *Father Damien* imbibed this faith in Christ's divinity with his mother's milk, in his family in Flanders. He grew up with it and later it led him to his brothers and sisters in the distant islands of Molokai. In order to give definitive confirmation to the truth of his witness, he offered his life in their midst. What could he have offered the lepers, who were condemned to a slow death, if not his own faith and this truth that Christ is Lord and God is love? *He became a leper among the lepers; he became a leper for the lepers.* He suffered and died like them, believing that he would rise again in Christ, for Christ is Lord!

9. Saint Paul also writes: "There are different gifts but the same Spirit; there are different ministries but the same Lord; there are different works but the same God who accomplishes all of them in everyone. To each person the manifestation of the Spirit is given for the common good" (1 Cor 12:4-7). With these words the Apostle presents a *dynamic vision of the Church, dynamic and at the same time charismatic.* In this charismatic vision, the Spirit manifests himself, the Spirit sent by the Father in Christ's name, upon the Apostles. Everything has its origin in the various gifts of grace which enable believers to carry out their activities and to fulfill their vocations and various ministries in the Church and in the world.

Paul's view is universal, *and, in this universal vision, we certainly find part of our blessed's life:* his charism, his vocation and his ministry. In all this the Holy Spirit has manifested himself for the common good. The beatification of Father Damien benefits the entire Church. It has particular importance for the Church in Belgium, as well as for the Church in the islands of Oceania.

10. It is providential that this beatification is taking place on the *Solemnity of Pentecost*. In the Letter to the Corinthians, Paul goes on to say: "The body is one and has many members, but all the members, many though they are, are one body; and so it is with Christ. It was in one Spirit that all of us... were baptized into one body. All of us have been given to drink of the one Spirit" (1 Cor 12:12-13). This Spirit has blown across the distant islands of Oceania, through the ministry of Father Damien; it finds an echo in your families, your parishes and your missionary congregations. In the history of your country, there have been a great number of *works* for the benefit and growth of the Church; worthy of particular note is the establishment of many religious congregations, which have had an important influence through their spiritual, charitable, intellectual and social activities. Moreover, individuals endowed with profound charisms began to achieve great works. One need only mention foundations such as the Catholic universities of Leuven and Louvain-la-Neuve, and the *Young Catholic Workers* (J.O.C.); suffice it to recall persons such as *Cardinal Mercier, a pioneer of ecumenism, or later, Cardinal Cardijn, founder of the Young Catholic Workers,* and many others through whom the Spirit worked for the good of the whole Church, not only in your country but throughout the world.

11. Blessed Damien, you let yourself be led by the Spirit as a son obedient to the Father's will. In your life and your missionary work, you show forth Christ's tenderness

and mercy for every man, revealing the beauty of his inner self, which *no illness, no deformity, no weakness can totally disfigure.* By your actions and your preaching, you remind us that Jesus took on himself the poverty and suffering of mankind, and that he has revealed its mysterious value. Intercede with Christ, physician of soul and body, for our sick brothers and sisters, so that in their anguish and pain they may never feel abandoned, but that, in union with the risen Lord and with his Church, they may discover that the Holy Spirit comes to visit them and they may receive the comfort promised to the afflicted.

12. "May the glory of the Lord endure forever; may the Lord rejoice in his works!" (Ps 104:31). It is with these words of the psalmist that I wish to end our meditation on this solemn, long-awaited day, when *the mature fruit of holiness — Father Damien de Veuster —* receives the glory of the altars in his homeland. Brothers and sisters, be docile to the Holy Spirit, so that through your life men can discover the God from whom every perfect gift comes!

The Cause for Canonization was brought to its completion with the formal approval of the required second miracle in 2008. An 80-year-old woman in Hawaii, Audrey Toguchi, was diagnosed with incurable liposarcoma and was cured after she asked for the intercession of Father Damien. In April 2008, the Holy See confirmed its acceptance of the second miracle, and on June 2, 2008, the Congregation of the Causes of Saints at the Vatican gave its recommendation that Father Damien should be canonized a saint. On July 3, 2008, a decree was promulgated by Pope Benedict XVI and Cardinal José Saraiva Martins that officially verified the miracle needed for canonization.

Finally, on February 21, 2009, Pope Benedict XVI held an ordinary consistory (the meeting of those Cardinals in Rome) at which the formal date was set for Damien's canonization, along with nine other beati who were also eligible for canonization. Damien was to be canonized on October 11, 2009, in Rome. That same day, the two Superiors General of the Congregation of the Sacred Hearts, Sister Rosa M. Ferreiro, SS.CC., and Father Javier Alvarez-Ossorio, SS.CC., announced the news to the congregation's member worldwide:

> It is with great joy that we write to tell you that the Holy Father has just announced the date of the canonization of our brother Damien. It will take place in Rome on Oct. 11th 2009.
>
> Now that we know the date, for which we have waited so long, the whole Congregation can intensify its preparation for this joyous and inspiring event, a preparation that has already begun in many places. Damien is a gift of God's goodness to the Congregation, the Church and all of humanity.
>
> At the time of the canonization the General Governments will host *three days of celebration in Rome*: a vigil of prayer on October 10, 2009 (the evening before), a festive gathering the day of the celebration at St. Peter's and a Mass of Thanksgiving on the following day, October 12, 2009. We will send you more information when we have the details.
>
> As part of our interior preparation, both personal and communal, we offer two prayers, one addressed to God the Father and the other to Damien. We ask you to use them and share them with others:
>
> > God of mercy,
> > We thank you for Damien,
> > brother to all,

father to lepers,
child of the Sacred Hearts.

You inspired in him
a passionate love for the life,
health and dignity
of those he found fallen
by the side of the road.

Thank you, for like Jesus
he knew how to love until the end.
Thank you, for like Mary
he knew how to give himself without reserve.

Thank you Father, for through Damien
you still inspire holiness
and passion for your kingdom.
Amen

Damien, brother on the journey,
happy and generous missionary,
who loved the Gospel more than your own life,
who for love of Jesus left your family, your homeland,
    your security and your dreams,

Teach us to give our lives
with a joy like yours,
to be lepers with the lepers of our world,
to celebrate and contemplate the Eucharist
as the source of our own commitment.

Help us to love to the very end
and, in the strength of the Spirit, to persevere in com-
    passion

for the poor and forgotten
so that we might be
good disciples of Jesus and Mary.
Amen.

May the Lord bless us with that same joy that filled the heart of Damien and may he pour forth on us his Spirit of love and courage so that we might respond generously to the gift of our brother, who died joyful to be a child of the Sacred Hearts.

Fraternally in the Sacred Hearts,
Sr. Rosa M. Ferreiro, sscc
Fr. Javier Alvarez-Ossorio, sscc
Superiors General

The following is from the Sacred Hearts Archives, courtesy of Father Christopher Keahi, SS.CC.

The last letter from the Sandwich Islands brought us the sad news of the death of Rev. Father Damien Deveuster [sic] on April 15 at Kalawao (Molokai).

The renown of this valiant missionary has become so universal that it seems almost useless to tell you about his life. Actually, can any place of some importance be found where his name is not known? Who has not admired the heroic charity and indefatigable zeal with which, for 16 years, he devoted himself to the spiritual care of the lepers of Molokai? He has been extolled in every language. Protestants and Catholics of all countries agree in proclaiming him a hero of Christian charity and in seeing him as an example of devotedness that is rare in the annals of the XIX century. As for us, we pray to increase our esteem and love for the religion that can inspire and sustain unto death such sublime virtue. And we do not cease to bless and thank the Sacred Hearts of Jesus and Mary for having drawn from our religious family such a noble example of Christian heroism.

It is undoubtedly thanks to the loving influence of the Sacred Hearts that the unreserved and unlimited dedication of dear Father Damien has produced a new growth in generosity among us, a generosity of which we are pleased to cite an example. A generous Protestant banker named Bishop founded (with the approval of the government), a home at Kalawao (Molokai) for leper girls under the direction of the Franciscan Sisters. Bishop Hermann [Koeckemann] (Bishop of Olba and Vicar Apostolic of the Sandwich Islands) needed to send a priest as chaplain there last year. Knowing that in virtue of the obedience due him, his priests would not refuse an appointment to that post, His Excellency wisely judged that he should not impose such a complete and heroic sacrifice on any of them. This is why he appealed (for a volunteer) to the devotedness of all his missionaries. And we have the happiness of telling you that all of them showed themselves to be true to their vocation as children of the Sacred Hearts. Aside from some who were somewhat offended by this appeal, as if their willingness to obey had been doubted, all responded with veritable enthusiasm. One of the first responded in a manner worthy of a religious and of a child of the Sacred Hearts: "My answer is in my Rule." He was the one chosen. But we like to think that the good dispositions of all the others will not fail to draw a great abundance of blessings on the mission in the Sandwich Islands and on all our Institute.

To return to Rev. Father Damien, we would like to mention the main stages of his life, so as to keep alive among us the memory of this worthy religious who pushed the spirit of sacrifice to the extremity of immolating himself.

Joseph Deveuster was born on January 3, 1840, at Tremelo, a small village between Louvain and Malines (Belgium). His solidly Christian parents, while being careful to train the heart of their young son in piety and virtue, also wanted to develop and embellish his education. This prompted them to send him first to the primary school at Wachter, recognized for its good course of studies and for the zeal of the teacher. Since the young Joseph always showed real interest in and serious application to his school work, and since moreover they did not think he was called to an ecclesiastical career, they had him continue his studies at the professional school in Braine-le-Comte. It was there that God sought this soul in order to make him a vessel of election.

Following a mission preached by some Redemptorists, the young man heard the voice of God in his heart. Urged by a desire to consecrate himself to God, he wrote to his elder brother who was then a novice in our house at Louvain. Shortly afterwards, he went himself to ask for admission to the novitiate. Since he had not studied Latin, he was admitted on February 2, 1859, only as a choir brother.

However, seeing his love for intellectual work and his great facility in learning, those in charge asked his brother, who in the meantime had made his profession, to teach him that language. When, on October 8, 1864, he made his vows in the chapel at Picpus and took the name of Brother Damien, he did so as an aspirant for the priesthood. After studying philosophy at Paris, he was sent by his superiors to Louvain to study in that city.

In 1863 his brother, Rev. Father Pamphile, fell ill just at the time when, by order of his superiors, he was to leave for the mission in the Sandwich Islands. Father Damien, who was then only in minor orders, asked and obtained permission to replace him. Contented and joyful, he sailed (from Bremerhaven) on October 29, 1863, and arrived at Honolulu on March 19, 1864. Ordained priest shortly afterwards (May 21) by Bishop Maigret, Bishop of Arathie and Vicar Apostolic, he expended his zeal in evangelization throughout the districts of Puna, Kohala, and Kamakua. Everywhere he left the reputation of an excellent confrere, a good religious, a laborious, active, and devoted missionary. An unexpected circumstance brought him, on May 16th, 1873, in the company of Bishop Maigret, to the leprosarium of Molokai. There, touched by the neglect in which hundreds of unfortunate lepers lived, completely isolated from the rest of humanity, he made a heroic resolution. Not waiting to be sent by his superiors he offered himself and asked that as a favor he be allowed to remain among them.

It was during the first days of June, 1873, that he arrived in that sad place, to begin a life of privation, work, and sacrifice — or, rather, to begin to die. He was only 33 years old and full of life, so that the small piece of land where he heard only the monotonous sound of the surf, where he saw only the frightfully disfigured bodies of the lepers, where he breathed only the infected odor emanating from the hideous wounds of the sick, must have seemed to him much more a tomb than an abode of living.

Nevertheless, without ever regretting his sacrifice, he lived constantly among the lepers whom he loved as his children. Without respite, he set to work to improve the material and spiritual conditions of his companions. He himself built chapels and houses; he often dug with his own hands the graves wherein he buried the dead. In agreement with the government, he founded an orphanage for the leper boys. He dressed the wounds of the sick, obtained for the lepers the best medicine available, and sought by beautiful religious ceremonies to raise the morale of those unhappy victims and to fill their hearts with hope. It is impossible to list here all that his charity inspired him to do, under the kindly gaze of God, Who has written all in the book of life.

Doctor G.W. Woods, chief surgeon of the American warship *Lakawana,* spent a week on Molokai in 1876 to make a special study of leprosy. In 1887 he wrote to Father Damien that he had visited all parts of the world where leprosy could be found, but he had never found a place where the lepers were so happy and where they were so well cared for than at the leper settlement of Molokai.

Even if the Hawaiian government helped the lepers with really royal generosity, Father Damien could well have claimed for himself a large part of this praise. Moreover, although strongly Protestant, the government always displayed a high esteem for him. In recognition of the immense services rendered by this charitable missionary to the Hawaiian people, it conferred on him in 1881 the title of Commander of the Royal Order of Kalakaua.

A long time ago, as you know, Rev. Father Damien contracted the terrible malady, which is incurable. But, without losing his natural gaiety and giving up his habitual activity, he continued to work and to care for the sick as was his custom. He rejoiced when he was able to have two priests with him on Molokai: Rev. Father Wendelin Moellers and Rev. Father Conrardy, and three Franciscan Sisters. Everyone hoped he would be able to live longer; but God decided otherwise.

On March 28 his strength failed and he had to remain in his room; he knew that death was approaching. Without fear, he offered God the sacrifice of whatever life yet remained. Stripped of everything, lying on a straw mattress laid on the ground, he prepared in a most edifying manner for his entrance into eternity. With religious calm and in the most profound peace, he awaited death. Finally, on April 15 at 8 a.m., his beautiful soul sped heavenward to receive, we are confident, the reward of his work and suffering. His death was really worthy of a child of the Sacred Hearts; it was the death of a saint....

In the Sacred Hearts,
Father Marcellin Bousquet, Superior General

Appendix 2

The following are excerpts of the open letter published by Robert Louis Stevenson in reply to the calumny of Rev. Mr. Hyde:

An Open Letter by Robert Louis Stevenson

SYDNEY, FEBRUARY 25, 1890.

SIR, — It may probably occur to you that we have met, and visited, and conversed; on my side, with interest. You may remember that you have done me several courtesies, for which I was prepared to be grateful. But there are duties which come before gratitude, and offences which justly divide friends, far more acquaintances.

Your letter to the Reverend H. B. Gage is a document which, in my sight, if you had filled me with bread when I was starving, if you had sat up to nurse my father when he lay a-dying, would yet absolve me from the bonds of gratitude. You know enough, doubtless, of the process of canonisation to be aware that, a hundred years after the death of Damien, there will appear a man charged with the painful office of the DEVIL'S ADVOCATE. After that noble brother of mine, and of all frail clay, shall have lain a century at rest, one shall accuse, one defend him.

The circumstance is unusual that the devil's advocate should be a volunteer, should be a member of a sect immediately rival, and should make haste to take upon himself his ugly office ere the bones are cold; unusual, and of a taste which I shall leave my readers free to qualify; unusual, and to me inspiring. If I have at all learned the trade of using words to convey truth and to arouse emotion, you have at last furnished me with a subject. For it is in the interest of all mankind, and the cause of public decency in every quarter of the world, not only that Damien should be righted, but that you and your letter should be displayed at length, in their true colours, to the public eye.

To do this properly, I must begin by quoting you at large: I shall then proceed to criticise your utterance from several points of view, divine and human, in the course of which I shall attempt to draw again, and with more specification, the character of the dead saint whom it has pleased you to vilify: so much being done, I shall say farewell to you for ever.

'HONOLULU,
'AUGUST 2, 1889.
'Rev. H. B. GAGE.

'DEAR BROTHER, — In answer to your inquiries about Father Damien, I can only reply that we who knew the man are surprised at the extravagant newspaper laudations, as if he was a most saintly philanthropist. The simple truth is, he was a coarse, dirty man, head-strong and bigoted. He was not sent to Molokai, but went there without orders; did not stay at the leper settlement (before he became one himself), but circulated freely over the whole island (less than half the island is devoted to the lepers), and he came often to Honolulu. He had no hand in the reforms and improvements inaugurated, which were the work of our Board of Health, as occasion required and means were provided. He was not a pure man in his relations with women, and the leprosy of which he died should be attributed to his vices and carelessness. Others have done much for the lepers, our own ministers, the government physicians, and so forth, but never with the Catholic idea of meriting eternal life. — Yours, etc.,

'C. M. HYDE.'
(From the Sydney PRESBYTERIAN, October 26, 1889.)

To deal fitly with a letter so extraordinary, I must draw at the outset on my private knowledge of the signatory and his sect. It may offend others; scarcely you, who have been so busy to collect, so bold to publish, gossip on your rivals. And this is perhaps the moment when I may best explain to you the character of what you are to read: I conceive you as a man quite beyond and below the reticences of civility: with what measure you mete, with that shall it be measured you again; with you, at last, I rejoice to feel the button off the foil and to plunge home. And if in aught that I shall say I should offend others, your colleagues, whom I respect and remember with affection, I can but offer them my regret; I am not free, I am inspired by the consideration of interests far more large; and such pain as can be inflicted by anything from me must be indeed trifling when compared with the pain with which they read your letter. It is not the hangman, but the criminal, that brings dishonour on the house.

You belong, sir, to a sect — I believe my sect, and that in which my ancestors laboured — which has enjoyed, and partly failed to utilise, an exceptional advantage in the islands of Hawaii. The first missionaries came; they found the land already self-purged of its old and bloody faith; they were embraced, almost on their arrival, with enthusiasm; what troubles they supported came far more from whites than from Hawaiians; and to these last they stood (in a rough figure) in the shoes of God. This is not the place to enter into the degree or causes of their failure, such as it is.

One element alone is pertinent, and must here be plainly dealt with. In the course of their evangelical calling, they — or too many of them — grew rich. It may be news to you that the houses of missionaries are a cause of mocking on the streets of Honolulu. It will at least be news to you, that when I returned your civil visit, the driver of my cab commented on the size, the taste, and the comfort of your home. It would have been news certainly to myself, had any one told me that afternoon that I should live to drag such matter into print. But you see, sir, how you degrade better men to your own level; and it is needful that those who are to judge betwixt you and me, betwixt Damien and the devil's advocate, should understand

246

your letter to have been penned in a house which could raise, and that very justly, the envy and the comments of the passers-by.

I think (to employ a phrase of yours which I admire) it 'should be attributed' to you that you have never visited the scene of Damien's life and death. If you had, and had recalled it, and looked about your pleasant rooms, even your pen perhaps would have been stayed.

Your sect (and remember, as far as any sect avows me, it is mine) has not done ill in a worldly sense in the Hawaiian Kingdom. When calamity befell their innocent parishioners, when leprosy descended and took root in the Eight Islands, a QUID PRO QUO was to be looked for. To that prosperous mission, and to you, as one of its adornments, God had sent at last an opportunity. I know I am touching here upon a nerve acutely sensitive. I know that others of your colleagues look back on the inertia of your Church, and the intrusive and decisive heroism of Damien, with something almost to be called remorse. I am sure it is so with yourself; I am persuaded your letter was inspired by a certain envy, not essentially ignoble, and the one human trait to be espied in that performance.

You were thinking of the lost chance, the past day; of that which should have been conceived and was not; of the service due and not rendered. Time was, said the voice in your ear, in your pleasant room, as you sat raging and writing; and if the words written were base beyond parallel, the rage, I am happy to repeat — it is the only compliment I shall pay you — the rage was almost virtuous.

But, sir, when we have failed, and another has succeeded; when we have stood by, and another has stepped in; when we sit and grow bulky in our charming mansions, and a plain, uncouth peasant steps into the battle, under the eyes of God, and succours the afflicted, and consoles the dying, and is himself afflicted in his turn, and dies upon the field of honour — the battle cannot be retrieved as your unhappy irritation has suggested. It is a lost battle, and lost for ever.

One thing remained to you in your defeat — some rags of common honour; and these you have made haste to cast away. Common honour; not the honour of having done anything right, but the honour of not having done aught conspicuously foul; the honour of the inert: that was what remained to you. We are not all expected to be Damiens; a man may conceive his duty more narrowly, he may love his comforts better; and none will cast a stone at him for that. But will a gentleman of your reverend profession allow me an example from the fields of gallantry? When two gentlemen compete for the favour of a lady, and the one succeeds and the other is rejected, and (as will sometimes happen) matter damaging to the successful rival's credit reaches the ear of the defeated, it is held by plain men of no pretensions that his mouth is, in the circumstance, almost necessarily closed.

Your Church and Damien's were in Hawaii upon a rivalry to do well: to help, to edify, to set divine examples. You having (in one huge instance) failed, and Damien succeeded, I marvel it should not have occurred to you that you were doomed to silence; that when you had been outstripped in that high rivalry, and sat inglorious in the midst of your well-being, in your pleasant room — and Damien, crowned with glories and horrors, toiled and rotted in that pigsty of his under the cliffs of Kalawao — you, the elect who would not, were the last man on earth to collect and propagate gossip on the volunteer who would and did.

I think I see you — for I try to see you in the flesh as I write these sentences — I think I see you leap at the word pigsty, a hyperbolical expression at the best. 'He had no hand in the reforms,' he was 'a coarse, dirty man'; these were your own words; and you may think it possible that I am come to support you with fresh evidence.

In a sense, it is even so.

Damien has been too much depicted with a conventional halo and conventional features; so drawn by men who perhaps had not the eye to remark or the pen to express the individual; or who perhaps were only blinded and silenced by generous admiration, such as I partly envy for myself — such as you, if your soul were enlightened, would envy on your bended knees. It is the least defect of such a method of portraiture that it makes the path easy for the devil's advocate, and leaves for the misuse of the slanderer a considerable field of truth. For the truth that is suppressed by friends is the readiest weapon of the enemy.

The world, in your despite, may perhaps owe you something, if your letter be the means of substituting once for all a credible likeness for a wax abstraction. For, if that world at all remember you, on the day when Damien of Molokai shall be named Saint, it will be in virtue of one work: your letter to the Reverend H. B. Gage.

You may ask on what authority I speak. It was my inclement destiny to become acquainted, not with Damien, but with Dr. Hyde. When I visited the lazaretto, Damien was already in his resting grave. But such information as I have, I gathered on the spot in conversation with those who knew him well and long: some indeed who revered his memory; but others who had sparred and wrangled with him, who beheld him with no halo, who perhaps regarded him with small respect, and through whose unprepared and scarcely partial communications the plain, human features of the man shone on me convincingly. These gave me what knowledge I possess; and I learnt it in that scene where it could be most completely and sensitively understood — Kalawao, which you have never visited, about which you have never so much as endeavoured to inform yourself; for, brief as your letter is, you have found the means to stumble into that confession.

'LESS THAN ONE-HALF of the island,' you say, 'is devoted to the lepers.'

Molokai — 'MOLOKAI AHINA,' the 'grey,' lofty, and most desolate island — along all its northern side plunges a front of precipice into a sea of unusual profundity. This range of cliff is, from east to west, the true end and frontier of the island. Only in one spot there projects into the ocean a certain triangular and rugged down, grassy, stony, windy, and rising in the midst into a hill with a dead crater: the whole bearing to the cliff that overhangs it somewhat the same relation as a bracket to a wall. With this hint you will now be able to pick out the leper station on a map; you will be able to judge how much of Molokai is thus cut off between the surf and precipice, whether less than a half, or less than a quarter, or a fifth, or a tenth — or, say, a twentieth; and the next time you burst into print you will be in a position to share with us the issue of your calculations.

I imagine you to be one of those persons who talk with cheerfulness of that place which oxen and wain-ropes could not drag you to behold. You, who do not even know its situation on the map, probably denounce sensational descriptions, stretching your limbs the while in your pleasant parlour on Beretania Street. When I was pulled ashore there one early morning, there sat with me in the boat two sisters, bidding farewell (in humble imitation of Damien) to the lights and joys of human life. One of these wept silently; I could not withhold myself from joining her.

Had you been there, it is my belief that nature would have triumphed even in you; and as the boat drew but a little nearer, and you beheld the stairs crowded with abominable deformations of our common manhood, and saw yourself landing in the midst of such a population as only now and then surrounds us in the horror of a nightmare — what a haggard eye you would have rolled over your reluctant shoulder towards the house on Beretania Street! Had you gone on; had you found every fourth face a blot upon the landscape; had you visited the hospital and seen the butt-ends of human beings lying there almost unrecognisable, but still breathing, still thinking, still remembering; you would have understood that life in the lazaretto is an ordeal from which the nerves of a man's spirit shrink, even as his eye quails under the brightness of the sun; you would have felt it was (even to-day) a pitiful place to visit and a hell to dwell in.

It is not the fear of possible infection. That seems a little thing when compared with the pain, the pity, and the disgust of the visitor's surroundings, and the atmosphere of affliction, disease, and physical disgrace in which he breathes. I do not think I am a man more than usually timid; but I never recall the days and nights I spent upon that island promontory (eight days and seven nights), without heartfelt thankfulness that I am somewhere else.

I find in my diary that I speak of my stay as a 'grinding experience': I have once jotted in the margin, 'HARROWING is the
word'; and when the MOKOLII bore me at last towards the outer
world, I kept repeating to myself, with a new conception of their
pregnancy, those simple words of the song -"Tis the most distressful country that ever yet was seen.'

And observe: that which I saw and suffered from was a settlement purged, bettered, beautified; the new village built, the hospital and the Bishop-Home excellently arranged; the sisters, the
doctor, and the missionaries, all indefatigable in their noble tasks.
It was a different place when Damien came there and made his
great renunciation, and slept that first night under a tree amidst his
rotting brethren: alone with pestilence; and looking forward (with
what courage, with what pitiful sinkings of dread, God only knows)
to a lifetime of dressing sores and stumps.

You will say, perhaps, I am too sensitive, that sights as painful abound in cancer hospitals and are confronted daily by doctors
and nurses. I have long learned to admire and envy the doctors and
the nurses. But there is no cancer hospital so large and populous
as Kalawao and Kalaupapa; and in such a matter every fresh case,
like every inch of length in the pipe of an organ, deepens the note
of the impression; for what daunts the onlooker is that monstrous
sum of human suffering by which he stands surrounded. Lastly,
no doctor or nurse is called upon to enter once for all the doors
of that gehenna; they do not say farewell, they need not abandon
hope, on its sad threshold; they but go for a time to their high calling, and can look forward as they go to relief, to recreation, and to
rest. But Damien shut-to with his own hand the doors of his own
sepulchre.

I shall now extract three passages from my diary at Kalawao.

A. 'Damien is dead and already somewhat ungratefully
remembered in the field of his labours and sufferings. "He
was a good man, but very officious," says one. Another tells

me he had fallen (as other priests so easily do) into something of the ways and habits of thought of a Kanaka; but he had the wit to recognise the fact, and the good sense to laugh at' [over] 'it. A plain man it seems he was; I cannot find he was a popular.'

B. 'After Ragsdale's death' [Ragsdale was a famous Luna, or overseer, of the unruly settlement] 'there followed a brief term of office by Father Damien which served only to publish the weakness of that noble man. He was rough in his ways, and he had no control. Authority was relaxed; Damien's life was threatened, and he was soon eager to resign.'

C. 'Of Damien I begin to have an idea. He seems to have been a man of the peasant class, certainly of the peasant type: shrewd, ignorant and bigoted, yet with an open mind, and capable of receiving and digesting a reproof if it were bluntly administered; superbly generous in the least thing as well as in the greatest, and as ready to give his last shirt (although not without human grumbling) as he had been to sacrifice his life; essentially indiscreet and officious, which made him a troublesome colleague; domineering in all his ways, which made him incurably unpopular with the Kanakas, but yet destitute of real authority, so that his boys laughed at him and he must carry out his wishes by the means of bribes. He learned to have a mania for doctoring; and set up the Kanakas against the remedies of his regular rivals: perhaps (if anything matter at all in the treatment of such a disease) the worst thing that he did, and certainly the easiest. The best and worst of the man appear very plainly in his dealings with Mr. Chapman's money; he had originally laid it out' [intended to lay it out] 'entirely for the benefit of Catholics, and even so not wisely; but after a long, plain talk, he admitted his error fully and revised the list. The sad state of the boys' home is in part the result of his lack of control; in part, of his own slovenly ways and false ideas of hygiene. Brother officials used to call it "Damien's Chinatown." "Well," they would say, "your China-town keeps growing." And he would laugh with perfect good-nature, and adhere to his errors with perfect obstinacy. So much I have gathered of truth about this plain, noble human brother and father of ours; his imperfections are the traits of his face, by which we know him for our fellow; his martyrdom and his example nothing can lessen or annul; and only a person here on the spot can properly appreciate their greatness.'

I have set down these private passages, as you perceive, without correction; thanks to you, the public has them in their bluntness. They are almost a list of the man's faults, for it is rather these that I was seeking: with his virtues, with the heroic profile of his life, I and the world were already sufficiently acquainted. I was besides a little suspicious of Catholic testimony; in no ill sense, but merely because Damien's admirers and disciples were the least likely to be critical. I know you will be more suspicious still; and the facts set down above were one and all collected from the lips of Protestants who had opposed the father in his life.

Yet I am strangely deceived, or they build up the image of a man, with all his weaknesses, essentially heroic, and alive with rugged honesty, generosity, and mirth. Take it for what it is, rough private jottings of the worst sides of Damien's character, collected from the lips of those who had laboured with and (in your own phrase) 'knew the man'; — though I question whether Damien would have said that he knew you. Take it, and observe with wonder how well you were served by your gossips, how ill by your intelligence and sympathy; in how many points of fact we are at one, and how widely our apprecia-tions vary. There is something wrong here; either with you or me. It is possible, for instance, that you, who seem to have so many ears in Kalawao, had heard of the affair of Mr. Chapman's money, and were singly struck by Damien's intended wrong-doing. I was struck with that also, and set it fairly down; but I was struck much more by the fact that he had the honesty of mind to be convinced.

I may here tell you that it was a long business; that one of his colleagues sat with him late into the night, multiplying arguments and accusations; that the father listened as usual with 'perfect good-nature and perfect obstinacy'; but at the last, when he was persuaded — 'Yes,' said he, 'I am very much obliged to you; you have done me a service; it would have been a theft.' There are many (not Catholics merely) who require their heroes and saints to be infallible; to these the story will be painful; not to the true lovers, patrons, and servants of mankind.

And I take it, this is a type of our division; that you are one of those who have an eye for faults and failures; that you take a pleasure to find and publish them; and that, having found them, you make haste to forget the overvailing virtues and the real success which had alone introduced them to your knowledge. It is a dangerous frame of mind. That you may understand how dangerous, and into what a situation it has already brought you, we will (if you please) go hand-in-hand through the different phrases of your letter, and candidly examine each from the point of view of its truth, its appositeness, and its charity.

Damien was COARSE.

It is very possible. You make us sorry for the lepers, who had only a coarse old peasant for their friend and father. But you, who were so refined, why were you not there, to cheer them with the lights of culture? Or may I remind you that we have some reason to doubt if John the Baptist were genteel; and in the case of Peter, on whose career you doubtless dwell approvingly in the pulpit, no doubt at all he was a 'coarse, headstrong' fisherman! Yet even in our Protestant Bibles Peter is called Saint.

Damien was DIRTY.

He was. Think of the poor lepers annoyed with this dirty comrade! But the clean Dr. Hyde was at his food in a fine house.

Damien was HEADSTRONG.

I believe you are right again; and I thank God for his strong head and heart.

Damien was BIGOTED.

I am not fond of bigots myself, because they are not fond of me. But what is meant by bigotry, that we should regard it as a blemish in a priest? Damien believed his own religion with the simplicity of a peasant or a child; as I would I could suppose that you do. For this, I wonder at him some way off; and had that been his only character, should have avoided him in life. But the point of interest in Damien, which has caused him to be so much talked about and made him at last the subject of your pen and mine, was that, in him, his bigotry, his intense and narrow faith, wrought potently for good, and strengthened him to be one of the world's heroes and exemplars.

Damien WAS NOT SENT TO MOLOKAI, BUT WENT THERE WITHOUT ORDERS.

Is this a misreading? Or do you really mean the words for blame? I have heard Christ, in the pulpits of our Church, held up for imitation on the ground that His sacrifice was voluntary. Does Dr. Hyde think otherwise?

Damien DID NOT STAY AT THE SETTLEMENT, ETC.

It is true he was allowed many indulgences. Am I to understand that you blame the father for profiting by these, or the officers for granting them? In either case, it is a mighty Spartan standard to issue from the house on Beretania Street; and I am convinced you will find yourself with few supporters.

Damien HAD NO HAND IN THE REFORMS, ETC.

I think even you will admit that I have already been frank in my description of the man I am defending; but before I take you up upon this head, I will be franker still, and tell you that perhaps nowhere in the world can a man taste a more pleasurable sense of contrast than when he passes from Damien's 'Chinatown' at Kalawao to the beautiful Bishop-Home at Kalaupapa. At this point, in my desire to make all fair for you, I will break my rule and adduce Catholic testimony.

Here is a passage from my diary about my visit to the Chinatown, from which you will see how it is (even now) regarded by its own officials: 'We went round all the dormitories, refectories, etc. — dark and dingy enough, with a superficial cleanliness, which he' [Mr. Dutton, the lay- brother] 'did not seek to defend. "It is almost decent," said he; "the sisters will make that all right when we get them here."' And yet I gathered it was already better since Damien was dead, and far better than when he was there alone and had his own (not always excellent) way. I have now come far enough to meet you on a common ground of fact; and I tell you that, to a mind not prejudiced by jealousy, all the reforms of the lazaretto, and even those which he most vigorously opposed, are properly the work of Damien.

They are the evidence of his success; they are what his heroism provoked from the reluctant and the careless. Many were before him in the field; Mr. Meyer, for instance, of whose faithful work we hear too little: there have been many since; and some had more worldly wisdom, though none had more devotion, than our saint. Before his day, even you will confess, they had effected little. It was his part, by one striking act of martyrdom, to direct all men's eyes on that distressful country. At a blow, and with the price of his life, he made the place illustrious and public. And that, if you will consider largely, was the one reform needful; pregnant of all that should succeed. It brought money; it brought (best individual addition of them all) the sisters; it brought supervision, for public opinion and public interest landed with the man at Kalawao. If ever any man brought reforms, and died to bring them, it was he. There is not a clean cup or towel in the Bishop-Home, but dirty Damien washed it.

Damien WAS NOT A PURE MAN IN HIS RELATIONS
WITH WOMEN, ETC.

How do you know that? Is this the nature of the conversation
in that house on Beretania Street which the cabman envied, driving
past? — racy details of the misconduct of the poor peasant priest,
toiling under the cliffs of Molokai?

Many have visited the station before me; they seem not to have
heard the rumour. When I was there I heard many shocking tales,
for my informants were men speaking with the plainness of the
laity; and I heard plenty of complaints of Damien. Why was this
never mentioned? and how came it to you in the retirement of your
clerical parlour?

But I must not even seem to deceive you. This scandal, when I
read it in your letter, was not new to me. I had heard it once before;
and I must tell you how. There came to Samoa a man from Honolulu; he, in a public-house on the beach, volunteered the statement
that Damien had 'contracted the disease from having connection
with the female lepers'; and I find a joy in telling you how the report
was welcomed in a public-house. A man sprang to his feet; I am
not at liberty to give his name, but from what I heard I doubt if you
would care to have him to dinner in Beretania Street. 'You miserable little — ' (here is a word I dare not print, it would so shock your
ears). 'You miserable little — ,' he cried, 'if the story were a thousand times true, can't you see you are a million times a lower — for
daring to repeat it?'

I wish it could be told of you that when the report reached you
in your house, perhaps after family worship, you had found in your
soul enough holy anger to receive it with the same expressions; ay,
even with that one which I dare not print; it would not need to have
been blotted away, like Uncle Toby's oath, by the tears of the record-
ing angel; it would have been counted to you for your brightest righ-
teousness. But you have deliberately chosen the part of the man from
Honolulu, and you have played it with improvements of your own. The
man from Honolulu — miserable, leering creature — communicated

the tale to a rude knot of beach-combing drinkers in a public-house, where (I will so far agree with your temperance opinions) man is not always at his noblest; and the man from Honolulu had himself been drinking — drinking, we may charitably fancy, to excess.

It was to your 'Dear Brother, the Reverend H. B. Gage,' that you chose to communicate the sickening story; and the blue ribbon which adorns your portly bosom forbids me to allow you the extenuating plea that you were drunk when it was done. Your 'dear brother' — a brother indeed — made haste to deliver up your letter (as a means of grace, perhaps) to the religious papers; where, after many months, I found and read and wondered at it; and whence I have now reproduced it for the wonder of others. And you and your dear brother have, by this cycle of operations, built up a contrast very edifying to examine in detail. The man whom you would not care to have to dinner, on the one side; on the other, the Reverend Dr. Hyde and the Reverend H. B. Gage: the Apia bar-room, the Honolulu manse.

But I fear you scarce appreciate how you appear to your fellow-men; and to bring it home to you, I will suppose your story to be true. I will suppose — and God forgive me for supposing it — that Damien faltered and stumbled in his narrow path of duty; I will suppose that, in the horror of his isolation, perhaps in the fever of incipient disease, he, who was doing so much more than he had sworn, failed in the letter of his priestly oath — he, who was so much a better man than either you or me, who did what we have never dreamed of daring — he too tasted of our common frailty. 'O, Iago, the pity of it!' The least tender should be moved to tears; the most incredulous to prayer. And all that you could do was to pen your letter to the Reverend H. B. Gage!

Is it growing at all clear to you what a picture you have drawn of your own heart? I will try yet once again to make it clearer. You had a father: suppose this tale were about him, and some informant brought it to you, proof in hand: I am not making too high an estimate of your emotional nature when I suppose you would regret the circumstance? that you would feel the tale of frailty the more keenly since it shamed the author of your days? and that the last thing you would do would be to publish it in the religious press? Well, the man who tried to do what Damien did, is my father, and the father of the man in the Apia bar, and the father of all who love goodness; and he was your father too, if God had given you grace to see it.

Robert Louis Stevenson

The following is an eyewitness account by Father Wendelin Moellers, SS.CC., of the final days, funeral, and burial of Father Damien.

On Saturday, March 23rd, he was as active as usual, going and coming. It was the last day I saw him like this.

After March 28th, he did not leave his room. On that day, he took care of his temporal affairs. After having signed his papers, he said to me, "How happy I am to have given everything to the Bishop; now I die poor; I no longer have anything of my own." On Thursday, March 28th, he remained in bed. On Saturday, the 30th, he prepared himself for death. It was truly edifying to see him; he appeared to be so happy. I heard his general confession and then made my own confession. Together we renewed our vows that bind us to the Congregation. The next day he received the Holy Viaticum. During the day he was as joyful as usual. "Do you see my hands?" he asked. "All my wounds are closing, and the crust is turning black. It's a sign of death, as you well know. Look at my eyes too; I have seen so many dying lepers that I cannot be mistaken. Death is not far off. I would very much have liked to see the Bishop once again, but the Good God is calling me to celebrate Easter with Him. May God be blessed." He did not think of anything else but of preparing himself to die. There was no mistaking the fact that death was indeed approaching.

On April 2nd he received Extreme Unction administered by Fr. Conrardy. "How good God is," he told me during the day, "to have let me live long enough to have two priests near me to help me in my last moments and then to know that the good Sisters of Charity are here at the leprosarium. That was my Nunc Dimittis [sic]. Work for the lepers is assured; I am no longer needed, so very soon I will go up there." "When you are up there, Father," I told him, "you will not forget those whom you are leaving orphans." "Oh, no," he responded, "if I have any influence with God, I will intercede for all who are in the leprosarium." I asked him to leave me his mantle, as Elijah did, so that I would have his big heart. "Eh! What would you do with it," he asked; "it is full of leprosy!" I then asked him for his blessing. He blessed me, with tears in his eyes, and also blessed the courageous daughters of St. Francis, for whose coming he had prayed so much.

The good priest was better during the following days; we even had some hope of keeping him with us a little longer. The good Sisters often came to visit him. What I most admired in him was his admirable patience. He who was so ardent, so alive, so strong... to be nailed in this way to his poor sickbed... but, however, without suffering very much. Like the simplest and poorest of lepers, he was lying on the ground on a poor straw mattress, and we had a lot of trouble getting him to accept a bed. And what poverty! He who had spent so much money to care for the lepers had been self-forgetting to the point of not having sheets or a change of underclothing.

His attachment to the Congregation was admirable. How often did he not say to me, "Father, you represent the Congregation for me here, don't you? Let us say together the prayers of the Congregation. How sweet it is to die a child of the Sacred Hearts!" He asked me several times to write to our Very Reverend Father to tell him that his sweetest consolation was to die a member of the Congregation of the Sacred Hearts.

On Saturday, April 13th, he became worse, and all hope of keeping him longer vanished. A little after midnight he received the Good Lord for the last time; he would soon see Him face to face. From time to time he would lose consciousness. When I went to see him, he recognized me, spoke to me, and we said "Goodbye," because I had to go to Kalaupapa for the next day, Sunday. The next morning I returned after Mass; I found him quite strong, but his mind wandered. In his eyes I read resignation, joy, satisfaction, but his lips could not articulate what was in his heart. Every once in a while he would press my hand affectionately.

On Monday, April 15th, I received a note from Rev. Fr. Conrardy that Damien was in agony. I hurried to him, but on the way

I met another messenger who was going to announce his death. Father had died without any effort, as if he were falling asleep; he passed away peacefully, after spending close to sixteen years amid the horrors of leprosy. The good shepherd had given his life for his sheep. When I arrived, he had already been dressed in his soutane. All signs of leprosy had disappeared from his face, and the wounds in his hands were dried.

About 11 o'clock we carried him to the church, where he remained on view until 8 a.m. the next day, surrounded by the lepers who prayed for their beloved Father. On Monday afternoon the Sisters had come to decorate his coffin; they nailed white silk on the inside and covered the exterior with black cloth on which they had sewn a white cross.

On April 16th I celebrated Holy Mass for our dear confrere. After Mass the funeral cortege made its way past the new church to enter the cemetery. First went the crossbearer, then the musicians and members of an association, followed by the Sisters with the women and young girls. The coffin was carried by eight white lepers, after which came the officiating priest, accompanied by Rev. Fr. Conrardy and acolytes, in turn followed by the Brothers with their boys and the men.

Fr. Damien had begun his life on Molokai in utter destitution, even having to spend his first nights under a large tree. Complying with his desire to be buried under the same pandanus tree, I had (during his illness) a grave dug at the spot indicated. It is there that his body reposes awaiting a glorious resurrection; he faces the altar. The grave is sealed by a strong bed of cement; therein lie the precious remains of good Father Damien, whom the world rightly calls the hero of charity.

Molokai, April 17th, 1889
Fr. Wendelin, SS.CC.

The following "Decree Concerning the Process of the Beatification and Canonization of the Servant of God Damien de Veuster" — which has been reset to ensure its legibility (and as closely as possible to the original typographical styles) — is from the Sacred Hearts Archives, courtesy of Father Christopher Keahi, SS.CC.

SACRED CONGREGATION FOR THE CAUSES OF SAINTS
DECREE
(MALINES)

CONCERNING THE PROCESS OF BEATIFICATION AND
CANONIZATION OF THE SERVANT OF GOD

Damien Joseph de Veuster

PROFESSED PRIEST
OF THE CONGREGATION OF THE SACRED HEARTS OF JESUS AND MARY
and
THE PERPETUAL ADORATION OF THE BLESSED SACRAMENT, (PICPUS)

ON THE QUESTION

whether or not he practiced the theological virtues of faith, hope and love for God and for his neighbors and the cardinal virtues of prudence, justice, temperance and fortitude, and all the other virtues related to them to a heroic degree.

"This has taught us love — that He gave up His life for us; and we, too, ought to give up our lives for our brothers." (I Jn 3, 16). Nobody can come to Christ if he does not feel compelled by holy necessity, to walk in love, following the One who *"loved us, giving Himself up in our place as a fragrant offering and a sacrifice to God" (Eph 5, 2).* He

came as a physician to heal the sick (see *Lk* 5, 31), He was tempted in every way that we are though He is without sin (see *Heb* 4, 15); *"He took our sicknesses away and carried our diseases for us"* (*Mt* 8, 17), and in the Easter mystery of His death and resurrection He gave proof of what He said during the Last Supper: *"A man can have no greater love than to lay down his life for his friends"* (*Jn* 15, 13). At the same time, He left us His commandment, to love one another as He loved us (see ibid. 12). The Servant of God, Damien de Veuster, professed priest of the Congregation of the Sacred Hearts of Jesus and Mary, took this commandment as the norm for his life; in fact, "he made himself weak to win the weak" (see *I Cor* 9, 22), "he laid down his life for his sheep" (see *Jn* 10, 11), and, by offering his life, he became a martyr of the charity of Christ.

The Servant of God was born on the 3rd of January 1840 in Tremelo, a small village in the diocese of Malines, Belgium. His parents were John Francis de Veuster and Ann Catherine Wauters. They had eight children; four of them became religious. He was baptized on the very day of his birth with the name of Joseph. He lived his childhood in his native home and he attended the school of Werchter. He made his First Holy Communion in 1850. He only began his secondary studies at Braine-le-Comte when he was 18; thus, he hoped to be able to give the help needed in the family business in which he had been involved during his adolescent years. In May 1858, after two months of study, he decided to follow the divine vocation; at the beginning of 1859, after much prayer and spiritual discernment, he asked to be admitted as a lay brother to the house at Louvain of the Congregation of the Sacred Hearts of Jesus and Mary and the Perpetual Adoration of the Blessed Sacrament, (Picpus). His brother August, in religion Pamphile, had already entered before him. He was admitted on the 3rd of January 1859, and on the 2nd of February he began his novitiate with the new name of Damien. Shortly after he was changed to the class of students. When the novitiate had been completed satisfactorily, he was admitted to profession; he pronounced his vows in Paris on the

7th of October 1860. After studying philosophy in Paris and theology in Louvain, he received minor orders in Malines during the month of September 1863.

In the same year 1863, when his brother Pamphile became ill and could not join the other messengers of the Gospel going to the Hawaiian Mission, Damien volunteered to take his place, asking to be sent to the very far islands of the Pacific Ocean. When his request was accepted, he left [Bremerhaven] on the 29th of October and arrived in Honolulu on the 19th of March 1864. There, he was ordained subdeacon, deacon and finally priest on the 21st of May 1864. Priest and victim, he wanted to be a disciple of Jesus and he had but one desire: to lay down his life for his brothers as Our Saviour did. And this he did, first in Puna (Hawaii) from 1864 to 1865, and then in Kohala-Hamakua, on the same island, with great apostolic zeal: he proclaimed the Gospel with confidence, he helped the weak and the poor, he lovingly cared for the sick and communicated to all the joy of Christ's love.

Until his death he persevered in this strong, admirable and apostolic love. He showed this same love in 1873 when a missionary was needed for the island of Molokai, where civil authorities were sending all the lepers. He volunteered spontaneously, and gladly gave himself, having from that moment on but one desire, namely, to bury himself with those unhappy people and to devote himself to the spiritual care of the lepers. He arrived in Molokai on the tenth of May, carrying only a cross and his Breviary. He wished to devote himself completely, to others, seeking every means to ease the sufferings of his brothers and sisters who were living in such terrible material and spiritual misery and who tried to forget their condition by living a life of licentiousness. Damien always showed himself to be a man of God. Forgetting himself, he was always full of happiness and understanding. His pure life, extreme poverty, kindness and firm character expressed in his life what he proclaimed in his preaching. In order to make the others feel, in a certain way, the presence of God, a God who is love (*I Jn* 4, 16), he tried to make them see the generous and omnipresent kindness of God: he was both doctor and nurse, carpenter and bricklayer, tailor and farmer. He comforted and served his lepers, seeing and revering Christ in them. In order to make their living conditions more human, he did not blush in asking for money and he was very happy when he could improve their situation. Very often he was the only priest and religious on the island of sorrow. He was ready to risk even his health for the sake of his apostolate. In this way, he attracted to religion those suffering brothers, and fortified their faith; he tried to make those precious children of Christ understand that their sorrows were a participation in the mystery of Jesus' passion.

In 1884 he shared in their suffering as he contracted leprosy; he accepted this disease with love as a gift coming from our Saviour, and he had had a premonition of it since the moment of his arrival to the island of death. However, even when he felt weakened by the disease, he tried to maintain the rhythm of his activities and his total devotion to the service of the sick. He addressed to them in terms such as "we, lepers" giving the example of faith in Divine Providence and complete abandon to the will of God. His disease progressed inexorably, and he was forbidden to leave Molokai, even if it was for sacramental confession. In his spiritual solitude, he abandoned himself more completely to the love and presence of God; his prayers were more profound and, as he himself wrote, he drew from Eucharist the strength which he needed to live his life of charity with great courage until the end and to bear his terrible disease as a true Christian. Furthermore, this man of God did not lack persecutions, slanders, and enmity on the part of jealous and envious people, sufferings which purified him, as he accepted these difficulties as something coming from the hands of God, who tests his good servants with temptation (see *Tob* 12, 13-14); so, his apostolate could become more fruitful through spiritual crosses. In 1888, after three years alone, a brother and a Belgian priest came to help him in his material and pastoral work, and they were with him in his last days. They, among many others, gave special testimony of

Damien's fervent, firm and simple godly life, of his prayerful spirit, of his fidelity to the obligations of his religious vocation, of his continual concern for the material and spiritual welfare of his brothers, and of his great spiritual peace. Dying with Christ, he was leading a hidden life with Him in God (see *Col* 3, 3). As he himself wrote in 1888: "I am always happy and content. Even if I am ill, I have no other desire than to accomplish God's will." He was preparing humbly to meet God, feeling more and more united with Him and bearing death in his own body. He passed from death to [everlasting] life on the 15th of April 1889.

When he was still alive, he had already been called "the apostle of charity" by [C]atholics and non- [C]atholics alike. When he died, the fame of his sanctity spread everywhere because in the "living grave" of Molokai — this was the name given to the island — where there was no law, he had shown the strong authority and power of the law of love, showing through his actions that love can do all things. This was the reason to begin the process, which has as its aim the raising of the Servant of God to the honour of the altars. The process took place in the archdiocese of Malines during the years 1938 to 1949, and supplementary processes were carried out in the dioceses of Paris, Northampton, Sandwich Islands and Hainan; on the 12th of May 1955, Pope Pius XII approved the introduction of the Cause of the Servant of God. According to the prescriptions of Pope Urban VIII, on the 17th of June of the same year, the Decree "de non-cultu" was published. Then, from 1956 to 1957, with the permission of the Holy See, the Apostolic Process on the Virtues of the Servant of God took place in the diocese of Malines, Nantes, Honolulu and Versailles. The Sacred Congregation of Rites published the Decree on the validity and juridical form of the Process on the 2nd of May 1959.

After having fulfilled all these obligations, the Sacred Congregation began to study the theological and cardinal virtues and all the other virtues related to them in the life of Damien de Veuster; this study took place during the "ante-preparatory" meeting called on the 4th of February 1969. In order to proceed further, the Historical-Hagiographical Department of the Sacred Congregation for the Causes of Saints (which had replaced the Congregation of Rites) had to prepare an official report on specific questions concerning the life of the Servant of God. This report was published in 1974. The study on virtues was resumed on the 19th of October 1976 during a special congress of the Official Prelates and Consultors. A short time later, on the 25th of January 1977, the Plenary Assembly of Cardinals gathered, and Cardinal Pietro Palazzini was the "Ponente" or Reporter. Everyone responded affirmatively to the question whether the Servant of God had practiced all the virtues heroically.

On the 17th of April 1977, the above mentioned Cardinal Prefect informed Pope Paul VI of the response of the Plenary Assembly, and His Holiness ordered that the Decree on the heroicity of the virtues of the Servant of God be prepared.

When everything had been carried out, His Holiness today, after having called the Cardinals, the Prefect who is signing the Decree, Pietro Palazzini, "Ponente" and Reporter of the Cause, me, Bishop Secretary, and everyone that had to be called, declared before those present: *It is a fact that the Servant of God Damien de Veuster lived heroically the theological virtues of Faith, Hope and Love, both with respect to God and his neighbor, and also the cardinal virtues of Prudence, Justice, Temperance and Fortitude, and all the other virtues related to them, in the case which was presented to us.*

He ordered this Decree to be made public and placed in the Acts of this Sacred Congregation.

Rome, July 7th of the Year of Grace 1977
Prefect Corrado Card. Bafile
Joseph Casoria, *Titular Bishop of Forum Novum, Secretary*

Appendix 5

The following is a copy of a letter from the Congregation for Divine Worship and the Discipline of the Sacraments to the Congregation of the Sacred Hearts informing its members that May 10 has been established as the feast day for Blessed Damien de Veuster and that the day may be celebrated by the congregation, in the church of his native city of Tremelo, Belgium, and in other locations, including the place of his death on Molokai, Hawaii, and in Louvain, Belgium.

CONGREGATIO DE CULTU DIVINO
ET DISCIPLINA SACRAMENTORUM

Prot. 1308/95/L

CONGREGATIONIS SACRORUM CORDIUM IESU ET MARIAE

Instante Reverendo Patre Angelo Lucas, Congregationis Sacrorum Cordium Iesu et Mariae Postulatore Generali, litteris die 10 iunii 1995 datis, vigore facultatum huic Congregationi a Summo Pontifice IOANNE PAULO II tributarum, libenter concedimus ut celebratio Beati Damiani De Veuster, presbyteri, in Calendarium proprium eiusdem Congregationis inseri valeat, die 10 maii gradu memoriae ad libitum in universa Congregatione, gradu vero memoriae obligatoriae in ecclesia loci eius nativitatis (Tremelo in Belgio), loci eius mortis (insula Molokai, Hawaii) et loci ubi eius exuviae coluntur (ecclesia S. Antonii in Lovanio, Belgium) quotannis peragenda.

Contrariis quibuslibet minime obstantibus.

Ex aedibus Congregationis de Cultu Divino et Disciplina Sacramentorum, die 22 iunii 1995.

(Antonius M. Card. Javierre)
Praefectus

(+ Gerardus M. Agnelo)
Archiepiscopus a Secretis

The following is the Address of Pope John Paul II to the King of the Belgians.

Sire,

I am deeply moved by the warm words of welcome that Your majesty has just addressed to me, and I wish to assure Him of my deep gratitude. I thank their presence Her majesty the Queen, as well as the high national, provincial and municipal Authorities who have taken part in this welcoming ceremony.

Last year, circumstances obliged me to postpone the visit that I wished to make to Belgium, to celebrate the beatification of Father Damien de Veuster amidst the people of whom he is such an illustrious son. It gives me great joy to be in your country today for this occasion.

I am happy to be here once again in this land, this crossroads, so rich in encounters and exchanges which have marked the European continent. I am happy to meet your people, who have contributed to shaping the history and culture of Europe and who today occupy such an important position. In greeting the persons who are present here, the inhabitants of Melsbroek as well as the military personnel of this base and their families, I address to all Belgians — whether they are members of the Catholic Church or belong to other traditions — the very cordial greetings of the Bishop of Rome. While the citizens of this country have proven capable of developing institutions by accepting their diversity, I offer them my fervent wishes for a future of prosperity and social progress in fraternal harmony.

Sire, ten years ago, it was your brother, King Baudouin, who welcomed me to Belgium. Upon my arrival, I wish to pay homage to his memory, recalling the personal meetings that I had with him, as well as the great esteem and affection in which he was held by the Belgians and countless persons beyond your borders. I salute in him the Christian who, very united with Queen Fabiola, was able to serve his compatriots with truly evangelical devotion.

I turn now to my Brothers in the Episcopate who have come to welcome me. I greet very warmly Cardinal Godfried Danneels, the Archbishop of Mechelen-Brussels, and the other Bishops of Belgium. I am also pleased to be accompanied on this pilgrimage by Cardinal Jean-Jérome Hamer and Cardinal Jan Pieter Schotte, your compatriots, who have placed their skills and devotion at the service of the Apostolic See.

In this brief stay, I cannot repeat the more extensive pastoral visit that I made among you in 1985. My pilgrimage has a very specific goal: the honor given by the Church to Damien de Veuster, an exceptional religious and priest, the force of whose spirit radiates throughout the world. The beatification of this Servant of God is a joy for the entire Church, in Belgium and far beyond. He inherited the qualities of his family and his people, from whom he was later separated by geographical distance, but never spiritually. He is an outstanding witness of the missionary zeal that many Belgians have displayed and demonstrated by their active assistance of disadvantaged peoples throughout the world. In the spirit of the Congregation of the Sacred Hearts, Father Damien combined a profound faith and spiritual experience with an active charity that respected human beings totally in their suffering and extreme weakness.

Dear Catholics of Belgium, in coming to celebrate among you in the beatification of Father Damien, I give him to you as an intercessor who will aid and inspire you. May he strengthen within you the fidelity of the faith and generosity of fraternal service, qualities that are deeply rooted in the centuries-old traditions of your families! I confide this wish to him for all of you.

At the start of this brief stay, devoted mainly to religious celebrations, I wish to thank the Authorities of the Kingdom and everyone who has kindly contributed to its organization. I remember also the numerous preparations which were undertaken last year for my planned visit, I would like to express my gratitude and offer my warmest greetings to those whom I will not see, notably the inhabitants of Tremelo, the compatriots of Father Damien. They have faithfully preserved his memory, celebrating with fervor, and I regret that I could not have been with them. I think also of the people of the diocese of Namur, who should have assembled at the tomb of Saint Mutien-Marie. To those whom I cannot name here, I give them my affectionate sympathy and my encouragement in their spiritual and social life.

Reiterating the expression of my gratitude to Their Majesties the King and Queen for their welcome, as well as to all the personalities gathered here, I invoke the abundance of divine Blessings for all.

The following has been made available through the courtesy of the Damien-Dutton Society.

The Damien-Dutton Society was founded in New Brunswick, New Jersey, in 1944 by Howard E. Crouch. While serving as a Staff Sergeant in the United States Medical Corps during World War II, he was assigned in August 1941 to a lend-lease base being established on the island of Jamaica in the British West Indies. The base was located near a Jamaican Government-run leprosarium in Spanish Town which was staffed by members of the Marist Missionary Sisters whose United States headquarters was located in Bedford, Massachusetts.

With the urging of the Base Chaplain, Sergeant Crouch visited the leprosarium and was impressed with the work the Sisters were doing under very difficult conditions. Leprosy at that time was considered highly contagious and feared. Anyone suspected of having the disease or diagnosed [with it] was incarcerated in the leprosarium compound by law. The sulfone drugs were unknown at the time so the only treatment was chaulmoogra oil obtained from the nut of a tree grown in India. It was a very ineffective drug and the patients had no hope. There were over two hundred patients at Spanish Town when the Sergeant first visited, some having been there for up to fifty years. The compound was separated into two sections, one for men and the other for women. All means of preventing escape were in place including barbed wire, cut glass shards cemented into the top of the walls, and guards.

It was at the leprosarium that Sergeant Crouch met Sister Mary Augustine, one of the members of the staff in charge of the one-room schoolhouse for the more than fifty children afflicted with the disease and barred from living with their parents or loved ones. Pledging to do what he could to assist in helping the patients to while away their time, he organized squads of servicemen and servicewomen who would visit the compound on their off-duty time. They presented shows, gave concerts with the army band, brought toys for their children and gifts for the adults. For the next three years he was ordered back to the United States to be assigned to a hospital ship bringing wounded back from the European front. While home on leave, he interested his family and friends to continue the work he had started in Spanish Town and thus the Damien-Dutton Society was founded. During the Society's early years, aid was confined to Jamaica, but after the war and [Sergeant Crouch's] discharge from the army, and with the original band of volunteers growing to several hundred, they branched out to assist other leprosy hospitals around the world. Likewise, the Nun, Sister Mary Augustine, returned to the United States and assisted in the project. The Sergeant went on to pursue his studies in Hospital Administration and continued the work of the Society on a part-time basis. A newsletter, the Damien-Dutton "Call" was started to inform members of the activities of the Society. Interest and membership continued to grow.

In 1953, the DAMIEN-DUTTON AWARD was established to be presented to an individual or group of individuals who had made a significant contribution to the conquest of leprosy, either by direct patient care, research, education, social rehabilitation or philanthropy. The Award, in the form of a bronze medallion with the sculptured faces of Blessed Damien and Brother Joseph Dutton, was designed by Sister Mary Augustine and cast by the well-known sculptor, Robert Amendola. The first recipient was Stanley Stein, a patient at the United States Government Leprosy Hospital in Carville, Louisiana, who organized the patients to declare their rights and founded THE STAR magazine. Since then, the Award has achieved international recognition and is considered to be the most prestigious award in the field of leprosy today. List of Award winners follows:

1953 Stanley Stein, UNITED STATES
1954 Reverend Joseph Sweeney, KOREA

1955 Sister Marie Suzanne, FRANCE
1956 Dr. Perry Burgess, UNITED STATES
1957 John Farrow, UNITED STATES
1958 Sister Hilary Ross, UNITED STATES
1959 Dr. H. Windsor Wade, PHILIPPINES
1960 Monsignor Louis Joseph Mendelis,
    UNITED STATES
1961 Dr. Kensuke Mitsuda, JAPAN
1962 Reverend Pierre de Orgeval, FRANCE
1963 Eunice Weaver, BRAZIL
1964 Dr. Robert G. Cochrane, UNITED KINGDOM
1965 President John F. Kennedy, UNITED STATES
1966 Peace Corps, UNITED STATES
1967 Dr. Howard A. Rusk, UNITED STATES
1968 Dr. Francis Hemerijckx, BELGIUM
1969 Dr. Victor George Heiser, UNITED STATES
1970 Dr. Dharmendra, INDIA
1971 Dr. Chapman H. Binford, UNITED STATES
1972 Dr. Patricia Smith, VIETNAM
1973 Dr. Jacinto Convit, VENEZUELA
1974 Dr. José N. Rodriguez, PHILIPPINES
1975 Dr. Oliver Hasselblad, UNITED STATES
1976 Dr. Yoshio Yoshie, JAPAN
1977 Drs. Paul and Margaret Brand, UNITED STATES
1978 Dr. Fernando Latapi, MEXICO
1979 Dr. Stanley G. Browne, UNITED STATES
1980 Robert Watelet, ZAIRE
1981 American Leprosy Missions, UNITED STATES
1982 Dr. Ma Haide, PEOPLE'S REPUBLIC OF CHINA
1983 Murlidhar Devidas Amte (Baba Amte), INDIA
1984 Mother Teresa, INDIA
1985 Dr. John H. Hanks, UNITED STATES
1986 Samuel J. Butcher, UNITED STATES
1987 Dr. W. Felton Ross, UNITED STATES

1988 Hermann Kober, WEST GERMANY
1989 Catholic Medical Mission Board, UNITED STATES
1990 Dr. Wayne M. Meyers, UNITED STATES
1991 Dr. Ruth Pfau, PAKISTAN
1992 Anwei Skinsnes Law, UNITED STATES
1993 Dr. C.K. Job, INDIA
1994 International Journal of Leprosy, UNITED STATES
1995 Dr. Jon Lew, SOUTH KOREA
1996 Richard Marks, UNITED STATES
1997 Dr. Roy Pfalzgraff, M.D., UNITED STATES
1998 Jean Margaret Watson, ENGLAND
1999 Dr. Margaret Anne Meyer, UNITED STATES
2000 Dr. K.V. Desikan, INDIA
2001 Michel F. Lechat, M.D., BELGIUM
2002 Dr. Yo Yuasa, M.D., JAPAN
2003 Gerard Kirchner, UNITED STATES
2004 Dr. Michael F. R. Waters, ENGLAND
2005 Eliazar T. Rose, INDIA
2006 Dr. E.P. Fritschi, INDIA
2007 Dr. Roland V. Cellona, PHILIPPINES
2008 The Nippon Foundation and the Sasakawa Memorial Health Foundation, JAPAN

In 1973, the Corporate Board of the Damien-Dutton Society was composed of well-known people in the fields of religious education and science, and an Advisory Board was added including well-known leprologists: Dr. Wayne Meyers, Dr. Margaret Brand, Dr. Paul Converse, Dr. Gerald Walsh, Dr. Felton Ross, and others.

In 1977, Howard Crouch retired from his position as an administrator at Kennedy High School on Long Island, New York, to assume full-time control of the operations of the Society.

In 1975 the Society opened a Gift Shop in Bellmore and later another in Port Jefferson, both on Long Island. The purpose of the shops was to raise funds to cover the administrative costs of operating the Society so that donated funds would be used exclusively for leprosy programs.

The Damien-Dutton Society's main purpose has always been to raise funds for medical care, education, research and social rehabilitation programs for leprosy patients, regardless of race, color or creed, in all corners of the globe.

Howard Crouch and the Society have been recipients of many honors, including GOOD SAMARITAN AWARD by the Alexian Brothers; THE CELTIC CROSS and the FOR COUNTRY AWARD by the Catholic war veterans; THE AMERICAN LEPROSY MISSIONS AWARD; THE CARITAS AWARD from the diocese of Rockville Centre of New York, and others.

Leprosy (Hansen's Disease)

Leprosy is a chronic infectious disease caused by the microorganism, "Mycobacterium leprae," acting primarily on the cooler areas of the body, the skin, upper respiratory tract, anterior segment of the eye, superficial portions of the peripheral nerves and testes, reports Dr. Wayne Meyers in his article, "Leprosy," published by the Armed Forces Institute of Pathology, Washington, D.C. Dr. Meyers, considered to be one of the leading leprologists in the world, serves on the Board of the Damien-Dutton Society. For decades humans have been considered to be the only reservoir of M. leprae, but recently it has been discovered that wild armadillos in Louisiana and Eastern Texas have acquired leprosy. Epidemiological data suggests that wild, infectious armadillos transmit leprosy to humans, perhaps by direct contact or by formites. Naturally acquired leprosy has also been found in some primates such as the mangabey monkey.

Modes of transmission of leprosy remain uncertain, but the naso-respiratory tract seems the most likely route. In adults, leprosy is found more common in men than in women. In children the ratio is close to one to one. Incubation periods vary to as long as 30 years but are usually two to five years. Much depends on the patient's immune response. The number of cases worldwide varies greatly, but it is estimated to be between 10 [million] to 12 million. Approximately 5,000 cases exist in the United States.

Leprosy and AIDS

Mycobacterium infections, particularly M. tuberculosis and M. avium are highly prevalent in patients with HIV infections in North America, Europe and elsewhere.

In the Spring 1996 issue of the Damien-Dutton "Call," Dr. Meyers writes that contrary to popular opinion, leprosy is far from eliminated. Many patients still suffer disabilities and stigma which are the greatest tragedies of this disease. More than two million patients are receiving the multi-drug therapy and approximately five million more need continued care for disabilities. There is leprosy in at least 100 countries and of these, 25 countries are significantly affected with 95 percent of all the world's leprosy patients in India, Nigeria, Burma, Bangladesh and Brazil. In the United States with about 5,000 patients, 140 new patients were diagnosed in 1995. Dr. Meyers states that many people are confused because of the publicity generated by the declaration in 1991 by the World Health Organization of their goal to eliminate leprosy as a public health problem by the year 2000. The declaration does not say that leprosy will disappear or be eradicated by the end of the century, or that millions of disabled people will need care for decades. Furthermore, the best estimates are that there will be 600,000 or so new cases each year.

There are other factors that may occur that will make this goal impossible to reach. Most of these factors are similar to those that make tuberculosis and other infectious diseases a renewed threat in our time. Some of these problems include: leprosy bacilli may show increased resistance to present-day therapeutic drugs; how HIV will influence the spread of leprosy remains obscure; increasing poverty in countries with leprosy reduces the ability of governments to support leprosy control programs, and war and political strife interrupt the flow of aid for the care of leprosy patients. Many governments, including the United States of America, have drastically reduced support of laboratory research on leprosy, and programs for the care of the patients are in jeopardy. False hopes can bring drastic consequences. Tuberculosis is again a major threat as is malaria and other diseases once believed controlled.

Dr. Paul Converse, a member of the Damien-Dutton Board who works in a research laboratory at Johns Hopkins, writes in the Summer 1996 issue of the Damien-Dutton "Call," of the need for a vaccine. Dr. Converse cites a meeting he attended where the question arose whether or not it was worthwhile carrying out a vaccine research since they were having so much success with the multi-drugs. Experience has taught us that bacilli can develop resistance to chemotherapy and if this happens with the present MTD (multi-drug therapy) program, where do we turn next? We are already seeing patient resistance to MDT drugs around the world. To be sure of the elimination of leprosy in the 21st century, we should remember that the ONLY successfully eradicated disease, smallpox, was done so by means of vaccination of EVERY exposed individual in the world. Only then could smallpox experts rest on their laurels. To rest too soon in [our quest to eradicate] leprosy would be a great disservice to the patients, their families, and to [future] patients....

(*Note:* The full text of these articles by Dr. Meyers and Dr. Converse may be obtained from the Damien-Dutton Society. Write or call: Damien-Dutton Society for Leprosy Aid, Inc., 616 Bedford Ave., Bellmore, Long Island, NY 11710; Telephone: 516-221-5829, Fax: 516-221-5909; www.damien-duttonleprosysociety.org).

Upon the shores of this forgotten place,
A little boat did land,
And from this craft he stepped with haste,
To meet a wretched band.

His eyes did meet an unusual sight,
Fear came upon this face,
So he brushed aside all signs of fright,
And vowed to serve this race.

At first they scorned the sight of him,
This stranger that had come,
For all their souls were touched with sin,
And unknowns they would shun.

But soon they learned to love this priest,
Who toiled by their side.
From sun to sun he did not cease,
And buried those who died.

He cleansed their souls and dressed their sores,
With love and gentle care,
And they in turn with open door,
Would have their food to share.

Of course in time this saintly man,
Like a wind-blown tree did bend.
For this cursed disease did grasp his hand,
And he was one of them.
This did not stop or cause any shame,
For much still had to be done.

He served and blessed and eased much pain,
Far past each setting sun.

But then alas came that sorrowful day,
When lepers bowed and cried.
This message came and what did it say,
Dear father Damien had died.

EARL W. GOMES *(MARCH 10, 1960)*

When I beheld thee in the far Pacific isles,
Taking a loving care of the leper unkept,
Sweetly looking at him to alleviate his pains
I shuddered with fear, and my heart then wept.

When I beheld thee choosing the narrow path
That Christ our Saviour for love of us had tread,
In simple obedience accepting the hard yoke
I felt thine anguish and my heart then bled.

When I beheld thee covered with dreaded sores,
Yet going to relieve the poor suffering folk,
From hut to hut dragging thine own weary frame,
I guessed thy martyrdom and my heart then broke.

When I beheld thee during thy last days here,
I had a vision of Calvary's deep shade,
For thou wert like our Crucified God,
Then I knelt down and oh! my heart prayed.

But when I heard the world blessing thy memory,
Put, on thy radiant brow, the great eternal seal,
And when Heaven itself crowned thy victory,
Oh! then I stood up and my heart did peal.

POEM USED IN THE DAMIEN DAY CELEBRATION,
MAY 1944, IN HONOLULU

Ka Haku e ahonui mai
Ka Haku e ahonui mai
Karisto e ahonui mai
Karisto e ahonui mai
Ka Haku e ahonui mai
Ka Haku e ahonui mai

The Kyrie Eleison in Hawaiian

E Ko makou Makua I loko o ka lani
E ho'ano 'ia Kou inoa.
E hiki mai Kou aupuni:
E malama'ia kou makemake ma ka honua nei,
E like me ia I malama'ia ma ka lani la.
E ha'awi mai ia makou I keia la, i'ai na makou no neia la;
E kala mai, ho'i ia makou I ka makou lawehala 'ana,
Me makou e kala nei I ka po'e I lawehala I ka makou.
Mai ho'oku'u 'oe ia makou I ka ho'o-wale-wale 'ia mai, aka.
E ho'opakele no na'e ia makou I ka 'ino;
No Ka Mea, nou ke aupuni,
A Me ke mana, a me ka ho'onani'ia, a mau loa aku.
Amene.

The Lord's Prayer in Hawaiian

On the shores of Kalaupapa
We stand with heads bent low;
Shut away by high barrier cliffs,
We recall our own vanished island.

Farewell, farewell, beloved home!
Never shall we see thee more.
Constantly we implore God
To lift this affliction laid upon us.

Hymn of Kalaupapa

SUGGESTED READING

Adler, Jacob, and Gwynn Barrett, eds. *The Diaries of Walter Murray Gibson*. Honolulu: University of Hawaii Press, 1973.

Bunson, Margaret. *The Damien Report* (a newsletter published from 1982 to 1984), Honolulu.

———. *Faith in Paradise*. Boston: Daughters of St. Paul, 1977.

Bunson, Margaret and Matthew. *John Paul II's Book of Saints*. Huntington: Our Sunday Visitor, 2007.

Case, Howard D., ed. *Joseph Dutton, His Memoirs*. Honolulu: Honolulu Star Bulletin, 1931.

Cicognani, Amleto G. *Father Damien, Apostle of the Lepers*. Washington, D.C., 1947.

Clifford, Edward. *Father Damien, A Journey from Cashmere to His Home in Hawaii*. London: Macmillan, 1889.

Committee on Leprosy and Department of Health, State of Hawaii. "Recommendations for Treatment of Leprosy in Hawaii." n.d.

Crouch, Howard. *Two Josephs on Molokai, Damien and Dutton*. Bellmore, New York: Damien-Dutton Society for Leprosy Aid, 1998.

Daws, Gavan. *Holy Man*. New York: Harper and Row Publishers, 1973.

———. *Shoal of Time: A History of the Hawaiian Islands*. New York: Macmillan, 1968.

Englebert, Omer. *The Hero of Molokai*. Boston: Daughters of St. Paul, 1977.

Eynikel, Hilde. *Molokai: The Story of Father Damien*. Staten Island: Alba House, 1999.

Farrow, John. *Damien the Leper*. New York: Sheed and Ward, 1937.

Hathaway, Joseph C. "Leprosy in Hawaii," *Hawaii Medical Journal* 29 (1970), 429-437.

Jacks, L.V. *Mother Marianne of Molokai*. New York: Macmillan, 1935.

Jourdan, Vital. *The Heart of Father Damien*. New York: Bruce Publishing Company, 1955.

Kent, Harold W. *Dr. Hyde and Mr. Stevenson*. Tokyo: Tuttle, 1973.

King Kamehameha I and Father Damien Memorial Statues. Washington, D.C.: U.S. Government Printing Office, 1970.

Kuykendall, Ralph S. *The Hawaiian Kingdom* (3 vols.). Honolulu: University of Hawaii Press, 1938-1963.

Larkin, Francis. *The Heart of Father Damien*. New York: Bruce, 1955.

Life and Letters of Father Damien, The Apostle of the Lepers. London: Catholic Truth Society, 1889.

Prindivill, Raymond. *Damien, Martyr of Molokai*. New York: Paulist Press, 1937.

Stevenson, Robert Louis. *Father Damien, An Open Letter to the Reverend Dr. Hyde of Honolulu*, 1890.

Stewart, Richard. *Leper Priest of Moloka'i*. Honolulu: University of Hawai'i Press, 2000.

Summers, Catherine C. *Molokai: A Site Survey*. Honolulu: Bishop Museum, 1971.

Yzendoorn, Reginald. *History of the Catholic Missions in the Hawaiian Islands*. Honolulu: Honolulu Star Bulletin, 1927.

Index

Index